access to history

The USA and Vietnam 1945–75 THIRD EDITION

access to history

The USA and Vietnam 1945–75 THIRD EDITION

Vivienne Sanders

HODDER EDUCATION
AN HACHETTE UK COMPANY

Study guides revised and updated, 2008, by Sally Waller (AQA), Angela Leonard (Edexcel) and Sheila Randall (OCR).

The publishers would like to thank the following individuals, institutions and companies for permission to reproduce copyright illustrations in this book: AFP/Getty Images, page 116; AP/EMPICS, page 70, 110, 112, 140; © Bettmann/CORBIS, page 10, 15, 18, 30, 32, 40, 41, 55, 58, 69, 83, 96(top), 96(bottom), 97, 119, 147, 177, 195; © Corbis, page 53, 60; Getty Images, page 44; © Hulton-Deutsch Collection/CORBIS, page 13; © JP Laffont/Sygma/Corbis, page 170; © Wally McNamee/CORBIS, page 168; Time & Life Pictures/Getty Images, page 115.
The publishers would also like to thank the following for permission to reproduce material in this book: Edexcel Limited for extracts used on page 156.
The publishers would like to acknowledge use of the following extracts: www.fortunecity.com/tinpan/parton/2/mylai2.html for an extract, page 159.
Every effort has been made to trace all copyright holders, but if any have been inadvertently overlooked the Publishers will be pleased to make the necessary arrangements at the first opportunity.

Hachette UK's policy is to use papers that are natural, renewable and recyclable products and made from wood grown in sustainable forests. The logging and manufacturing processes are expected to conform to the environmental regulations of the country of origin.

Orders: please contact Bookpoint Ltd, 130 Milton Park, Abingdon, Oxon OX14 4SB. Telephone: (44) 01235 827720. Fax: (44) 01235 400454. Lines are open 9.00–5.00, Monday to Saturday, with a 24-hour message answering service. Visit our website at www.hoddereducation.co.uk

First published in 2007 by
Hodder Education,
An Hachette UK Company
338 Euston Road
London NW1 3BH

Impression number 11
Year 2014

Cover photo courtesy of Tim Page/Corbis
Typeset in Baskerville 10/12pt and produced by Gray Publishing, Tunbridge Wells
Printed and bound by CPI Group (UK) Ltd, Croydon, CR0 4YY

A catalogue record for this title is available from the British Library

ISBN: 978 0340 929308

Contents

Dedication vii

Chapter 1 Introduction: The United States and Vietnam 1

1 Introduction 1
2 Overview of the War 2
3 Overview of the Debates on the Vietnam War 3

Chapter 2 Vietnam and Foreigners Before 1953 7

1 Ho Chi Minh and Vietnamese Nationalism 8
2 The United States and Vietnam, 1941–5 14
3 The Reasons for the Early American Involvement in Vietnam 17
4 'These Situations … Have a Way of Snowballing' 20
5 Key Debates on the Truman Years 21

Chapter 3 Eisenhower and Two Vietnams 24

1 Ho, Giap and the French Failure in Indochina 25
2 Dienbienphu – The Debate over American Intervention 29
3 The Geneva Conference on Indochina, 1954 34
4 Two Vietnams and Two Leaders 39
5 Assessment of Eisenhower's Policy 46
6 Key Debates 48

Chapter 4 'Vietnam is the Place' – The Kennedy Crusade (1961–3) 51

1 Introduction: Kennedy's War? 52
2 Kennedy's Early Ideas about Vietnam 52
3 The President and his Advisers 54
4 Kennedy's Actions in the Third World 61
5 Kennedy and Diem 63
6 Conclusions 75
7 Key Debates 76
Study Guide 79

Chapter 5 'Johnson's War'? 80

1 Why Johnson Continued US Involvement in the War 81
2 How Johnson was Able to Escalate the War 87
3 Why Did Johnson Escalate the American Involvement in Vietnam? 90
4 'Where Are We Going?' 95
5 Historians and 'Johnson's War'? 100
Study Guide 102

Chapter 6 Why the USA Failed: I – The People in Vietnam 109
1 The Vietnamese 109
2 The Americans 122
3 Key Debates 130

Chapter 7 Why the USA Failed: II – US Politicians and People 132
1 Problems with Johnson's Aims and Methods 133
2 Why and How Johnson was Forced to Retreat 135
3 Johnson's Last Months 150
4 Conclusions about Johnson and the War 152
Study Guide 154

Chapter 8 1969–73: Nixon – Diplomatic Genius or Mad Bomber? 162
1 The Transformation of a Cold Warrior? 163
2 President Nixon 167
3 1969–71 171
4 1972 – Getting Re-elected 179
5 Assessment of Nixon's Vietnam Policy 185
6 Key Debate 188
Study Guide 190

Chapter 9 Conclusions 192
1 Summarising the Debates 192
2 The Effects of the War 194
3 The Lessons of the Vietnam War 200

Glossary 201

Index 206

Dedication

Keith Randell (1943–2002)

The *Access to History* series was conceived and developed by Keith, who created a series to 'cater for students as they are, not as we might wish them to be'. He leaves a living legacy of a series that for over 20 years has provided a trusted, stimulating and well-loved accompaniment to post-16 study. Our aim with these new editions is to continue to offer students the best possible support for their studies.

1 Introduction: The United States and Vietnam

POINTS TO CONSIDER

From 1954 to 1973, the United States of America was deeply involved in a war in Vietnam. This chapter gives an overview of the debates on:

- Why the United States got involved and remained in Vietnam
- Why the United States failed to defeat Communism in Vietnam
- The results of the Vietnam War

Key dates

Late 1800s	French conquered Vietnam
1946–54	Vietnamese Communists led struggle for independence from France
1954	Era of French domination ended. Two Vietnamese governments: North Vietnam (Communist) and South Vietnam
1954–68	United States gave ever-increasing aid to unpopular anti-Communist South Vietnamese regimes
1968–73	United States gradually withdrew from Vietnam
1975	Vietnamese Communists took over the whole of Vietnam

1 | Introduction

Many who were born after the American involvement in the Vietnam War ended (1973) have vivid mental images of Americans in Vietnam, thanks to memorable scenes in Hollywood movies: Robin Williams as a DJ trying to win the hearts and minds of the Vietnamese people in *Good Morning Vietnam*; Robert de Niro trying to stop his Vietnam veteran buddy playing Russian roulette with a gun against his head in *The Deer Hunter*; Charlie Sheen prowling through the jungle with a war-crazed sergeant in *Platoon*; Sylvester Stallone going back to Indochina to defeat the Communists single handedly in a *Rambo* film; Tom Cruise barely recognisable as a crippled veteran in *Born on the Fourth of July*.

The Vietnam War is still very much alive in the memories and actions of Americans today. I spent Christmas 1995 with my uncle and aunt in California. A career soldier in his younger days, my uncle was a helicopter pilot in the American army in Vietnam in 1966–8. I wanted to hear his recollections of Vietnam. 'When Bob [his son] comes', my uncle said, 'don't mention the war. It is not the sort of thing I want to talk about in front of my kids.' I knew the great issues that historians debate about America and Vietnam, but many were painfully immediate that Christmas. My uncle was a professional soldier in the army of the richest and most powerful nation in the world in 1966. Why did he have to fight in a small, poor country in Southeast Asia? Why did he think his children were embarrassed about his participation in the war? What impact did the war have on him and his family? Answers to the first two questions are given in this book. The answer to the third question is that it greatly damaged his family life and that he now has the kind of terminal cancer that is exceptionally common amongst Vietnam veterans exposed to **Agent Orange**.

Key terms

Agent Orange
A herbicide used by the US in Vietnam, in order to defoliate the trees to destroy enemy cover.

Communist
One whose ideology (set of beliefs) is anti-imperialist (against countries that try to conquer or dominate others) and pro-equal distribution of wealth.

Guerrilla
A soldier who tries to avoid conventional warfare (that is, one army directly confronting another), preferring methods such as sabotage to counter the enemy's superior conventional forces.

2 | Overview of the War

From 1946 to 1954 the Vietnamese people struggled for independence against their French colonial masters. When the French left Vietnam in 1954 the country was temporarily divided into two. Almost immediately the Americans moved in, helping to create and support an anti-**Communist** Vietnamese regime in the south against the **Communist** Vietnamese regime in the north. Although Vietnamese struggles against foreigners before 1954 are briefly discussed, this book concentrates on the years of American involvement in Vietnam (1954–73). From 1954, the United States made increasingly strenuous efforts to support the government of South Vietnam in its struggle against Communist **guerrillas** who were supported by North Vietnam, China and the USSR. However, by 1973 the United States had given up the struggle against the Vietnamese Communists. The latter proceeded to take over the whole of Vietnam in 1975. The causes, course and consequences of American involvement are much debated by historians.

Key dates

The Vietnamese war of independence against France: 1946–54

USA deeply involved in Vietnam: 1954–73

Vietnam became fully Communist: 1975

Summary diagram: Overview of the Vietnam War

1946–54	Vietnamese v French
1954	French out USA and two Vietnams in
1954–73	USA and South Vietnam v (Communist) North Vietnam
1973	USA out
1975	Vietnam united and Communist

Key question
When was the United States at war?

3 | Overview of the Debates on the Vietnam War

Historians disagree about almost every aspect of US involvement in Vietnam. There is not even agreement about the dates between which the US was at war. This is because American diplomatic and military intervention was gradual. It escalated slowly, over a long period of time from 1945 onwards. Furthermore, the US never actually declared war on anyone. There was little direct involvement between 1945 and 1954 when France was attempting to re-establish colonial rule over the country following the Second World War (see Chapters 2 and 3). However, from 1954 onwards, the US became more and more embroiled in the region (Chapters 4–8).

a) A key debate: why did the US get involved and remain in Vietnam?

This is one of the most hotly debated issues.

i) The official explanation

The official American government position was that the US was fighting against an aggressive and evil Communist movement, and that the Vietnamese Communists were the puppets of the USSR and China. Washington said that if Vietnam fell to Communism, other Southeast Asian countries would probably follow (for this 'domino theory' see page 31). Unless the US stopped Communism, American national security and liberty and free enterprise throughout the world would be threatened. There were different emphases as circumstances changed. In the 1950s it was stressed that America's ally France needed help (Chapters 2 and 3). In the 1960s South Vietnam's need for freedom and democracy was emphasised (Chapters 4–8). It was said that the US had an obligation to continue its commitment in Vietnam and that American international credibility would be damaged if the US withdrew (see, in particular, Chapters 5, 7 and 8).

ii) Idealism, economic self-interest or militarism?

While some historians (for example, G. Lewy) see idealism behind American anti-Communist crusading, others (for example, Gabriel Kolko) think that American economic self-interest was the most important motivating force. Many companies did well out of war, and many Americans thought it vital that America should continue to have access to the raw materials and markets of Southeast Asia – something they thought would cease if Southeast Asia became Communist (see page 17). Many Vietnamese today attribute US involvement in Vietnam to American economic greed and militarism.

iii) The role of presidents

Historians argue over how the blame for the involvement and its continuation should be apportioned between the various presidents who held office during this period. Truman was the first to get involved but is rarely blamed. Some historians blame Eisenhower, more blame Kennedy but most blame Johnson. Many revile Nixon for not getting the US out quickly enough.

US presidents in the era of American involvement in Vietnam

President	Dates	Chapters
Harry Truman	1945–53	2
Dwight Eisenhower	1953–61	3
John Kennedy	1961–3	4
Lyndon Johnson	1963–9	5–7
Richard Nixon	1969–73	8

iv) The 'quagmire theory'

Some historians (for example, Arthur Schlesinger Jr) favour the 'quagmire' interpretation of American involvement. According to the **quagmire theory**, successive presidents took one step after another, thinking each step would be the one to solve the Vietnam problem. The US then got deeper and deeper into the quagmire (literally, a muddy marsh).

v) The stalemate theory

Some historians (for example, L. Gelb and R. Betts) bitterly accuse American presidents of knowing that they could not win yet continuing the war so that they would not be 'the first president to lose a war'. That is known as the **stalemate theory**.

vi) The commitment trap

Many historians, whether implicitly or explicitly, argue that the commitment made to Vietnam by the previous president(s) made it harder for each president's successor(s) to exit without the US and the president(s) losing face.

vii) Shared responsibility

Other historians (for example, Vaughn Davis Bornet) feel that it is unfair to blame the presidents alone. They argue that the responsibility is shared by the presidents' advisers, the **State Department**, the **Defence Department**, the **Joint Chiefs of Staff** (JCS), the **Central Intelligence Agency** (CIA), and ambassadors to Vietnam. Presidents normally make decisions after hearing the advice of all the above. Furthermore, in order to finance any fighting, the president needed to get money from **Congress**. The president and Congress were elected by the people. Some historians claim that Congress, the public, and the press who kept them informed bear some responsibility for American involvement because it is clear that presidents responded to what they thought the electorate did or did not want.

Key terms

Quagmire theory
Belief that the US got slowly and increasingly stuck in Vietnam.

Stalemate theory
Belief that the US continued to fight an unwinnable war in Vietnam, simply to avoid being seen to be defeated.

State Department
The US equivalent of Britain's Foreign Office – the section of the federal bureaucracy with responsibility for US relations with foreign powers.

Defence Department
The section of the federal bureaucracy with responsibility for US defence.

Joint Chiefs of Staff
Established during the Second World War – US army, navy and air force chiefs.

Central Intelligence Agency
Established in 1947 – responsible for collecting and evaluating intelligence data for the federal government.

Congress
The US equivalent of Britain's parliament – passes laws and votes money for the president to spend.

Summary diagram: Why did the US get involved and remain in Vietnam?

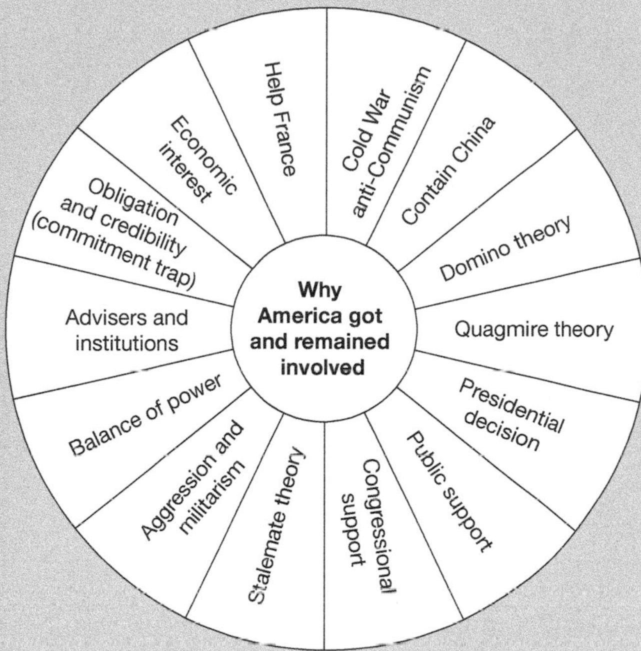

b) A key debate: why did the US fail in Vietnam?

The other central debate concerns why America failed in the war (Chapters 6 and 7). Despite tremendous American efforts, the state of South Vietnam collapsed in 1975 after an invasion by the North. The American military (for example, William Westmoreland) tend to blame the civilians for the loss of the war. Had the US immediately employed all its military power, they argue, it would have won. They are bitter about the politicians who 'lost their nerve' in the face of mounting protests from the American public.

However, some historians (for example, S. Stanton) blame the military as much as the civilians, saying they failed to adopt the appropriate **counter-insurgency** tactics. Instead of 'search and destroy' operations against the Communist guerrillas, the US should have concentrated forces on the 17th parallel to divide the North and South (see the map on page 37), and worked harder to win the hearts and minds of the South Vietnamese people. Some (such as Eric Bergerud) believe the war was unwinnable because of the strength and stubborn conviction of the North Vietnamese (helped by the USSR and China) and the hopelessness of America's South Vietnamese allies.

Key term

Counter-insurgency When faced with irregular (guerrilla) warfare conducted against the South Vietnamese government by discontented South Vietnamese rebels (insurgents), some Americans urged special tactics (for example, propaganda) to counter those insurgents.

Summary diagram: Why did the US fail in Vietnam?

c) The results of the Vietnam War

The results of the war are less debated. It is unanimously agreed that Americans and Vietnamese suffered physically, emotionally and economically (Chapters 6–8). There are still visible reminders of the war. Limbless veterans and war memorials can be seen in both countries. The physical landscape in Vietnam has not yet recovered. Lush tropical forests have not yet grown back. So many Vietnamese emigrated to America that one area of Los Angeles is known as 'Little Saigon'. In both countries, some remain embittered, although more are keen to forget the war and get on with their lives. Perhaps the final great debate about 'Vietnam' is what, if any, lessons the US (and others) can learn from it (Chapter 8).

Some key books in the debates

E. Bergerud, *Dynamics of Defeat* (Boulder, 1991).
V. Davis Bornet, *The Presidency of Lyndon B. Johnson* (Kansas, 1983).
L. Gelb and R. Betts, *The Irony of Vietnam* (Washington, 1979).
H. Kissinger, *White House Years* (Boston, 1979).
G. Kolko, *Anatomy of a War* (Pantheon, 1985).
G. Lewy, *America in Vietnam* (Oxford University Press, 1978).
A. Schlesinger Jr, *The Bitter Heritage* (Boston, 1966).
S. Stanton, *The Rise and Fall of an American Army* (Dell, 1985).
W. Westmoreland, *A Soldier Reports* (Dell, 1976).

2 Vietnam and Foreigners Before 1953

POINTS TO CONSIDER

There are three particularly controversial questions regarding American involvement in Vietnam: 1) Why did the United States get involved? 2) Which presidents were responsible for that involvement? 3) Why did the United States fail there?

This chapter helps to answer those three questions, through the following sections:

- Ho Chi Minh and Vietnamese nationalism
- The United States and Vietnam, 1941–5
- The reasons for early American involvement in Vietnam
- 'These situations … have a way of snowballing'
- Key debates on the Truman years

Key dates

1887		Indochina (Vietnam, Cambodia and Laos) under French domination
1911		Ho Chi Minh left Vietnam
1919		Paris Peace Settlement at end of First World War
		President Wilson ignored Ho Chi Minh's pleas for greater Vietnamese freedom
1924		Ho Chi Minh visited USSR
1929		Ho Chi Minh established Indochinese Communist Party
1939–45		Second World War
1941		Japanese completed conquest of French Indochina
		Ho returned to Vietnam
		Vietnam Independence League (Vietminh) established
1941–5		USA at war with Japan
1945	April	President Roosevelt died; Truman became president
	September	Ho Chi Minh declared Vietnamese independence, but US and Britain allowed French to return to Vietnam
1945–9		Start of Cold War between USA and USSR

1946	November	Outbreak of Franco-Vietminh War
1949		France established 'independent' Associated State of Vietnam under Bao Dai
	October	China became Communist
1950	January	USSR and China recognised Ho's Democratic Republic of Vietnam
	February	Start of 'McCarthyism'
		USA recognised Associated State of Vietnam and promised aid
	September	Military Assistance Advisory Group (MAAG) established
1954		United States paid 80 per cent of French costs in Indochina

1 | Ho Chi Minh and Vietnamese Nationalism

Two of the most important reasons why the Americans were to fail in Vietnam were (a) Vietnamese **nationalism** and (b) the leadership of Ho Chi Minh (1890–1969).

a) Vietnamese nationalism before 1900

Key question
Who and what had inspired Vietnamese nationalism?

Captain John White was the first American to set foot on Vietnamese soil. Seeking trade, he arrived in the port of Saigon in 1820. He found a small country very different from the United States of America. The vast majority of Vietnamese were peasant farmers producing rice on the fertile deltas of the Red River in the north and the Mekong in the south. The growing of rice was a communal activity carried out by the people of each village. Their community spirit and nationalism had been vital in fending off frequent Chinese attempts to conquer Vietnam. China was at least a hundred times larger in both area and population, but during their centuries of struggle against the Chinese the Vietnamese had generally been successful because they had perfected guerrilla warfare techniques (see page 2). Vietnamese guerrillas abandoned the towns, avoided frontal attacks, and harassed the Chinese into confusion and exhaustion.

Key terms

Nationalism
In the case of Vietnam, patriotic enthusiasm for an independent Vietnam.

Indochina
The countries now known as Vietnam, Cambodia and Laos.

During the nineteenth century the French replaced the Chinese as the greatest threat to Vietnamese independence. In their search for souls, trade, empire and glory, the French began attacking Vietnam in the mid-nineteenth century. By 1887 the countries subsequently known as Vietnam, Cambodia and Laos were under the control of the French, who referred to them collectively as **Indochina**. Vietnamese internal squabbles had facilitated the French triumph.

Key date
Indochina under French domination: 1887

However, the economic and political humiliations of French colonial rule soon caused articulate Vietnamese nationalists to unite to consider how to turn national resentment into rebellion. One nationalist who changed his name many times (partly to avoid detection) eventually became known throughout the world as Ho Chi Minh.

Key question
Who and what shaped and inspired Ho Chi Minh's nationalism and Communism?

b) The shaping of a Vietnamese leader

Ho Chi Minh's patriotism was shaped and inspired by Vietnamese history and by his father. His Communism was initially inspired by the **Russian Revolution** and then by the Chinese Communist Party.

i) Family background

Ho Chi Minh's father worked his way up to the rank of **mandarin**, then abandoned his family and became a travelling teacher and doctor. Ho inherited that service ethos and the urge to wander, free of family commitments.

Key terms

Russian Revolution
Began in 1917. It made Russia into the world's first Communist country, called the Union of Soviet Socialist Republics (USSR).

Mandarin
A high-ranking civil servant.

Self-determination
When a people has the right to decide how they will be governed.

ii) Years abroad

In 1911 Ho sailed away from Vietnam on a French merchant ship and it was 30 years before he returned. A major aim of these travels was to help to prepare himself for the eventual struggle for Vietnamese independence. On his travels he studied Westerners with interest and admiration. He was particularly impressed by the wealth and dynamism of New York City. He took any job, whether assistant pastry cook in London's five-star Carlton Hotel or painter of 'genuine' Chinese antiquities in France!

Intoxicated by French culture during a six-year stay in Paris, he denounced the corruption of the French language by English words such as '*le manager*'. He mixed with political radicals who discussed the Communist revolution currently convulsing Russia. Ho discovered that he shared many Communist beliefs, especially opposition to the colonialism whereby white nations dominated Asians and Africans.

Key dates

Ho Chi Minh out of Vietnam: 1911–41

Paris Peace Settlement at end of the First World War: 1919

President Wilson ignored Ho Chi Minh's pleas for greater Vietnamese freedom: 1919

iii) At the Paris Peace Conference (1919)

In 1919 US President Woodrow Wilson was in France masterminding the peace settlement at the end of the First World War. Wilson emphasised that all people had the right to **self-determination**. Ho was impressed by Wilson's ideas and the words of the American Declaration of Independence (1776), which said that all men were created equal and entitled to a say in who governed them. Although Ho was aware that these fine words could not always be taken literally and that Americans did not always apply them to non-European peoples, he nevertheless petitioned Wilson for democratic reforms in Vietnam. Although Wilson ignored him, Ho never ceased to call upon the Western democracies to live up to their declared principles. Meanwhile, he was optimistic that his fellow Vietnamese would soon revolt against their French oppressors just as ordinary Russians seemed to have rejected their upper-class government. 'It was patriotism and not Communism that originally inspired me', Ho said later.

iv) 'A professional revolutionary'

In 1924 Ho went to Moscow, where he met Soviet leaders such as Stalin, but he found that they were disappointingly uninterested in little Vietnam.

Profile: Ho Chi Minh 1890–1969

1890	–	Born to a Vietnamese nationalist of the mandarin class in central Vietnam
1911–41	–	In exile from Vietnam
1941	–	Returned to Vietnam and established League for the Independence of Vietnam (Vietminh) to combat Japanese occupation of Vietnam
1943	–	Contacted United States units in southern China, suggested co-operation against Japan. US officers helped to train Vietminh
1945	–	Declared newly independent Democratic Republic of Vietnam (DRV)
1945–6	–	Unsuccessful negotiations with the French. Increased Franco-Vietminh military clashes (the First Indochina War or the Franco-Vietminh War)
1950	–	DRV recognised by USSR and People's Republic of China
1950–3	–	Most of Vietnamese countryside under Vietminh control
1954	–	French decisively defeated at Dienbienphu. Geneva Accords 'temporarily' divided Vietnam (with Ho's Vietminh dominant in the North, and Bao Dai in the South), and promised elections in a reunified Vietnam in 1956
1959	–	Communist guerrillas (Vietcong) caused increased problems for Ngo Dinh Diem, ruler of South Vietnam. Ho increasingly in the background, but his followers dominated the North Vietnamese government in Hanoi. As 'Uncle Ho', he was increasingly the symbol of nationalism and national unity
1969	–	Died

Ho Chi Minh was one of the most influential Communist leaders of the twentieth century. He was the prime mover in the establishment of the unusually nationalistic Communist Party of Vietnam, which he led for three decades. He led the Vietnamese people to victory over the Japanese and the French, and then towards victory over the United States.

In an age when alternative Vietnamese leaders ruined their nationalist credentials by association with foreign powers, Ho Chi Minh's main appeal lay in his patriotism. Significantly, in the 1920s and 1930s, other Communists criticised him as too nationalistic.

He was willing to dilute or even ignore Communist ideology in order to maximise support. He successfully cultivated the 'common touch'. In the 1950s, American observers reported that the bulk of the population supported 'Uncle Ho', as he called himself. He was to be seen everywhere – villages, rice fields, meetings and the battlefront. As he never married and paid little attention to his blood relations, he really seemed like 'uncle' Ho to many of his fellow countrymen.

A Vietnamese nationalist cartoon from the early 1930s showed peasants driving out French colonial troops. The peasants shout 'Wipe out the gang of imperialists, mandarins, capitalists and big landlords!'

Key dates

Ho Chi Minh visited USSR: 1924

Ho Chi Minh established Indochinese Communist Party: 1929

Later in the year he visited China. By now he was fluent in Russian, Chinese, French and English, as well as Vietnamese. Ho began to organise Vietnamese students in China into a revolutionary league. 'I have become a professional revolutionary', he told a French friend in 1927.

Meanwhile back home, Vietnamese nationalists clashed with their French colonialist oppressors. Believing that the time would soon be ripe for revolution, Ho established the Indochinese Communist Party in Hong Kong in 1929.

Throughout the 1930s, Ho's writings were smuggled into Vietnam while he continued travelling carefully observing Communism in China and the Soviet Union, mentally preparing himself for the struggle for Vietnamese independence. That struggle was brought to a head by the actions of the Emperor Bao Dai, the French and the Japanese, all of whom gave Ho Chi Minh revolutionary opportunities.

Key question
How did Bao Dai increase Ho Chi Minh's popularity?

c) Bao Dai – the French puppet

One of the main reasons why Ho Chi Minh was a popular leader was because of the dearth of appealing alternatives. One such unappealing alternative was the Emperor Bao Dai, whose association with the French compared unfavourably with Ho's patriotism.

After Bao Dai was crowned emperor at the age of 12 in 1925, his French colonial masters sent him to Paris for a French education. Bao Dai returned to Vietnam aged 19. He attempted to govern through a cabinet of nationalists, but he lacked the forceful personality necessary to shake off French tutelage. He could not even stand up to his own mother, a formidable harridan addicted to gambling and betel nuts (a sort of Vietnamese chewing gum that rotted and blackened teeth). Powerless and bored, Bao Dai devoted himself to hunting animals and women. An American described him as a 'short, slippery-looking customer rather on the podgy side and freshly dipped in oil' who 'wore a fixed, oily grin that was vaguely reptilian'. When accused of spending too much time watching movies, he said it was in order to improve his English.

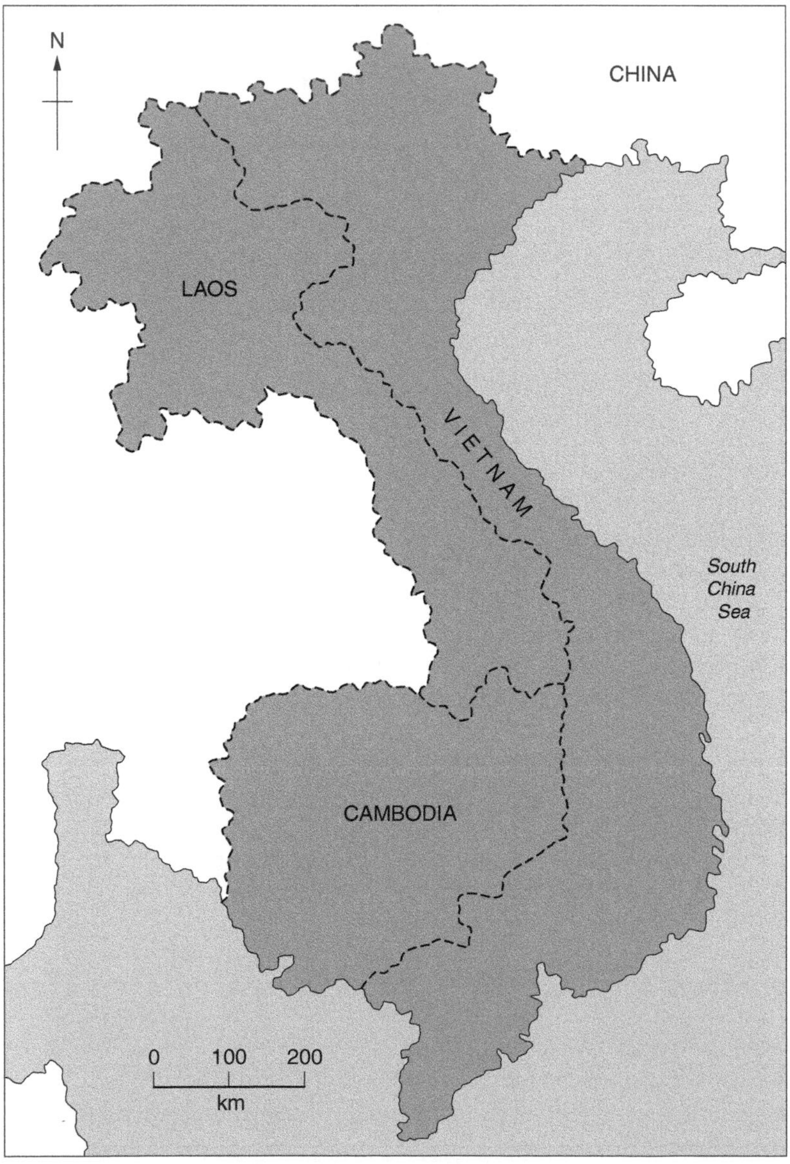

French Indochina.

Key dates

Second World War: 1939–45

Japan completed conquest of French Indochina; Ho Chi Minh returned to Vietnam: 1941

Vietnam Independence League (Vietminh) established: 1941

During the Second World War (1939–45) Bao Dai exchanged French domination for Japanese domination. The outbreak of war in Europe distracted European colonial powers such as France. When Hitler defeated France in June 1940, the expansionist Japanese demanded the right to have Japanese soldiers and bases in northern French Indochina (Vietnam). The French had to agree. In July 1941 the Japanese invaded southern Indochina and in December 1941 they attacked the United States and took over the colonial possessions of Britain and America.

i) The Vietnamese nationalists' search for leadership

Exasperated by Bao Dai's collaboration with foreign imperialists, Vietnamese nationalists desperately sought effective leadership. Many looked to Ho Chi Minh to provide it. In early 1941 Ho finally returned to his native land. He told other nationalists that all Vietnamese should unite to fight both the Japanese and their French collaborators in Indochina. Ho and his friends called their movement the Vietnam Independence League but it became more commonly known as the **Vietminh**. The Vietminh were both nationalists and Communists. They treated ordinary Vietnamese civilians with respect and promised a fairer distribution of wealth and power and freedom from foreigners. It was now that Ho changed his name. His new name of Ho Chi Minh meant 'Bringer of Light'.

Key term

Vietminh
Ho's Vietnamese nationalist followers were known as the Vietminh after 1941.

Profile: Emperor Bao Dai 1913–97

1913	– Born to the French puppet emperor of Vietnam. Educated in France
1926	– Succeeded to throne of Vietnam
1939–45	– During the Second World War, dominated first by the French colonial regime, then by the Japanese conquerors
1946	– Distrusted both the French and Ho Chi Minh, so fled to Hong Kong
1949	– French enticed him back, promising him greater independence and power. Known as 'Playboy Emperor'
1954	– By Geneva Accords, Vietnam 'temporarily' divided into Ho's Communist North and Bao Dai's non-Communist South. Bao Dai appointed Diem his prime minister
1955	– When national referendum called for South Vietnam to become a republic, he retired to France
1997	– Died in France

Bao Dai was the last reigning emperor of Vietnam. Had he been more able and hard-working, Vietnamese history might have been different. As it was, albeit reluctantly, he accepted domination by the Japanese, the French, and then Diem, and never exercised any real power or gained any real popularity.

Summary diagram: Ho Chi Minh and Vietnamese nationalism

2 | The United States and Vietnam, 1941–5

a) American ideas about Vietnam, 1941–5

Key question
What did President Roosevelt envisage for post-war Vietnam?

During their struggle against the Japanese (1941–5) the Americans had not given much thought to French Indochina. **President Roosevelt** was critical of French colonialism but uncertain about what to advocate for French Indochina after Japan was defeated.

In 1942 he wanted to inspire the French to fight against the Germans, so he talked of allowing France to retain colonies such as Indochina after the war. However, in 1943 he said that France had 'milked' Indochina for 100 years and left the Vietnamese people 'worse off than they were in the beginning', which made him feel that an **international trusteeship** would be the best thing for Indochina. He felt that Indochina offered strategically important naval bases so he proposed that America should be one trustee, along with Chiang Kai-shek's China and the USSR. Soon afterwards he changed his mind again and suggested that the French could retain Indochina if they promised to steer it towards independence. Finally, just before his death in 1945, he offered Indochina to Chiang. Already overburdened with problems, Chiang explained the traditional Vietnamese hatred of China and politely declined.

There are several possible explanations for Roosevelt's apparent inconsistency over the fate of French Indochina. He tended to think out loud, to test his ideas on people, and to speak to win favour with a particular audience. He was also preoccupied with winning the war: 'I still do not want to get mixed up in any Indochina decision', he told a colleague on 1 January 1945. 'Action at this time is premature.' The experts in his State

Key figure

Franklin Roosevelt
1882–1945; US president 1933–45. In his fourth and final term he gave some thought to the best post-war government for Vietnam, but made no practical impact on that country.

Key term

International trusteeship
President Roosevelt envisaged several countries, including the US, guiding post-war Vietnam towards independence.

Department disagreed amongst themselves and offered him conflicting advice: the Far East division criticised French rule and claimed that unless France allowed self-government in Indochina there would be bloodshed and unrest there for years; the European specialists were pro-French, seeing France as an ally in Europe, and they urged the president to refrain from any policy towards Indochina that might alienate the French.

Key question
Was US hostility to Ho Chi Minh inevitable?

b) Ho's early relations with the Americans

i) Ho and the Americans in the Second World War

One of the main reasons the Americans got involved in Vietnam was their dislike of Ho Chi Minh. It is therefore important to trace the early relationship between Ho and America in order to see whether their enmity was inevitable and justifiable.

Ho was impressed by the military and economic might of the United States, and hoped that he could gain American support for Vietnamese independence. Ho's Vietminh co-operated with the Americans in the fight against the Japanese. An American doctor saved Ho's life in July 1945. A group of Americans had found Ho looking like 'a pile of bones covered with dry yellow skin', suffering from dysentery, malaria and several other tropical diseases for which the doctor gave him treatment. At this time, the Americans admired Ho's Vietminh troops and their brilliant General Giap.

Profile: General Giap c. 1911–

c. 1911	– Born to an anti-colonialist scholar-gentry family in North Vietnam
1920s	– Educated at University of Hanoi, became a history teacher
1926	– Joined Communist movement
1930	– Arrested by French for supporting student strikes
Mid-1930s	– Joined ICP (see page 10). Read books on guerrilla tactics; decided slow, patient 'people's war' was best
1937	– Gained a law degree
1945	– Minister of the Interior in Ho Chi Minh's new Democratic Republic of Vietnam (DRV)
1954	– Defeated French at decisive battle of Dienbienphu, which brought French colonialist regime to an end. Became deputy prime minister of North Vietnam
1960s	– Vital work in defeating American forces supporting anti-Communist regime in South Vietnam
1973	– United States' departure from Vietnam owed much to Giap
1976–80	– Defence Minister of newly united Communist Vietnam
1982	– Retired from government

Giap was important in that his military strategy and tactics played a vital role in defeating first the French and then the United States, which brought about an independent Communist Vietnam.

ii) Ho's declaration of independence

Ho knew how to flatter Americans. He enlisted their aid in drafting the speech he made before hundreds of thousands of his fellow countrymen on 2 September 1945 after the Japanese surrender in the Second World War. In that speech Ho declared the independence of the Democratic Republic of Vietnam. He began by quoting from the American Declaration of Independence:

> 'All men are created equal. They are endowed by their Creator with certain inalienable rights; among these are Life, Liberty and the pursuit of Happiness.' This immortal statement was made in the Declaration of Independence of the United States of America in 1776 ... The Declaration of the French Revolution made in 1791 ... also states: 'All men are born free and with equal rights ...'. Those are undeniable truths ... The French have fled, the Japanese have capitulated, Emperor Bao Dai has abdicated. Our people have broken the chains which for nearly a century have fettered us and have won independence for the Fatherland. The whole Vietnamese people, animated by a common purpose, are determined to fight to the bitter end against any attempt by the French colonialists to reconquer our country. We are convinced that the Allied nations [led by America, Britain and the Soviet Union] have acknowledged the principles of self-determination and equality of nations ... [and] will not refuse to acknowledge the independence of Vietnam ... The entire Vietnamese people are determined to mobilise all their physical and mental strength, to sacrifice their lives and property, in order to safeguard their independence and freedom.

It is difficult to say whether Ho was genuinely optimistic that the Americans would support him. In the summer of 1941 President Roosevelt announced that he wanted 'to see sovereign rights and self-government restored to those who have been forcibly deprived of them'. During the Second World War, as Ho pointed out in his declaration of independence, Roosevelt frequently repeated these sentiments.

Key dates

Ho declared independence of Democratic Republic of Vietnam (DRV): 2 September 1945

Death of President Roosevelt; succeeded by Vice-President Harry Truman: April 1945

iii) Ho and Truman

In April 1945 Roosevelt died in office and was succeeded by Vice-President Harry Truman. Truman sided with the European specialists in the State Department. He assured the French that America recognised their pre-eminent position in Indochina, while expressing the hope that they would grant more self-government to the Vietnamese. In August 1945 General Giap had told the Hanoi crowds that America was a 'good friend', being 'a democracy without territorial ambitions'. However, at the end of the year, in conversation with Bao Dai (who had abdicated in favour of Ho and agreed to be Ho's 'supreme adviser') Ho was cynical:

> They [the Americans] are only interested in replacing the French ... They want to reorganise our economy in order to control it. They are **capitalists** to the core. All that counts for them is business.

Between October 1945 and February 1946 eight messages from Ho to Washington went unanswered. Due to ever-increasing American anti-Communism, the US had stopped co-operating with Ho, even though the USSR still recognised French rule over Vietnam.

Key term

Capitalists
Those who believe in a free market economy with no state intervention – the opposite of the Communist economic philosophy.

Summary diagram: The United States and Vietnam 1941–5

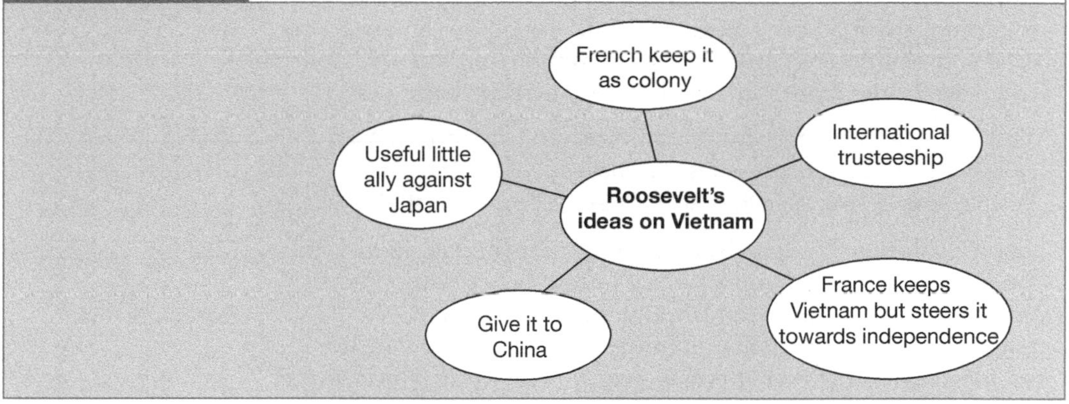

Key question
Why did Truman get involved in Vietnam?

3 | The Reasons for the Early American Involvement in Vietnam

Although American intelligence agents in Hanoi reported to Truman in September 1945 that the traditionally nationalistic Vietnamese were 'determined to maintain their independence even at the cost of their lives', the Truman administration helped to restore French rule. Why?

a) US motives: an overview

Americans believed after the Second World War that Communism threatened international free trade and the democratic ideals which were important to American well-being and security. Therefore, America became involved in Vietnam for a mixture of economic and ideological reasons. Individuals were also important.

As a new and non-elected president, Truman felt he had to appear tough and decisive in foreign policy. Relatively ignorant about the rest of the world, he relied heavily upon men like Dean Acheson, whom he made Secretary of State in 1949. Acheson believed in standing up to Communists. Truman and Acheson's interpretation of events in Europe and the Far East led to the first significant American commitment to Vietnam. It is therefore necessary to look at those events.

b) Events in Vietnam in 1945–6

During the Second World War America and its allies had agreed that Chiang's Chinese Nationalists would take the surrender of the Japanese forces in northern Vietnam, while the British would take their surrender in southern Vietnam. Japan surrendered in August 1945 and the Chinese and British moved into Vietnam as agreed. Vietnam was in chaos; Japanese troops waited to be returned home, Chinese Nationalists pillaged the north, while Ho declared Vietnamese independence and struggled for power with other Vietnamese factions. In September 1945 some Vietminh clashed with French soldiers released by the Japanese in Saigon and some consider this the outbreak of the first Vietnam War (others date it from November 1946). During 1945 fighting between Ho's

Vietminh and the French escalated as increasing numbers of French troops were transported to Indochina by the British, who sympathised with France's desire to retain its empire. America went along with this because Truman did not want to alienate the French. Ho preferred the French to the Chinese. The French, he said:

> are weak. Colonialism is dying. The white man is finished in Asia. But if the Chinese stay now, they will never go. I prefer to sniff French shit for five years than eat Chinese shit for the rest of my life.

Chiang's Chinese Nationalist forces soon returned home to deal with the Chinese Communists, but fighting between the French and the Vietminh continued throughout 1946. Keen to compensate for her humiliation during the Second World War and to retain wealthy southern Vietnam, France was reluctant to give in and get out altogether.

Key date

Outbreak of Franco-Vietminh War: November 1946

Profile: Harry Truman 1884–1972

1884		– Born to a mule trader and farmer in Missouri
1935		– Elected senator for Missouri (Democrat)
1941–5		– United States in the Second World War – Truman excelled on Senate Committee investigating National Defence
1945	April	– Roosevelt died, Truman became president
1947		– Effectively declared Cold War in 'Truman Doctrine' speech: said United States would help any country that resisted Communism
1949		– Set up NATO (North Atlantic Treaty Organisation), the Western anti-Communist military alliance. When China became Communist, Republicans accused Truman and the Democrats of 'losing China'
1950		– Senator Joseph McCarthy (Republican) said Truman's State Department contained Communists; beginning of paranoid Cold War period
		– When Communist North Korea invaded non-Communist South Korea, Truman sent United States forces to restore the *status quo*
1950–3		– Korean War, often known as 'Truman's War'; increasingly unpopular
1953		– Retired to Missouri
1972		– Died

Harry Truman was important in relation to Vietnam because he made the decision to oppose Communism throughout the world and began the United States' involvement in the Cold War against the USSR and the People's Republic of China. With aid to the French in their struggle to defeat the Communist Ho Chi Minh's fight for Vietnamese independence, he started the American involvement in Vietnam, although it could be argued that the commitment was still reversible at his death.

Key terms

Containment
Truman's policy whereby the US would attempt to contain or halt any further spread of Communism.

Kremlin
The headquarters of the Soviet government in Moscow.

Cold War
The struggle between the USA and USSR from the mid-1940s to the mid-1980s. US and Soviet forces never met in combat – hence the 'cold' war.

United Nations
Set up in 1945 to try to keep world peace.

c) US hostility to the USSR

The French appealed to a sympathetic President Truman for aid, cleverly maintaining that Ho was part of a worldwide Communist conspiracy orchestrated by Moscow and likely to lead to Soviet domination everywhere. America feared and loathed Communism and had long been suspicious of the Soviet Union.

After the Second World War, the US feared the actual Soviet domination of Eastern Europe, and the possible Soviet domination of Iran, Greece and Turkey. This convinced the Truman administration to adopt the policy of '**containment**' of Communism.

By 1947 the Truman administration felt that Ho was probably a puppet of the **Kremlin**. This was the main reason why America gave increasing support to the French in Vietnam. Some State Department specialists feared that the administration was over-simplifying matters and during 1948 pointed out that Ho had made friendly gestures to America and that the Vietnamese Communists were *not* subservient to the Kremlin, but the general atmosphere in early **Cold War** America was not conducive to such subtleties of analysis.

In 1949 Acheson said that it was 'irrelevant' to ask whether Ho was 'as much nationalist as Commie' for 'all Stalinists in colonial areas are nationalists'. This American conviction that what was at stake in Vietnam was the expansion of Communism (rather than a Vietnamese war for independence) was eventually to embroil America in a bloody and disastrous war there. However, the distinction between Ho's nationalism and Communism *was* relevant. Ho was always a nationalist first. Stalin recognised this. The Americans did not.

Key dates

Start of Cold War between the USA and USSR: 1945–9

China became Communist: October 1949

French established 'independent' Associated State of Vietnam under Bao Dai: 1949

USSR and China recognised Ho's Democratic Republic of Vietnam: January 1950

Start of 'McCarthyism' (fanatical anti-Communism in the USA); USA recognised Associated State of Vietnam: February 1950

MAAG established: September 1950

d) US hostility to Communist China

Late in 1949 Mao Zedong's Communists took over China. Under attack from the Republicans for having 'lost' China and fearing further Communist expansion in Asia, Acheson persuaded Truman to give more money to help French forces in Indochina. US fears of a worldwide Communist offensive seemed justified when Ho (having failed to obtain American recognition in exchange for a promise of neutrality in the Cold War) persuaded China and the Soviets to recognise his Democratic Republic of Vietnam in January 1950. In the next month, the United States finally recognised the supposedly independent 'Associated State of Vietnam' that had been set up by the French in 1949.

e) The McCarthy hysteria and the Korean War

In February 1950 Senator Joseph McCarthy began whipping many Americans into an anti-Communist frenzy. When Communist North Korea attacked South Korea in 1950 the United States mobilised the **United Nations** in a war to halt Communist aggression in the Far East.

According to America's military leaders, the Joint Chiefs of Staff (JCS), the world balance of power was at stake in Southeast Asia, an area full of strategically vital materials (see page 31), where American allies such as Japan and Australia might be vulnerable to Communist attack. When Chinese troops poured into Korea, American fears of Chinese expansionism were confirmed. In this situation and atmosphere it is not surprising that the Truman administration decided that Indochina must not be allowed to fall into Communist hands.

f) US support for France

Even before the Korean War, the Truman administration concluded that the French were invaluable allies against Communism in both Indochina and Europe, and therefore deserving of American assistance. Acheson and Truman were very conscious that France was important to the stability of the Western alliance in Europe and to **NATO**. When France linked Franco-American co-operation in Europe with American aid in Indochina, it served to confirm the US belief that they must become more involved in that region. In May 1950, Truman offered $10 million to support the French military effort, and established a US Military Assistance Advisory Group (MAAG) in Saigon. Although at this stage there were only 15 American military officers in MAAG, by the end of 1950, the US had given France $100 million, along with aircraft, patrol boats, **napalm bombs** and ground combat machinery.

Key terms

NATO
The North Atlantic Treaty Organisation was an anti-Communist Western military alliance, established by the USA in 1949.

Napalm bombs
Bombs containing jellied petrol.

Summary diagram: Reasons for early American involvement in Vietnam

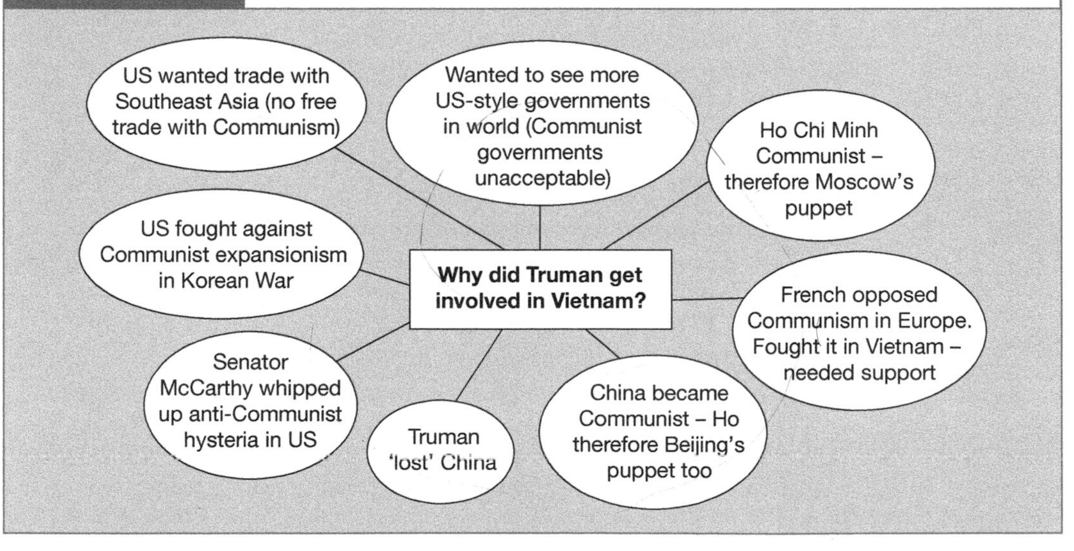

4 | 'These Situations … Have a Way of Snowballing'

Key question
To what extent had Truman committed the USA in Vietnam?

By 1954 the Americans were more convinced than the French of the importance of Vietnam in the global struggle against Communism, and America was paying nearly 80 per cent of the French bill for Indochina. Truman had given over $2 billion to the French war effort and $50 million for economic and technical aid to the Vietnamese people.

Franco-American relations were not always smooth: some Americans in Vietnam saw the French rather than the Vietminh as the enemy. In order to keep the anti-colonialist Americans happy, the French in 1949 had recognised Vietnam's 'independence' under their feeble puppet emperor, Bao Dai, on whose behalf they kept control of Vietnam's army, finance and foreign policy. Bao Dai expended most of his limited energy in a long-running dispute with the French High Commissioner over which of them should use the presidential palace in Saigon. He told an American diplomat that after his brief co-operation with Ho and exile he had returned to Vietnam only because the French had promised independence. Near to tears he asked: 'This independence, what is it? Where is it? Do you see it?'

This French unwillingness to grant real independence caused anxiety within the Truman administration. Some criticised Bao Dai and feared that France and America were being distracted from the more important issue of European defence against Communism by this involvement in Indochina. One State Department Far East specialist admitted that 'the trouble is that none of us knows enough about Indochina'.

A Defence Department official warned in November 1950 that America was becoming dangerously and deeply involved:

> we are gradually increasing our stake in the outcome of the struggle … we are dangerously close to the point of being so deeply committed that we may find ourselves completely committed even to direct intervention. These situations, unfortunately, have a way of snowballing.

That official was right. Fearful of the Communist governments of Russia and China, and believing that Ho was their puppet, the Truman administration had got the United States involved in French-dominated Vietnam.

5 | Key Debates on the Truman Years

As the United States did not consider Vietnam important before the Second World War, historians are interested in why the region became so important after the Second World War.

Key terms

Orthodox historians
American historians of the Cold War who see their country as bravely and idealistically standing up to the 'evil' of Communism.

Revisionist historians
American historians who criticise US motives in the Cold War as aggressive and acquisitive.

a) A key debate: why did the US become involved in the Cold War?

The United States' involvement in French Indochina under Truman is part of the wider debate on the origins of the Cold War.

i) The orthodox interpretation

Orthodox historians of the Cold War see the United States resisting Communist aggression and expansion. They usually emphasise US ideological motivation.

ii) The revisionist interpretation

Revisionist historians emphasise the United States' desire to shape the world in its own image. Revisionists emphasise the economic motivation behind US foreign policy, and criticise it as aggressive and acquisitive.

iii) The post-revisionist interpretation

Post-revisionist historians refuse to blame everything on the USSR, recognising that both great powers were ambitious, aggressive, with security concerns and frequent mutual misunderstandings.

Key term

Post-revisionist historians Historians who consider the USA and the USSR equally responsible for the Cold War.

iv) Vietnam in the Cold War context

It was the Cold War context that made little Vietnam important to the United States: State Department official Dean Rusk (see page 60) knew at the time that 'this is part of an international war'. 'Had American leaders not thought that all international events were connected to the Cold War there would have been no American war in Vietnam' (Schulzinger, 1997).

b) A key debate: what was Truman's motivation?

i) Orthodox interpretations

Orthodox historians, such as Herring (1979), Schulzinger (1997), and Duiker (2000), considered Truman's involvement in Vietnam to be part of his containment strategy. Having told the American public in his Truman Doctrine speech of 1947 that the world was divided into two very different spheres, and indicated that some kind of conflict was inevitable, there was great public pressure (Blum, 1982) on Truman to continue to hold the line against any Communist advance.

Some historians (such as Shaplen, 1966) emphasise that as part of the containment policy, the Truman administration felt it had to support its ally, France, in the French struggle to retain Indochina, as a strong France was essential to help contain Communism in Europe. However, Leffler (1997) insists that the Truman administration's policy was, 'not determined by the imperative of their European policy … but by their conviction that the West could not afford to lose Indochina'. While Leffler sees Truman motivated primarily by the desire for security for the United States, he criticises Truman for exaggerating the Soviet threat and the failure to see that the nationalistic Ho Chi Minh was a very different leader from the Soviets puppet rulers of Eastern Europe.

ii) Revisionist interpretations

Revisionist historians such as Kolko (1985) say that it was the markets and raw materials of Southeast Asia that motivated Roosevelt then Truman's interest in Vietnam. According to Kolko, the United States aimed, 'to create an integrated, essentially capitalist world framework out of the chaos of the Second World War and the remnant of the colonial system' – Vietnam became important because a Communist, nationalist revolution there posed a threat to this global capitalist system. If this revolution succeeded, others might follow. Some historians, such as Schaller (1985), stressed that the United States did not want those markets simply for itself, but wanted its important trading partners France, Britain and Japan to have continued access to those markets.

Key term

Geopolitical Political positions governed by the United States' geographical location in the world.

iii) Post-revisionist interpretations

Historians such as Anderson (2005) recognise that there were many factors involved in Truman's involvement in Vietnam. By the end of Truman's presidency, says Anderson, '**geopolitical** strategy, economics, domestic US politics, and cultural arrogance shaped the growing in American involvement in Vietnam'.

c) A key debate: to what extent had Truman committed the United States in Vietnam?

'The Vietnam war was not an American war' during the Truman years, according to Anderson (2005). Although a Vietminh victory would constitute 'an unacceptable strategic gain' for the Communist world, says Anderson, American dislike of French colonialism 'restrained US involvement. US policy decisions had defined Indochina as strategically important, but those decisions had not yet committed the United States to the Vietnam War.'

While Anderson apparently exonerates Truman from blame for what became a highly unpopular American involvement, Herring felt the Vietnam involvement was the virtually inevitable result of Harry Truman's containment policy. 'It was the mind set of the Truman administration which ultimately led to that tragic and misguided war', agreed Byrnes (2000).

Some key books in the debates

D. Anderson, *The Vietnam War* (New York, 2005).
R.M. Blum, *Drawing the Line: The Origins of the American Containment Policy in East Asia* (New York, 1982).
M. Byrnes, *The Truman Years* (London, 2000).
W. Duiker, *Ho Chi Minh* (New York, 2000).
G. Herring, *America's Longest War* (New York, 1979).
G. Kolko, *Anatomy of a War* (New York, 1985).
M. Leffler, *A Preponderance of Power: National Security, the Truman Administration, and the Cold War* (Stanford, 1997).
M. Schaller, *The American Occupation of Japan: the Origins of the Cold War in Asia* (New York, 1985).
R.D. Schulzinger, *A Time for War: The United States and Vietnam, 1941–75* (New York, 1997).
R. Shaplen, *The Lost Revolution: The United States in Vietnam, 1946–68* (New York, 1966).

Summary diagram: Vietnam and foreigners

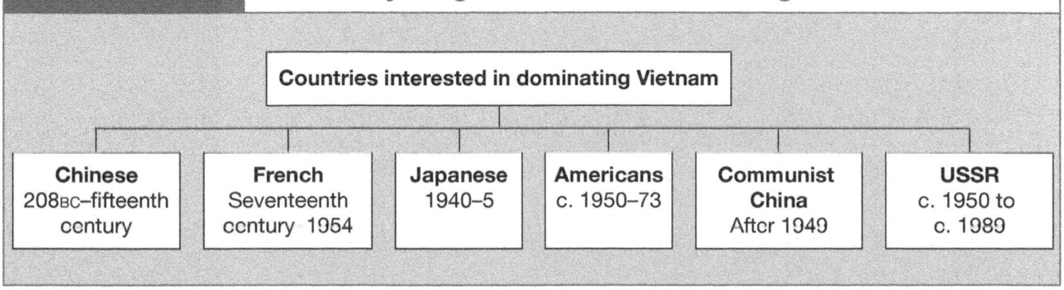

3 Eisenhower and Two Vietnams

POINTS TO CONSIDER

A century of French involvement in Indochina ended in 1954, at a conference held at Geneva in Switzerland. Laos, Cambodia and a divided Vietnam emerged from this conference. Truman's successor, President Eisenhower, became the sponsor of the southern part of Vietnam, while Ho Chi Minh led the north. This chapter looks at:

- Ho, Giap and the French failure in Indochina
- Dienbienphu – the debate over American intervention
- The Geneva Conference on Indochina, 1954
- Two Vietnams and two leaders
- Assessment of Eisenhower's policy
- The key debates

Key dates

1949		China became Communist
1950		Diem made influential friends in the United States
1954	Spring	Eisenhower decided against US intervention to help French at Dienbienphu
	April	Eisenhower's domino theory
	May	French defeated at Dienbienphu
		International conference discussed French Indochina at Geneva
	July	Geneva Accords: Vietnam 'temporarily' divided
	September	Establishment of Southeast Asia Treaty Organisation
	November	Eisenhower sent General Collins to help/assess Diem
		Creation of Military Assistance Advisory Group (MAAG) to help South Vietnam
1955	May	Diem decisively defeated religious sects in South Vietnam
	October	Diem held 'fair' elections in South Vietnam

1956	Date set at Geneva for national elections in Vietnam – these never happened, due to American interference Ho Chi Minh's government brutally suppressed revolts in North
1957	USSR proposed admission of North and South Vietnam to the United Nations
1960	Communist disruption of South Vietnam had dramatically increased The second Indochina War or Vietnam War began

Key question
Why was France unable to keep control of Vietnam?

1 | Ho, Giap and the French Failure in Indochina

Eisenhower inherited Truman's commitment to the French and their puppet emperor, Bao Dai. He continued to finance the French military effort and the extravagant emperor whose other sources of revenue included gambling casinos, brothels and opium dens in Saigon. However, the French continued to lose ground. Why?

a) Bao Dai's unpopularity and Ho's popularity

The French puppet emperor, Bao Dai (see page 13), was never popular in Vietnam. In late 1951 a US official said Bao Dai's government:

> is in no sense the servant of the people. It has no grass roots. It therefore has no appeal whatsoever to the masses … Revolution will continue and Ho Chi Minh will remain a popular hero so long as 'independence' leaders with French support are simply native mandarins [the Vietnamese ruling class] who are succeeding foreign mandarins [the French].

The extravagant emperor and his French puppet masters were simply too unpopular to remain in power. In sharp contrast, Ho was seen by many Vietnamese as a patriot who cared about the ordinary people of Vietnam (see page 11). His fairer redistribution of land and educational and health care programmes helped to win over the Vietnamese peasantry.

b) Vietnamese rebel strengths

Ho Chi Minh compared the struggle between the French and the Vietminh to a fight between an elephant and a grasshopper. Although the French seemed more powerful, Ho's Vietminh proved elusive and determined. 'You can kill ten of my men for every one I kill of yours', Ho told one Frenchman, 'but even at those odds, you will lose and I will win'. The French had more men and materials but Vietminh guerrilla tactics utilised the physical geography of the country. The Vietminh would make surprise attacks then retreat to Western Vietnam's jungle and mountains, which were enveloped by monsoon mist for half the year. 'If only the Vietnamese would face us in a set battle', lamented one French officer, 'how we should crush them'.

The Chinese supplied Ho with weapons, including the latest American ones, captured from Chiang's defeated nationalists (see pages 18–19). Most important of all, the Vietminh fought for an inspiring cause, a free and more **egalitarian** Vietnam. Vietnamese rebel strengths were such that the French, despite all their apparent advantages, found it very difficult to win the war.

Key term

Egalitarian
In this context, a Vietnam in which people had greater social, economic and political equality.

c) Vo Nguyen Giap

The brilliant Vietminh military commander, Vo Nguyen Giap (see page 15), was of great importance in the defeat of the French. It is important to look at what shaped, inspired and sustained him in the long, hard fight against the French that few outside Vietnam expected him to win.

i) The making of a fanatical nationalist and Communist

Giap's father was a mandarin who had participated in anti-French uprisings in the 1880s. Both he and one of his daughters were 'subversives' who died in French prisons. Like Ho, Giap admired French culture but loathed French colonialism. The French had Giap on their list of revolutionary nationalists from the time he was 13 years old. He attended Vietnam's only university, at Hanoi, and in 1937 joined the Indochinese Communist Party. Another of his sisters was shot by the French for being a Communist. Giap felt the Communist emphasis on co-operation and sharing fitted in with Vietnamese traditions and was therefore appropriate for Vietnam. He read widely on Vietnamese history, Communism and military strategy.

ii) Building up the Vietminh forces

In 1940 Giap met Ho and impressed him with his military knowledge. Giap and Ho collected dedicated individuals known as cadres around them. By 1944 Giap had trained several hundred military cadres. Hiding from the Japanese and the French in the jungles, they were sometimes forced to survive on insects, roots and tree bark. In true Communist fashion, all had to contribute to community life in these years: Giap became chief dishwasher, having been voted out of the chef's job. In 1943 the French killed his wife, which added to his fanaticism. From 1944 he commanded the Vietnamese Liberation Army or Vietminh (see page 13). His Vietminh forces numbered around 5000. At this time, he got on well with the Americans who gave him his first modern weapons for use against the Japanese. He made pro-American references in his speech on 'independence day' after the Japanese defeat. During 1946 he continued to improve the armaments of the 5000-strong army of Ho's Democratic Republic of Vietnam.

iii) Giap and personal discipline

Ho was alarmed when Giap had a public and passionate love affair with a famous dancer, attended night clubs and began wearing fashionable Western dress. He quickly introduced Giap to a serious and well-educated woman from a distinguished family. Giap married her and the embarrassing criticisms ceased.

iv) War against the French

In November 1946 the Vietminh officially declared war on the French. Giap improved military training and set out plans for revolutionary war. He would start with guerrilla warfare to wear down the enemy, then slowly move to set-piece battles as his army grew stronger. Like Ho, Giap paid great attention to winning over the ordinary people.

By 1952 Giap commanded over a quarter of a million regular soldiers and a militia nearing two million. Each army division was supported by 40,000 porters carrying rice or ammunition along jungle trails and over mountain passes. Many of the porters were women, the so-called 'long-haired army', whom the Vietminh found to be more effective than the male porters. Giap's soldiers willingly suffered for their country and their freedom:

> We had to cross mountains and jungles, marching at night and sleeping by day to avoid enemy bombing. We slept in foxholes [bomb craters], or simply alongside the trail. We each carried a rifle, ammunition and hand grenades, and our packs contained a blanket, a mosquito net and a change of clothes. We each had a week's supply of rice, which we refilled at depots along the way. We ate greens and bamboo shoots, picked in the jungle, and occasionally villagers would give us a bit of meat. By then I had been in the Vietminh for nine years, and I was accustomed to it.

Units held self-criticism sessions, during which errors were admitted and forgiven.

Key term

Diplomatic
In international relations, 'diplomacy' means relations between nations; a diplomat represents his nation abroad; nations that fully recognise each other have diplomatic relations.

v) Winning the hearts and minds of the people

Giap's soldiers followed set rules when dealing with civilians: be polite; be fair; return everything borrowed; do not bully; do not fraternise with women; try not to cause damage and if you do, pay for it.

Key date

China became Communist: 1949

vi) Chinese support

Mao's 1949 triumph (see page 19) had transformed the situation. Mao gave Giap and Ho **diplomatic** recognition, more armaments, advice, and sanctuary in China if Vietnamese soldiers were in trouble.

vii) Conclusions

The French inability to win in Vietnam owed much to Giap's fanatical determination to defeat them, and to the way he trained, deployed and inspired his army. Chinese aid was also important. It then took a crucial battle to make the French give up.

d) Dienbienphu (1954)

While Ho and Giap went from strength to strength, the French had problems. They tried what they called 'yellowing' their army (enlisting native Vietnamese) but did not trust these new recruits and gave them little responsibility. The Vietminh strategy exasperated the French. 'If only', one French officer said, 'the Vietnamese would face us in a set battle, how we should crush them'. In France itself, many people were beginning to lose heart and interest in Indochina, which gave great importance to the great military struggle between the French and the Vietminh at **Dienbienphu**.

Key term

Dienbienphu Site of decisive Vietminh military victory over France in 1954.

In 1954, the French decided to concentrate their efforts on Dienbienphu, which was located in a valley in the north of Vietnam. The French seized Dienbienphu intending to cut off Vietminh supply lines into the neighbouring Kingdom of Laos, a French ally. They built a fortress there in the hope of drawing the Vietminh into a set-piece battle. Both the French and the Americans thought that Dienbienphu could be held indefinitely. The French and the Americans failed to anticipate that, with great ingenuity, Giap's forces would be able to bombard the fortress from the surrounding high ground. Thousands of peasant volunteers had dismantled heavy, long-range guns and taken them piece by piece up into the surrounding hills. There, they successfully camouflaged the guns

Ho Chi Minh (centre) and Vo Nguyen Giap (on Ho's far left) plan the attack on Dienbienphu.

Key date
French defeated at Dienbienphu: May 1954

until they were ready to be fired. Despite (or because of) the comfort afforded by 18 prostitutes and 49,000 bottles of wine, the French garrison did badly in the several months' struggle at Dienbienphu.

Thus, French arrogance and Vietnamese ingenuity played an important part in the French failure in Indochina.

Summary diagram: Ho, Giap and the French failure in Indochina

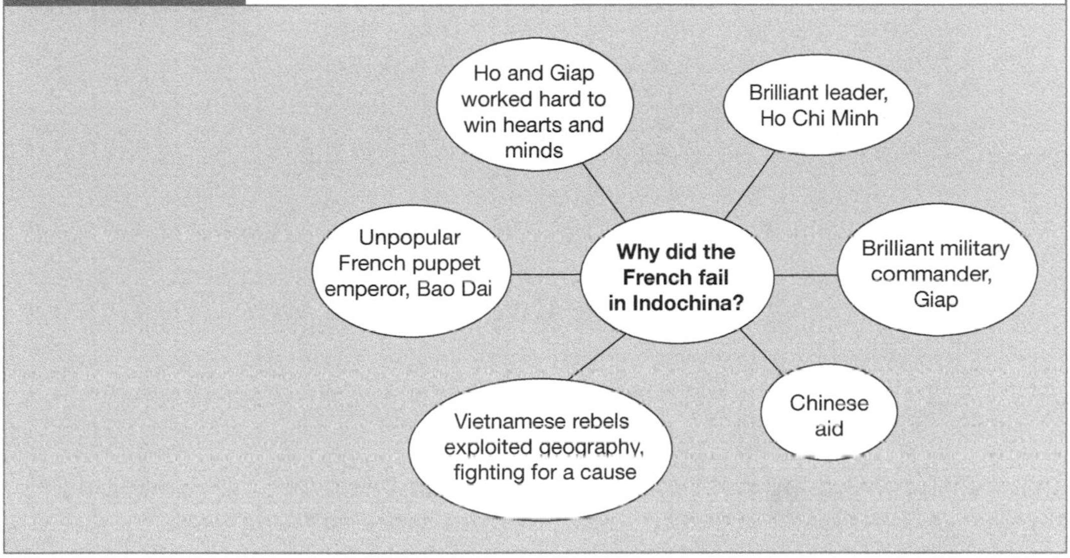

Key question
To what extent was Eisenhower committed to helping the French in Vietnam before Dienbienphu?

2 | Dienbienphu – The Debate over American Intervention

a) Eisenhower and the French before Dienbienphu

Not long before the showdown at Dienbienphu, Eisenhower had given the French $385 million worth of armaments for an offensive against the Vietminh. In return the French promised to grant Indochina greater independence. There was a considerable debate raging within the Eisenhower administration about the extent to which America should be involved in Vietnam. Many questions were being asked:

- Was Southeast Asia vital to US security?
- If Southeast Asia was vital to US security, should America get involved in Indochina?
- If America did get involved in Indochina, should that involvement take the form of financial aid to the French, US military advisers assisting the French, US air and/or sea support for the French, or the sending of US ground troops to Indochina?

Profile: Dwight D. Eisenhower 1890–1969

1890	–	Born to a poor family in Texas; moved to Kansas
1917–18	–	Distinguished service in First World War
1942–5	–	Supreme Commander of US troops in Europe in Second World War
1945–8	–	Army Chief of Staff
1950	–	Truman appointed him Supreme Commander of NATO
1952	–	Elected president (Republican); main campaign promises included ending the Korean War and '**rollback**'
1953	–	Ended Korean War; refused to speak out against McCarthyism
1954	–	Rejected Geneva Accords and helped to establish 'independent' state of South Vietnam. Set up Southeast Asia Treaty Organisation (SEATO)
1956	–	Did nothing when USSR quashed anti-Communist uprising in Hungary; re-elected president
1961	–	Retired to Pennsylvania
1969	–	Died

Eisenhower's importance in the Vietnam War is that he continued and increased American involvement there. Initially, he continued Truman's policy of helping the French to fight Communism in Vietnam. As the French withdrew, he helped to set up the South Vietnamese state, in defiance of the Geneva Accords (see page 36). American prestige was thereby committed to the maintenance of South Vietnam. However, he only sent in military advisers to help South Vietnam, not combat troops.

Key term

Rollback
The Eisenhower administration talked a great deal about going beyond President Truman's containment of Communism to a pushing back of Communism in places where it was already established.

- Did the US have enough troops to make a difference in Indochina?
- Was victory possible in Indochina in conjunction with the French or if America were there alone?
- Was America willing to risk a clash with China over intervention in Indochina?
- How much was America willing to do without allied (including UN) support?

Like most of the men in his administration, Eisenhower believed that Southeast Asia was vital to US security. However, he was more moderate than many in his views on what America should do there. He considered it easier and cheaper to pay other countries to help defend America: Communism threatened America and the French were fighting Communism, so it was better to pay the French to fight Communism than to send American boys to do it. However, when the French got into trouble early in 1954 Eisenhower responded to their pleas for extra help by sending US bombers accompanied by 200 American technicians. Eisenhower had now put the first American personnel into Vietnam. He told Congress in February 1954 that he disliked putting these Americans in danger but that 'we must not lose Asia'.

By March, the situation at Dienbienphu was beginning to look hopeless, so France requested a US air strike against the Vietminh in order to strengthen the French negotiating position at Geneva. Eisenhower gave the request serious consideration. Meanwhile, throughout the weeks of struggle at Dienbienphu, American schoolchildren prayed for the French to defeat the atheist Communists.

Key question
What were the American arguments for helping the French at Dienbienphu?

b) Arguments for American intervention at Dienbienphu

Eisenhower was concerned about Vietnam and Dienbienphu for several reasons:

- French strength was being drained away in Vietnam and Eisenhower wanted France to be a strong NATO member to help defend Western Europe against the Soviet threat.
- The French threatened to be unhelpful about European defence arrangements and to get out of Indochina unless America aided them there.
- In the presidential election campaign Eisenhower had rejected Truman's policy of containment of Communism and had advocated liberation of Communist countries ('rollback'). As yet he had not 'liberated' a single soul from Communism.
- Eisenhower knew that Truman's popularity had suffered greatly because he had 'lost' China and he did not want the Democrats to say he had 'lost' Vietnam.
- In a speech broadcast on TV and radio in March 1954, Secretary of State John Foster Dulles (see page 32) made it clear that the administration feared Chinese expansion in Indochina. He pointed out that the Vietminh were trained and equipped by the Chinese.
- Most important of all, Eisenhower felt that the loss of Vietnam to Communism would affect the global balance of power. He feared that if the US allowed Vietnam to fall to Communism, other Southeast Asian countries would follow. At a press conference in April 1954 Eisenhower explained that Vietnam was vitally important to America:

> You have the specific value of a locality in its production of materials [rice, rubber, coal, iron ore] that the world needs. You have the possibility that many human beings pass under a dictatorship that is inimical to the free world. You have the broader considerations that might follow what you would call the 'falling domino' principle … You have a row of dominoes set up, you knock over the first one, and what will happen to the last one is the certainty that it will go over very quickly. So you could have the beginning of a disintegration that would have the most profound influences … You are talking about millions and millions of people.

Key date
Eisenhower's domino theory: April 1954

Eisenhower privately said that 'in certain areas at least we cannot afford to let Moscow gain another bit of territory' and that Dienbienphu might be such a place. He briefly toyed with the idea of a lightning American air strike – in unmarked planes because 'we would have to deny it for ever'.

Profile: John Foster Dulles 1888–1959

1888	– Born to a Presbyterian minister
Early 1900s	– Attended top schools and universities, including Princeton
1910s–30s	– Wall Street attorney
1919	– Expertise in foreign affairs recognised by President Woodrow Wilson, who named Dulles legal counsel to US delegation at Paris Peace Conference
1941	– Said in a speech: 'The great trouble with the world today is that there are too few Christians'
1941–5	– Helped to prepare UN Charter
1945–51	– Negotiated Japanese peace treaty
1953	– Appointed Secretary of State by Eisenhower Said US would face any Soviet aggression with 'massive nuclear retaliation'
1954	– Probably played decisive role in Bao Dai's appointment of Diem as his prime minister. Initiated SEATO to counter Communism. One contemporary said he suffered from 'pactomania'! In a speech in April, said that the United States had Jesus Christ on its side, and needed allies that believed likewise
1959	– Died in office

The militantly anti-Communist Dulles was an exceptionally important figure in the early years of the Cold War and in the shaping of the Vietnam involvement. Foreign observers often considered him inflexible, but some contemporaries felt he had effectively contained the USSR. The historian Arthur Schlesinger Jr called him 'the high priest of the Cold War'. Eisenhower called him 'One of the truly great men of our time'.

The historian Seth Jacobs called Dulles 'the most unapologetically religious man to superintend American foreign policy since Woodrow Wilson'. Dulles believed the decisive 'battle between Christianity and Communism' would be fought in Asia. Jacobs emphasised that Dulles' Christianity contributed massively to his support of the Christian Diem and to his failure to understand the predominantly Buddhist country of Vietnam. Dulles' biographer, Townsend Hoopes, described him as 'magnificently ignorant of Vietnamese history and culture'. Dulles helped to ensure that the US rejected the Geneva Accords and supported Diem and the new, artificial creation, South Vietnam.

Key question
What were the American arguments against helping the French at Dienbienphu?

c) Arguments against American intervention

Not every influential American agreed that something should be done about Vietnam:

- Some disliked the domino theory, doubting whether the loss of a relatively small country to Communism would cause the loss of others.
- Some of the military and the Secretary of Defence felt that Indochina was 'devoid of decisive military objectives' and that any US intervention there would be pointless, 'a serious diversion of limited US capabilities'.
- One vice-admiral insisted that 'partial' involvement through air and sea forces alone would be a delusion. 'One cannot go over Niagara Falls in a barrel only slightly', he said.
- Even Eisenhower, while he was commander of NATO, had said that 'no military victory is possible in that kind of theatre' and in the early 1960s he would write in his memoirs that 'the jungles of Indochina would have swallowed up division after division of US troops'. He pointed out the dangerous possibility that the US could find itself fighting Communists everywhere and felt he could not put US troops on the Asian mainland again just a year after he had gained massive popularity by getting them out of Korea.
- Even if Eisenhower had wanted to send US troops, there were none readily available. The Republicans' **'new look'** defence policy emphasised nuclear weaponry at the expense of manpower.
- Many Americans were uncertain about the wisdom of being too closely entangled with the French in Indochina. Eisenhower privately described the French as 'a hopeless, helpless mass of protoplasm'! The French themselves disliked the American conditions for involvement. France did not want to grant total independence to Vietnam and then carry on fighting there under a US commander.
- Eisenhower wrote in his memoirs that 'the strongest reason of all' for America to stay out 'is the fact that among all the powerful nations … the United States is the only one with a tradition of anti-colonialism … an asset of incalculable value … The moral position of the United States was more to be guarded than … all of Indochina'. Eisenhower clearly recognised the danger of replacing French colonialism with American colonialism.
- Perhaps more importantly, Eisenhower and Dulles tried but failed to get the British support that Congress required before they would approve American military intervention. Prime Minister Churchill said the struggle was not winnable and might trigger World War Three. Ironically, one unenthusiastic senator was Lyndon Johnson, who said, 'We want no more Koreas, with the United States furnishing more than 90 per cent of the manpower'.

Key term

'New look'
Republican policy emphasising nuclear weaponry rather than conventional forces for defence.

Faced with all this uncertainty, Eisenhower decided against direct American intervention in Vietnam. Without American intervention, the French were doomed to defeat at Dienbienphu. That defeat would ensure that the French government and people were finally ready to give up and get out of Indochina.

Key date
Eisenhower decided against US intervention to help French at Dienbienphu: Spring 1954

Summary diagram: Dienbienphu – the debate over American intervention

Arguments for and against US intervention at Dienbienphu

For	Against
Eisenhower had continued to invest money/honour in Vietnam	US could get out and say, 'The French lost it'
Communism had to be stopped – and Eisenhower had talked of 'rollback' and 'dominoes'	Losing a small country full of peasants to Communism would not greatly affect the balance of power Only just out of unpopular Korean War
Good to let French soldiers do the fighting against Communism	The French were 'hopeless' Few conventional forces ('new look') Congress and Britain said 'No'
France's help needed in NATO – have to support France in Vietnam	Impossible to win in Vietnam with French imperialists Might lead to World War Three with China

3 | The Geneva Conference on Indochina, 1954

a) Reasons for the International Conference at Geneva in 1954

Key question
Why was the 1954 Geneva conference held?

While the French and Vietminh battled at Dienbienphu, an international conference was called to discuss Indochina. Why was the conference called?

Key term
Armistice
Halt to fighting, but not yet a peace treaty.

- An **armistice** had finally ended three years of bitter fighting in Korea, so the time seemed ripe to try to end the fighting in French Indochina.
- Stalin had died and the new Soviet leaders wanted to show that they were keen to decrease Cold War tension.
- Keen to woo France away from the Western alliance, Moscow was willing to give France concessions over Indochina.
- In France many were tiring of the struggle and/or were aware of worldwide expectation that the war ought to be brought to an end.
- Communist China favoured negotiations because it wanted to forestall American involvement in Indochina and it judged that

participation in the peace talks would gain it increased international recognition and respectability.

Not everyone was enthusiastic about negotiations:

- Ho Chi Minh and the Vietnamese Communists were clearly winning the struggle for Vietnam. They feared and distrusted the French and did not expect to gain by talking to them.
- Bao Dai's new prime minister Ngo Dinh Diem feared and distrusted both the French and Ho and did not want to negotiate with either of them. Diem simply wanted the French out of Vietnam and a chance to concentrate on defeating the Communists.
- The Eisenhower administration in the United States feared that in their eagerness to get out of Vietnam the French might concede too much to the Communists.

Key date
International conference discussed French Indochina at Geneva: May 1954

The Chinese and Russians put great pressure on Ho to negotiate, but even before he said 'yes' the Russians agreed to a conference. Talks on the future of French Indochina were to begin on 8 May 1954 at Geneva. In the meantime the struggle for Dienbienphu continued.

Key question
What did the participants hope to gain from the Geneva conference?

b) The Geneva conference (1954)

i) Differing aims at Geneva

On 7 May 1954 the victorious Vietminh raised their red flag over Dienbienphu. The next day delegations representing France, Bao Dai, the Vietminh, Cambodia, Laos, the United States, the Soviet Union, the People's Republic of China and Great Britain assembled in Geneva to discuss ending the war in Indochina. Each delegation had different aims:

- Ho's Vietminh aimed to take over as much of Vietnam as possible and get foreigners out and, because of war weariness, they hoped for some kind of temporary truce.
- Bao Dai sought Vietnamese independence and an easy life.
- The French wanted to end their colonial war while trying to retain some influence in Indochina.
- America sought to contain Communism in Southeast Asia and to avoid elections in Vietnam, knowing that Ho Chi Minh would win. America rejected the idea of Communists in the government of Vietnam, and hoped for a united non-Communist Vietnam.
- The Chinese aimed at peace in Indochina to keep Western powers away from China's borders while she recovered from civil war. China also wanted to appear impressive and to gain diplomatic recognition and trade contacts.
- The Soviets aimed to divide both the French and Americans, and Ho and the Chinese. They were anxious to defuse troublesome situations that could hurt the USSR.
- The British wanted to stop the advance of Communism and prevent a wider war.

ii) Proceedings at Geneva

Occasionally the proceedings at Geneva resembled a French farce. Prime Minister Zhou Enlai of China was keen to make a dramatic impact. He arrived complete with the largest retinue (200) and Chinese antiques and carpets to decorate his lavish lodgings, all of which elicited pointed remarks from his comrades from the Soviet Union. The Vietminh studiously ignored the delegations of Bao Dai, Cambodia, Laos and France. Dulles refused to shake hands with the Communist Zhou. The French were impatient with the American refusal to recognise the Chinese, while the Americans found the French secretive and the British weak. The British Foreign Secretary said he had never known a conference like it. It is not surprising that it did not produce a durable settlement. The Americans were unwilling to commit themselves to any agreements made, partly to avoid giving any concessions to the Communists, partly to avoid being linked to any settlement that was unlikely to work. Back in Washington the intervention debate was raging again but Congress proved unwilling to intervene.

At first no agreement seemed possible at Geneva, but then a new French government, which was determined to settle the affair, came to power. Meanwhile, Zhou was equally determined to gain a settlement that would keep the Americans out of Indochina and as far away from China as possible. Zhou was willing to sacrifice comrade Ho in the interests of China, especially when it made him and his country look peace-loving, moderate and statesmanlike.

c) The Geneva Accords (1954)

Key question
What was agreed at Geneva in 1954?

In the **Geneva Accords**, the Vietminh, in effect represented by Zhou, agreed with France that:

- There would be Communist rule in the north of Vietnam while Bao Dai and his new prime minister, Diem, would govern the south. Ho's Vietminh would have to give up the territory which they occupied south of the 17th parallel (the line of partition between what would soon become North and South Vietnam was fixed at the latitude of 17 degrees north of the Equator, known as the 17th parallel). There would be a 10-km Demilitarised Zone (DMZ) above that parallel.
- The French forces would withdraw from the north and Ho's Vietminh forces from the south. There would be a truce between them.
- There would be democratic elections for a single Vietnamese government in 1956, when Vietnam would be re-unified.
- Neither the northern nor the southern Vietnamese were to make any military alliances with foreign powers, nor were they to allow foreign military bases in their territories. The French would remain in the south only in order to help prepare for the elections in 1956.

Other than the ceasefire, no documents were signed.

Key term

Geneva Accords
Agreements reached at Geneva in 1954 by France, China, Ho Chi Minh and the USSR, that Vietnam should be temporarily divided, with national elections held in 1956.

Key dates

Geneva Accords: Vietnam 'temporarily' divided: July 1954

Date set for nationwide elections in Vietnam that would never happen: 1956

Redrawing the map at the Geneva Conference (1954).

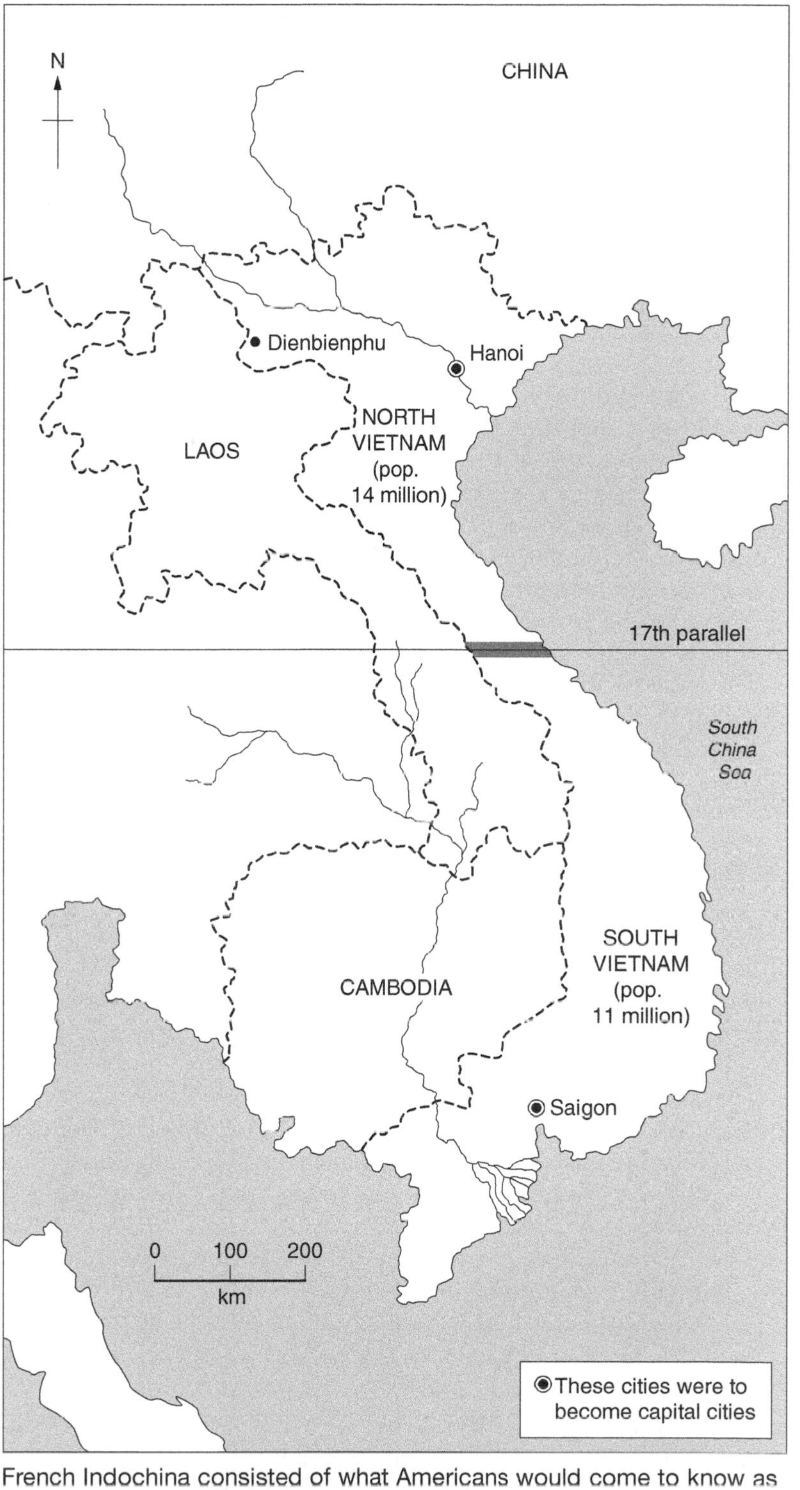

French Indochina consisted of what Americans would come to know as Vietnam, Laos and Cambodia. At Geneva, Vietnam was temporarily (supposedly) divided along the 17th parallel into a Communist North (under Ho) and a non-Communist South (under Bao Dai and Diem). Elections would (supposedly) be held in 1956 to reunite the country. Laos and Cambodia gained independence.

d) The significance of the Geneva Accords

Key question
What was the significance of the Geneva Accords?

The Geneva agreements were highly significant. While they appeared to recognise Vietnamese aspirations, they actually reflected great power wishes. Why did Ho accept a settlement that forced the Vietminh to retreat?

- He might have agreed in advance of the Geneva conference to accept the settlement in exchange for crucial Chinese aid at Dienbienphu.
- Like most of the other nations at Geneva, he wanted to forestall American intervention in Vietnam, and accepting a supposedly internationally supported agreement would hopefully ensure that.
- He needed time for consolidation in the north and peace would give him time for that.
- He needed Soviet aid and the Soviets wanted peace.
- He believed that the agreement that there would be nationwide elections in 1956 would be respected and knew that as the most popular Vietnamese national figure he was virtually certain to win (Eisenhower wrote in his 1963 memoirs that Ho would have won 80 per cent of the vote in a fair election).
- The negotiations had shown him that Communist China and the Soviet Union were not uncompromisingly supportive of his Democratic Republic of Vietnam. They had urged him to retreat.

The Geneva Accords were significant in several ways:

- They had shown that the two Communist giants were willing to sacrifice Ho Chi Minh if it suited them.
- The United States was significantly slow to pick up and/or exploit those divisions within the Communist world. Dulles knew there were **Sino-Soviet** tensions yet did not use them to advantage at Geneva.
- The ceasefire in Vietnam was between the French and the Vietminh – not between the Vietminh and any South Vietnamese government. New premier Diem of South Vietnam rejected the agreements as they put half of Vietnam under Communist control. He rightly predicted that 'another more deadly war' lay ahead.
- Owing to unwillingness to recognise the People's Republic of China and Communist control of the northern half of Vietnam, the Eisenhower administration agreed to respect, but would not sign, the Geneva agreements, saying 'the United States has not itself been a party to or bound by the decisions taken', and warning that America would view 'any renewal of aggression' with 'grave concern'. America chose to misinterpret the temporary ceasefire line of the 17th parallel as a permanent division between two states, a northern one which was Communist and a southern one which was friendly. The Geneva settlement and Vietnam had become victims of the Cold War.

Key term

Sino-Soviet
Another way of saying Chinese-Soviet. Sino pertains to Chinese.

Summary diagram: The Geneva conference on Indochina, 1954

	What did they want?	What did they get?
USA	No Communist gains	Half of Vietnam was not Communist, half was
USSR	Decreased Cold War tension	Settlement that did not last
China	Keep US out. Gain international recognition	Recognition, but US stayed in Southeast Asia
France	Respite. Retain some influence in Indochina	Got out. Hardly retained any influence
Ho Chi Minh	Control over as much of Vietnam as possible	Got half of Vietnam
Diem	Control over as much of Vietnam as possible	Got half of Vietnam, but soon lost it
UK	Peace in Southeast Asia. Halt spread of Communism	Uneasy, temporary peace. Communism not halted

4 | Two Vietnams and Two Leaders

After the Geneva conference, Ho and the Communists governed North Vietnam (from Hanoi) while Diem governed South Vietnam (from Saigon). Like all Vietnamese nationalists, Ho and Diem would have preferred a united Vietnam. One great question was whether either of them had the necessary skill and support to bring about national unification. Another great question was whether the Vietnamese would at last be able to decide their own destiny without foreign interference.

Key question
Did Diem have the ability, power and support to unite Vietnam?

a) Ngo Dinh Diem – background

i) Diem before 1950

Diem's ancestors came from central Vietnam, where they had been converted to Christianity by Portuguese missionaries in the seventeenth century. Generations of them had served as mandarins at the imperial Vietnamese court. Diem was the third of the Ngo family's six sons. The young Diem had considered becoming a priest but had decided that it would require too much self-discipline. As it turned out, the delicate-featured Diem never married and lived a more monk-like life than his older brother, who was a worldly archbishop of the Catholic Church.

Trained in a French school for Vietnamese bureaucrats, Diem successfully continued the family tradition of government service until he clashed with his French masters in 1933. A nationalist, he resented French unwillingness to give the Vietnamese any real power. Diem skulked around his mother's home for the next

Profile: Ngo Dinh Diem 1901–63

1901 – Born into a noble Vietnamese Catholic family in central Vietnam
1933 – Minister of the Interior to Emperor Bao Dai, but resigned because of French domination
1933–45 – Lived quietly in Hue
1945 – Captured by Communist forces; declined to join Ho Chi Minh's government and went into exile
1954 – Returned at Bao Dai's request, to be prime minister of US-backed government in South Vietnam
1955 – Defeated Bao Dai in government-controlled referendum; made himself president of newly declared Republic of South Vietnam
1956 – Refused to carry out Geneva Accords' planned nationwide elections; increasingly autocratic
1963 – Persecution of Buddhist majority led United States to withdraw support and collude in his assassination by his army generals

Diem was important in that many influential Americans perceived him as the only non-Communist who was anywhere near capable of running Vietnam. While he frequently showed considerable political cunning, his US-supported South Vietnamese government was always unpopular. The fact that there was no clear alternative non-Communist leader suggests that South Vietnam was not a viable state.

decade. He had high hopes of the Japanese allowing Vietnam to declare its independence during the Second World War, but they rejected his ideas.

A few months after the Vietminh shot his brother, Diem met Ho Chi Minh. Ho asked Diem to join his government and the fight for independence and a better life for the people of Vietnam. Diem replied that Ho's followers were murderers, and that he would fight for the freedom of the people in his own way. Subsequently some Communists criticised Ho for letting Diem go at this point.

ii) Diem's visit to the United States, 1950

In 1950 Diem went to the US, where he helped at a seminary for training priests. Disdainful of material comforts, he willingly scrubbed floors. He also met prominent American Catholics such as Senators John Kennedy and Mike Mansfield.

Key date: Diem made influential friends in the United States: 1950

Mansfield is an important figure in the history of the US involvement in Vietnam. He illustrates the importance of the role of Congress, American ignorance of Vietnam, and finally, how there was influential opposition to the involvement during the 1960s.

Mansfield knew virtually nothing about Vietnam ('I do not know too much about the Indochina situation. I do not think that anyone does'). However, Mansfield played a vitally important part in the continued support of Diem after 1955, as his congressional colleagues considered him to be their Indochina specialist.

The South Vietnamese presidential family in 1963. Diem is second from the right.

Key date

Establishment of SEATO: September 1954

iii) Diem as Bao Dai's premier

Bao Dai had been living on the French Riviera with a wife, a mistress, and a variety of French prostitutes who kept him occupied in between visits to the gambling casinos. As the French prepared to leave Vietnam, Bao Dai prepared to return. He thought that the American contacts might make Diem useful, so in 1954 he made Diem his prime minister. By that time the vast majority of Vietnamese nationalists with leadership qualities were Vietminh. Any non-Communist nationalists with potential either had been killed by the French or the Vietminh, or had given up political activities. Diem thus slid into a leadership vacuum.

Meanwhile, Eisenhower felt that Ho had triumphed at Geneva and that the United States had to do something to 'restore its prestige in the Far East'. Dulles therefore masterminded the Southeast Asia Treaty Organisation (SEATO), which combined America, Britain, France, Australia, New Zealand and Pakistan in a defensive alliance. **SEATO** members agreed to protect South Vietnam, Cambodia and Laos under a separate **protocol** – a transparent American device to circumvent the Geneva agreement, which had said that the Vietnamese must not enter into foreign alliances or allow foreign troops on their soil.

Key terms

SEATO
Defensive alliance between USA, Britain, France, Australia, New Zealand and Pakistan, 1954.

Protocol
In this context, an agreement between signatory nations.

b) Diem and American 'nation building'

i) Diem and the Americans in 1954

For nearly a decade, the short, plump and chain-smoking Diem, usually wearing the white sharkskin suits that were a status symbol for Vietnamese officials, was the titular leader of South Vietnam.

However, as he struggled and failed to control this artificial political creation, so his American patrons struggled and failed to control him.

According to the Geneva agreements, the French were supposed to stay in South Vietnam to enforce the ceasefire until the nationwide elections were held in July 1956. Diem, whom the French prime minister described as incapable and mad, rejected the idea of nationwide elections because he knew Ho would win. Soon after Geneva, Diem had decided to turn his back on the French and to rely instead on the Americans, who quickly pledged him their support. When the French finally left in April 1956, Dulles said 'We have a clean base there now, without the taint of [French] colonialism'. He referred to Dienbienphu as 'a blessing in disguise'.

Diem and his American patrons agreed that the Communist menace must be halted and that one way to do this was to build a stable, non-Communist South Vietnamese state. In November 1954, Eisenhower sent his Second World War associate General 'Lightning Joe' Collins to implement a 'crash programme' to maintain Diem's regime. Collins urged **land reform** as Saigon's main priority, but the United States created a Military Assistance Advisory Group (MAAG) to direct and, as it turned out, dominate US assistance.

Key dates

Eisenhower sent General Collins to help/assess Diem; creation of Military Assistance Advisory Group (MAAG) to help South Vietnam: November 1954

Diem decisively defeated religious sects in South Vietnam: May 1955

Diem held 'fair' elections in South Vietnam: October 1955

Key term

Land reform
Even anti-Communist Americans saw the need for a more equal distribution of land in Vietnam: an estimated 1 per cent of the population owned all the cultivable land in the south.

ii) American doubts about Diem

From the beginning, however, the Americans were not entirely happy with their new South Vietnamese ally.

According to Vice-President Richard Nixon, the problem was that 'the [South] Vietnamese lacked the ability to conduct a war by themselves or govern themselves'. With his high-pitched voice and capacity for endless talking rather than listening, Diem did not impress those Americans to whom he gave audience. One US diplomat called him a 'messiah without a message'. Dulles admitted that America supported Diem 'because we knew of no one better': he was simply the best of a bad bunch. The leaders of America's armed forces, the Joint Chiefs of Staff (JCS), were unenthusiastic about involvement with Diem, believing that his government was unstable.

Although Dulles contended that helping Diem to train his army would make his government stable, General Collins reported that Diem's regime was hopeless. Another old friend of Eisenhower's doubted whether the US could make 'a synthetic strong man' out of Diem. The Eisenhower administration nearly withdrew their support, but in the spring of 1955 Diem's effective action against Bao Dai and other non-Communist opponents halted them.

iii) Diem's defeat of Bao Dai

In October 1955, Diem held an election in South Vietnam, now clearly a separate state. Those voting for Bao Dai were punished: some were held down to have pepper sauce poured into their nostrils. Diem claimed 98.2 per cent of the vote, rejecting his sympathetic American adviser Colonel Edward Lansdale's proposals that 60 or 70 per cent was a more credible figure. Out of 450,000 registered voters in Saigon, Diem claimed that 605,025 had voted for him! Through a combination of force, fraud and friendship with America, Diem appeared to have made himself undisputed leader of the new state of South Vietnam. There was no real rival: Bao Dai remained in France and had refused to contest the election.

iv) MAAG and the Catholic migration south

The Eisenhower administration now increased aid to Diem. MAAG gave him hundreds of millions of dollars and advice on politics, land reform and covert operations against the Vietminh. American recommendations included sabotage and the recruitment of fortune tellers to predict doom under Communism. America had helped to transport around a million Vietnamese from the north to the south. Most of the refugees were middle-class, educated and Catholic. Some of the Catholics had been persuaded to go south by their priests telling them that 'Christ has gone to the South'. The Catholics were (initially) supportive of Diem, but their arrival made Diem even less popular amongst the predominantly Buddhist southerners.

v) The nature of Diem's regime

Diem visited America in 1957, when Eisenhower praised him as the 'miracle man' of Asia. Unfortunately, Diem's belief in his own infallibility and rectitude was so strengthened by such words that when Americans advised him that his repressive and unpopular administration needed to reform to survive, Diem dug his heels in and did nothing. His government had become a family operation and while Diem himself lived frugally, his family squabbled amongst themselves in their struggle to get rich.

Diem favoured his fellow Catholics from the north and the wealthy landowner class. He never appealed to the ordinary people as Ho did. Like the Americans who supported him, Diem did not understand the appeal of the Vietminh. He simply saw them as rebels and failed to comprehend how their ideas about greater economic equality could win so many peasant hearts. Diem disliked meeting his people and only reluctantly toured South Vietnam at the behest of his American patrons who rightly feared that unlike 'Uncle Ho' he lacked the common touch.

Key date

Ho Chi Minh's government brutally suppressed revolts in North: 1956

c) Support for Ho and Communism

Key question

Did Ho Chi Minh have the ability, power and support to unite Vietnam?

i) Ho's ruthlessness

In many ways Ho's regime in the North was as unpleasant as that of Diem in the South. Ho's Communists liquidated thousands of landlords and opponents and even loyal Vietminh by mistake. In 1956 Ho's soldiers (**People's Army of Vietnam** or PAVN) had to put down a revolt: 6000 peasants were killed or deported. Subsequently Ho and Giap admitted having wrongfully resorted to terror. On the other hand, Ho's egalitarian regime, free from apparent foreign domination, often won the hearts of the people in a way that Diem's never did.

Key term

People's Army of Vietnam
Formal name of Ho's North Vietnamese Army by 1956.

President Ngo Dinh Diem (front left) with Donald Quarles, Deputy Secretary of Defence, reviewing a guard of honour outside the Pentagon in honour of the president's visit, 16 May 1957.

ii) Ho's popularity

Joseph Alsop was one of the few Americans who had toured rural South Vietnam when it was still occupied by the Vietminh. He wrote about his 1954 travels for the *New Yorker* magazine in 1955:

> I would like to be able to report – I had hoped to be able to report – that on that long, slow canal trip to Vinh Binh [Mekong Delta] I saw all the signs of misery and oppression that have made my visits to East Germany like nightmare journeys to *1984* [a reference to the descriptions of a **totalitarian** state in George Orwell's novel titled *1984*]. But it was not so.
>
> At first it was difficult for me, as it is for any Westerner, to conceive of a Communist government's genuinely 'serving the people'. I could hardly imagine a Communist government that was also a popular government and almost a democratic government. But this is just the sort of government the palm-hut state actually was while the struggle with the French continued. The Vietminh could not possibly have carried on the resistance for one year, let alone nine years, without the people's strong, united support.

Key term

Totalitarian
An all-controlling, dictatorial government.

Many southerners remained quietly loyal to Ho after Vietnam was divided in 1954. A large number of southern peasants disliked both the corrupt regime of Diem and the Communists, although many began to turn to the latter.

iii) Communist activism in South Vietnam

Key date

The second Indochina War or Vietnam War began: 1960

Before 1959 Ho had discouraged supporters in the South from attacking Diem's regime. Hanoi wanted to be seen to be abiding by the Geneva agreements and was bitterly divided about whether consolidation in the North should take priority over liberation of the South. This gave Diem the opportunity to arrest and execute many southern Communist activists, whose numbers dropped from around 10,000 in 1955 to nearer 2000 by 1959. That forced the South's Communists into open revolt. By 1960 Hanoi had decided to give liberation equal priority to consolidation. Diem responded by concentrating even more on military solutions.

Key terms

National Liberation Front
From 1960, Ho's southern supporters gave themselves this name.

Vietcong
After 1960, Diem called the National Liberation Front 'Vietcong' (Vietnamese Communists or VC).

People's Liberation Armed Forces
The name by which Ho's southern supporters called their forces after 1960.

Agrovilles
New and well-defended villages set up by Diem's regime to keep Communists out.

From 1960 Ho's southern supporters called themselves the **National Liberation Front** (NLF), but Diem called them **Vietcong** (Vietnamese Communists or VC). Like the Vietminh in 1945, the NLF emphasised national independence rather than social revolution and contained non-Communists. The NLF organised itself into the **People's Liberation Armed Forces** (PLAF). The second Indochina War or Vietnam War had begun.

One of the great Vietnam War debates concerns the southern insurgents. Was the opposition to Diem:

- from indigenous southerners who had always remained in the South?
- from southerners who had moved north after Geneva and now returned?
- primarily from indigenous northerners?
- orchestrated by Hanoi?

There is an element of truth in all these suggestions. One thing is indisputable: the level of violence and disruption increased dramatically in South Vietnam from 1958 onwards. Diem responded by relocating peasants to army-protected villages called **agrovilles**. The peasants hated forced, expensive removals from their homes, lands and sacred ancestral tombs. Dissatisfaction with the regime of 'American Diem' was ever-increasing. In 1960 18 prominent Vietnamese nationalists petitioned Diem for moderate reform, but he became even more repressive in response. US ambassador Elbridge Durbrow recommended that Diem introduce political and social reform rather than concentrate on the use of military force, but MAAG disagreed.

d) Diem's situation in 1961

By 1961 Diem had received over a billion dollars from the Eisenhower administration. 'We bet pretty heavily on him', said Eisenhower, while Senator Kennedy described Diem as 'our offspring'. One exasperated US official in Saigon described Diem as 'a puppet who pulled his own strings – and ours as well'. While many knowledgeable Americans warned from the first that the struggle could not be won with Diem in power, others disagreed. Diem's American supporters were often those who saw the conflict in Vietnam in simple military terms, believing that Diem's battles were against unpopular Communists and could be won simply by pouring in more military aid and money ($7 billion between 1955 and 1961). The problem was that the Communists had a fair amount of popular support in South Vietnam and that Diem had to deal with so much non-Communist opposition. Even his army (Army of the Republic of Vietnam or **ARVN**) contained opponents, some of whom unsuccessfully rebelled against him in 1960. By 1961 America was supporting a very unpopular regime in South Vietnam.

Key term

ARVN
Diem's Army of the Republic of Vietnam.

Interestingly, at this stage, neither the USSR nor the People's Republic of China was as committed to Ho Chi Minh as the United States was to Diem. In 1957, the USSR had even suggested that both North Vietnam and South Vietnam be admitted to the United Nations.

Key date

USSR proposed admission of North and South Vietnam to the United Nations: 1957

Summary diagram: Two Vietnams and two leaders

Diem	Ho
Massively dependent on US aid	Some help from China and USSR
Unpopular with ordinary people	Popular with ordinary people
Unwilling to redistribute landed wealth	Willing to redistribute landed wealth
Lacked appealing personality	Charismatic, common touch
No supporters in North	Many supporters in South
Both nationalistic	
Both ruthless with opponents	

5 | Assessment of Eisenhower's Policy

a) Historians' consensus

Key question
To what extent was Eisenhower responsible for the US involvement in Vietnam?

While campaigning for the presidency, Eisenhower had emphasised the importance of liberating people from Communism. By those self-imposed standards he had failed. North Vietnam became a Communist state during his presidency. However, historians generally consider his Vietnam policy to have been a success. They tend to judge presidents by the extent to which they got America committed. Eisenhower did not send thousands of American troops to Vietnam as Johnson did, so Eisenhower is judged to have been relatively successful in dealing with Vietnam.

b) Had Eisenhower greatly increased the commitment?

Eisenhower inherited a limited involvement in Vietnam. Truman had financially aided the French in their struggle to retain influence in Vietnam because he believed that Vietnam was important in the Cold War. All members of the Eisenhower administration agreed that Vietnam was important. Some (including Vice-President Nixon and, possibly, Dulles) were even willing to use atomic bombs to help the French there, but Eisenhower said:

> You boys must be crazy. We can't use those awful things against Asians for the second time in less than 10 years. My God.

Eisenhower deserves credit for rejecting the atomic option. He recognised that the use of atomic bombs would probably lead to conflict with the Soviets and China. Nonetheless, Eisenhower's **administration** made Vietnam even more important than Truman's had.

Key term

Administration
Rather than refer to a president's 'government', Americans refer to a president's 'administration'.

Some historians praise Eisenhower for refusing to send Americans into combat in Vietnam. His memoirs suggest that he realised this was militarily and politically unwise. However, it must be remembered that Eisenhower gave a great deal of support to the French attempts at a military solution. Furthermore, it was probably only congressional leaders and the reluctance of his British allies that stopped him increasing direct American involvement during the struggle for Dienbienphu. In defiance of the Geneva Accords, Eisenhower effectively made the United States the guarantor of an independent state of South Vietnam and committed the US to the defence of a particularly unpopular leader in Diem. He gave Diem billions of dollars worth of aid and 1500 American advisers, nearly half of whom were military. Once such a commitment was undertaken, it was arguable that America had incurred an obligation to see it through. From that point it would prove to be but a short step to putting American soldiers into Vietnam.

Significantly, no one in the Eisenhower administration was urging reconsideration of the commitment to Vietnam, simply arguing about its nature. Ambassador Eldridge Durbrow urged political reform, to make South Vietnam a democracy, but the State Department and Dulles favoured concentration upon a strong government in Saigon to combat Communism.

c) Questions to think about

In order to come to conclusions about Eisenhower's responsibility for the American involvement in Vietnam, several questions need to be answered. Could any American president be seen to ignore any 'threat' from Communism in the Cold War era? When one president had committed American foreign policy in a certain direction was it feasible for another to reverse it? Once America had greatly aided the anti-Communists in South Vietnam could it legitimately then just dump them? Those who would answer 'no' to any of those questions would seem to suggest that Eisenhower was right, and that what was right would inevitably lead to American involvement in Vietnam.

However, much depends on the sort of questions one asks. Was Communism really such a threat to America? Was Vietnam going Communist really going to affect the course of the Cold War? Did America have any right to intervene in what was in effect an internal debate about what kind of government Vietnam should have? Negative answers to these questions would suggest that Eisenhower was mistaken in his policies. On the other hand, many Americans agreed with him, raising final questions. Can any president transcend the prejudices and preoccupations of his time? And if he does, will he and his party get re-elected?

6 | Key Debates

Some issues historians argue over are:

a) why the United States became and remained involved in Vietnam
b) the extent to which Eisenhower should be blamed for increasing the commitment
c) the legality of the creation and support of South Vietnam
d) whether the United States was in a no-win Cold War situation.

a) Why did the United States get involved and remain in Vietnam?

Once several presidents were involved in trying and failing to defend Communism in Vietnam, it was clear that the United States was stuck in a very difficult situation. As successive presidents got more and more involved, Halberstam (1964) published *The Making of a Quagmire*, from which the so-called 'quagmire theory' of US involvement developed. According to this theory, because of their ignorance of the Vietnamese people and situation, and their overconfidence in American power and ideals, US leaders let the United States get gradually trapped in an expensive commitment in an unimportant area, unable to exit without losing credibility. In the early 1970s, Halberstam and Fitzgerald wrote critically of US arrogance and ignorance of the appeal of Communism in Vietnam.

An alternative theory, the 'stalemate theory', emerged in the 1970s. First Daniel (1972) then Gelb and Betts (1979) claimed that the United States held to the commitment and even escalated in order not to win but to avoid being seen to lose by the American voters.

By the early 1980s, the 'flawed containment' (Divine, 1988) historians combined the quagmire interpretation with the global containment viewpoint, which said that in trying to halt Communism, the United States got bogged down in a no-win situation.

b) Should Eisenhower be blamed for increased American involvement in the Vietnam war?

Some historians absolve Eisenhower of responsibility for the American war in Vietnam. 'Eisenhower revisionists' such as Ambrose (1984) point out his statesmanship in not getting entangled in Dienbienphu. Gardner and Anderson (2005) on the other hand, contend that John Foster Dulles welcomed the end of French **neocolonialism** after Dienbienphu and gladly took the opportunity effectively to replace it. Short (1989) blames years of conflict in Vietnam on the US refusal to accept the Geneva Accords, while some historians criticise the Eisenhower administration either for its unwillingness to look beyond the Christian Diem in Vietnam or for its failure to consider promising non-Communist politicians in Southeast Asia (Kaiser, 2000 and Nashel, 2005). Anderson (1991 and 2005) rejected those who claimed that Eisenhower's decision not to help the French at Dienbienphu shows his statesmanship, claiming that Eisenhower had tried hard to get Congressional and British support for that aid. Anderson emphasises that both Eisenhower and Dulles continued to see Vietnam as vital in the Cold War context, and concludes that 'Eisenhower left Kennedy a policy of unequivocal support for Diem that had kept the domino from falling, but had not produced a self-sufficient nation in the South'. Anderson concluded that, 'the Eisenhower administration trapped itself and its successors into a commitment to the survival of its own counterfeit creation', that is, the non-viable South Vietnamese state.

Key term

Neocolonialism
Whereas old-style colonialism was usually openly exploitative, neocolonialism had a kinder face as, for example, when France claimed to be granting greater independence to Vietnam after the Second World War.

c) Were US actions legal?

Historians debate the legality of the US position in relation to the Geneva Accords. LaFaber (1989), for example, claimed that 'US officials used this supposed collective security pact [SEATO] to justify the unilateral American commitment to Vietnam'. Weinstein (1967) criticised the United States for supporting Diem's refusal to consult with North Vietnam on the elections, which freed North Vietnam to defy the Accords too. Defenders of the Eisenhower administration said that Saigon was not obliged to hold the elections as Bao Dai's representatives at Geneva had not signed the relevant parts of the Geneva Accords. They claimed that no country should be bound to an agreement made by a past colonial oppressor (France) and that free elections were impossible in the Communist North.

A second 'legal' issue concerns the outbreak of the second Indochina War or Vietnam War around 1960. Kahin and Lewis (1969), in a popular textbook, said that the initiative came from southern dissidents, driven to desperation by Diem's repression. Here, the blame for the war lay with Saigon, not Hanoi. The significance of this interpretation is that it rejected the claim of successive US administrations and other historians (for example, Pike, 1966) that this war was not a civil war, but an invasion from the North. Duiker (1998) rejected both 'extreme views', saying that what broke out at the end of the 1950s was 'an insurgent movement inspired by local conditions in the South but guided and directed from Hanoi'.

d) A no-win Cold War situation?

Naturally, American historians write America-centred histories of the conflict, although some try to place American decision-making in a more international context (Logevall, 2001), often emphasising the contemporary viewpoint of other nations. For example, the British rejected the 'falling dominoes' theory, convinced that what happened in Vietnam would have no impact on British Malaya. Logevall gives a balanced argument, both critical of the Eisenhower administration but also recognising that:

> making a stand in the Southern parts of Vietnam was not an illogical move in 1954, given the globalisation of the Cold War, given the domestic political realities, and most of all perhaps, given that the costs seemed reasonable – a few thousand American advisers on the ground, a few hundred million dollars in aid.

This would help to explain Dulles' candid assessment that the chances of success for the creation of the South Vietnamese state were only 10 per cent. The Eisenhower administration, says Duiker, 'went into the Diem experiment with its eyes wide open'.

Some key books in the debates

S. Ambrose, *Eisenhower: The President* (New York, 1984).
D. Anderson, *Trapped by Success: The Eisenhower Administration and Vietnam* (New York, 1991) and *The Vietnam War* (New York, 2005).
R. Divine, 'Vietnam reconsidered', *Diplomatic History* (1988).
W. Duiker, *US Containment Policy and the Conflict in Indochina* (Stanford, 1994) and *Sacred War* (New York, 1995).
D. Ellsberg, *Papers on the War* (New York, 1972).
F. Fitzgerald, *Fire in the Lake* (Boston, 1972).
L. Gardner, *Approaching Vietnam* (New York, 1988).
L. Gelb and R. Betts, *The Irony of Vietnam* (Washington DC, 1979).
D. Halberstam, *The Making of a Quagmire* (New York, 1964).
S. Jacobs, *America's Miracle Man in Vietnam* (Duke, 2004).
G. Kahin and J. Lewis, *The United States in Vietnam* (New York, 1969).
D. Kaiser, *An American Tragedy* (Harvard, 2000).
W. LaFaber, *The American Age* (New York, 1989).
F. Logevall, *The Origins of the Vietnam War* (London, 2001).
D. Pike, *Viet Cong* (Cambridge, Massachusetts, 1966).
A. Short, *The Origins of the Vietnam War* (London, 1989).
F. Weinstein, *Vietnam's Unheld Elections* (New York, 1967).

4 'Vietnam is the Place' – The Kennedy Crusade (1961–3)

POINTS TO CONSIDER

During the presidency of John Fitzgerald Kennedy (1961–3), American involvement in Vietnam dramatically increased. This chapter invites consideration of the following questions:

- Why did Kennedy continue the American commitment to Vietnam?
- Had Kennedy lived longer, would he have got out of Vietnam?
- Was it Kennedy's (as opposed to Johnson's) war?
- Were Kennedy's Vietnam policies wise?

This chapter examines these questions through sections on:

- Kennedy's early ideas about Vietnam
- The president and his advisers
- Kennedy's actions in the Third World
- Kennedy and Diem
- Conclusions
- The key debates

Key dates

1960		Kennedy advocated greater Cold War activism during presidential election campaign
1961	January	Kennedy became president
	April	Kennedy humiliated by failure to overthrow Fidel Castro in Cuba (Bay of Pigs)
	May	Vice-President Johnson visited Diem, urging reform; de Gaulle warned Kennedy of Vietnamese quagmire
1962		12,000 American advisers in Vietnam Strategic hamlets programme
	February	Kennedy created MACV
	May	After visiting South Vietnam, McNamara said United States was winning the war
	Summer	Unsuccessful unofficial peace talks with Hanoi
	October	Cuban Missiles Crisis

1963	January	Vietcong defeated ARVN and Americans at Battle of Ap Bac
	Spring	Anti-Diem protests by Buddhists
	September	Kennedy said the South Vietnamese had to win the war themselves, but that it would be a mistake for the United States to get out
	November	Diem assassinated Kennedy assassinated

1 | Introduction: Kennedy's War?

Key question
Was it 'Kennedy's war'? Or 'Johnson's war'?

The last two chapters focused on what was happening in Vietnam and explained the US response to it. For Truman and Eisenhower, Vietnam was a minor side-show in the Cold War. It was during the Kennedy presidency that Vietnam became far more important, although it was only under President Johnson that it became a national obsession.

There can be no doubt that the Kennedy presidency saw an increased commitment to South Vietnam. However, since Kennedy's death there has been considerable debate over his policy. The debate has been affected by the knowledge that during the presidency of his successor, the Vietnam War became highly controversial and unpopular. Kennedy's supporters have been inclined to argue that the Vietnam War was 'Johnson's war' and that just before his assassination Kennedy was planning to get America out. Similarly, the Johnson administration was much criticised for its apparent lack of understanding of Vietnam and for reliance upon military solutions to the problems there. However, the study of the Kennedy administration's policies reveals similar failures of perception as well as a massive increase in the American commitment in Vietnam. These issues are sometimes forgotten by those who concentrate upon Johnson's presidency in isolation.

Key terms

Congressman
Each of the 50 US states elects a number of congressmen to represent them in Congress.

Third World
Cold War era name for developing nations.

2 | Kennedy's Early Ideas about Vietnam

Key question
Did Kennedy's pre-presidential career and beliefs make greater involvement in Vietnam inevitable?

By the time Kennedy became president in January 1961 his ideas on Vietnam had already been shaped and demonstrated. Kennedy's Catholic family loathed Communism. The fanatically anti-Communist Senator Joseph McCarthy was a good friend of Kennedy's father and even dated the future president's sister. As a young Democratic **Congressman**, Kennedy believed that the expansion of Communism must be 'contained' by America.

Key date
Kennedy became president: January 1961

Although both Kennedy and Truman were Democrats, Kennedy attacked President Truman for 'losing' China in 1949 (see page 19). Like most Americans, Kennedy believed in Eisenhower's domino theory. However, Kennedy criticised President Eisenhower for allowing the rise of Communism in the newly emergent nations of the **Third World**. Kennedy considered the Third World to be the new Cold War battleground. He criticised French colonialism in Indochina. He believed that unless France granted

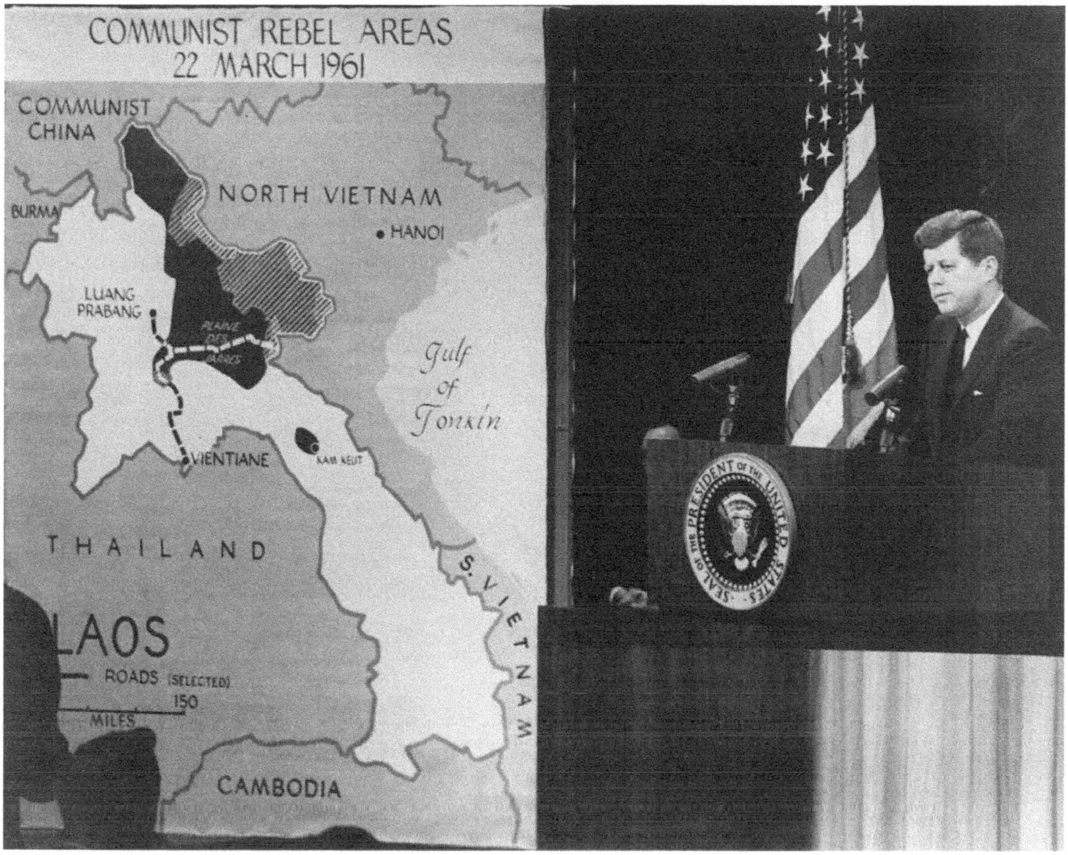

President Kennedy explaining the situation in Vietnam.

independence to the people of Indochina, thwarted nationalism might turn the Indochinese to Communism and the remainder of Southeast Asia could well follow. After the 1954 Geneva agreements Kennedy believed that democracy could thrive in South Vietnam but he rejected the idea of nationwide elections, which he thought Ho would win. His fears of Third World Communism clearly outweighed his sympathy for nationalism and true democracy. In a 1956 speech to the American Friends of Vietnam he reiterated the domino theory, calling South Vietnam:

> [the] cornerstone of the free world in Southeast Asia, the keystone of the arch, the finger in the dike. Burma, Thailand, India, Japan, the Philippines, and obviously Laos and Cambodia … would be threatened if the red tide of Communism overflowed in Vietnam … [which is] a proving ground for democracy in Asia … [and] a test of American responsibility and determination in Asia … [where] the relentless pressure of the Chinese Communists [must be stopped] … No other challenge is more deserving of our effort and energy … Our security may be lost piece by piece, country by country.

Key date
Kennedy advocated greater Cold War activism during presidential election campaign: 1960

Kennedy criticised Eisenhower for losing the initiative in foreign policy and during his 1960 presidential election campaign

Kennedy said that the country needed a president 'to get America moving again'. Militant anti-Communism was a keynote of his campaign **rhetoric**:

> The enemy is the Communist system itself – implacable, insatiable, unceasing in its drive for world domination … This is not a struggle for supremacy of arms alone. It is also a struggle for supremacy between two conflicting **ideologies**: freedom under God versus ruthless, godless tyranny.

So, although most Americans were unaware of events in Vietnam when Kennedy became president, his background suggested that he might be even more interested in and committed to Vietnam than his predecessors. This is why we must now shift our focus from Vietnam to Washington, DC.

Key terms

Rhetoric
Stylised speech, designed to impress and persuade.

Ideology
A set of principles or beliefs. The USSR's ideology was Communism, the USA's, liberal capitalism.

Summary diagram: Kennedy's early ideas about Vietnam

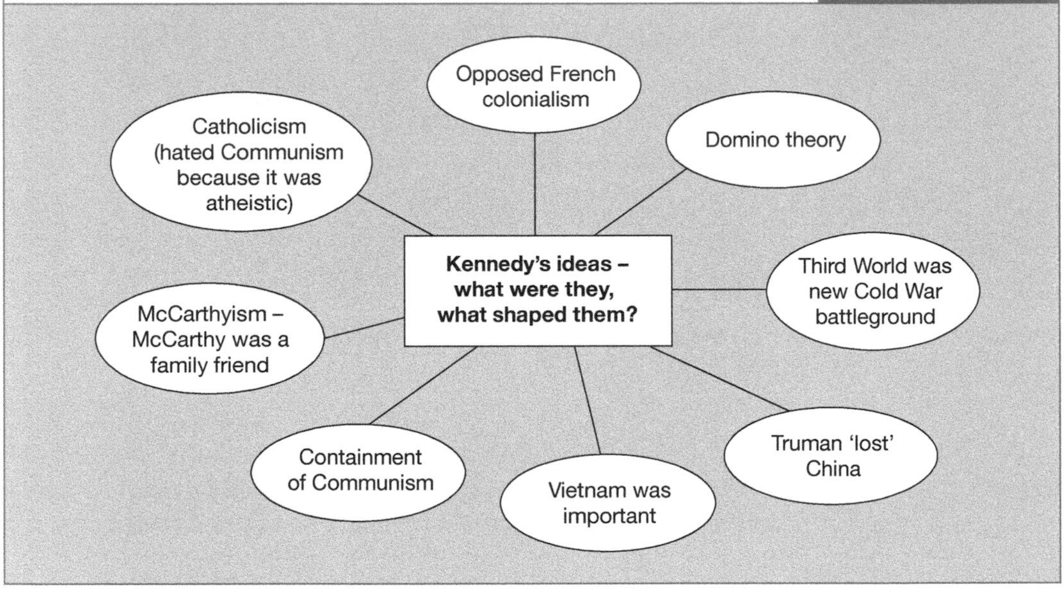

3 | The President and his Advisers

a) Kennedy – the impatient crusader in the Third World

Key question
What shaped Kennedy's Vietnam policy?

How did the interests, emphases and characters of President Kennedy and his chosen advisers shape US policy towards Vietnam?

i) Campaign rhetoric

Kennedy's **inaugural address** was entirely devoted to foreign policy. It contained inspirational and now famous phrases:

> let every nation know, whether it wishes us well or ill, that we shall pay any price, bear any burden, meet any hardship, support any friend, oppose any foes to assure the survival and the success of liberty.

Key term

Inaugural address
When the US President is sworn into office, he makes a speech setting out his ideas and plans.

Profile: John Fitzgerald Kennedy 1917–63

1917 – Born to a wealthy, Irish Catholic, Democrat family in Boston, Massachusetts

1938 – Acted as his father's secretary when Joseph Kennedy was ambassador to the UK

1940 – Graduated from Harvard; wrote the bestselling *Why England Slept*, which criticised British unpreparedness for war

1941 – Joined US Navy in the Second World War

1943 – Decorated for service in the Pacific

1946 – Successfully ran for Congress

1947–53 – Served three terms in the House of Representatives; criticised Truman administration for 'losing' China

1952 – Bobby, John's 27-year-old brother, successfully ran senatorial campaign against popular incumbent, Republican Henry Cabot Lodge Jr

1953 – Ambivalent towards fanatical anti-Communist Senator Joseph McCarthy – 'Half my people in Massachusetts look upon McCarthy as a hero'

1954 – Spent six months strapped to a board in family home in Florida, recovering from back surgery; wrote *Profiles in Courage*, about eight US political leaders who had defied public opinion on matters of conscience

Late 1950s – Served on Senate Foreign Relations Committee; advocated massive aid to emerging Third World nations; said France should grant independence to Algeria

1958 – Re-elected Senator for Massachusetts

1960 – Campaigned for president, with Lyndon Johnson as running mate. His campaign was characterised by Cold War rhetoric and Kennedy family glamour. Narrowly elected

1961 – Embarrassed by Bay of Pigs fiasco (unsuccessful attempt to overthrow left-wing ruler of Cuba). The more experienced Soviet leader Khrushchev seemed to bully/dominate Kennedy at the Vienna summit

1962 – Made Khrushchev back down over the Cuban Missiles Crisis

1963 – Signed nuclear test ban treaty
Assassinated

John F. Kennedy is important in the Cold War context in that his presidency was full of crises, for which he and/or Soviet leader Khrushchev clearly bore some blame. In many speeches, Kennedy advocated greater US militancy in the Cold War. He is important in the Vietnam context in that he dramatically increased US involvement there.

In some ways Kennedy was a prisoner of his own Cold War campaign rhetoric – designed to win votes, it served to limit his foreign policy options once in the White House. Having made much of the so-called '**missile gap**' in 1960 and the need for a more dynamic foreign policy, Kennedy was duty-bound to increase defence expenditure and foreign involvement.

Key term

Missile gap
In the late 1950s, Khrushchev claimed that the USSR had more missiles than the USA.

ii) Youth and inexperience

Kennedy was particularly sensitive about references to his youth and inexperience and this made him keen to be assertive in foreign affairs. An autumn 1961 White House luncheon was brought to a horrified standstill when a newspaper editor challenged Kennedy:

> We can annihilate Russia and should make that clear to the Soviet government … you and your Administration are weak sisters … [America needs] a man on horseback … Many people in Texas and the Southwest think that you are riding [your daughter] Caroline's tricycle.

A red-faced Kennedy who retorted 'I'm just as tough as you are' was clearly a president who thought he had much to prove. He was well aware that the nation was more likely to rally around a narrowly elected president during a time of national crisis. His campaign slogan had been 'a time for greatness' and he well knew that great presidents are not easily made in tranquil times. In his book *Profiles of Courage* Kennedy had said that 'great crises make great men'.

iii) Third World insurgency

Kennedy was convinced that the Third World was likely to be the main future arena of the struggle between the US and the Soviet Union. Khrushchev's rhetoric confirmed Kennedy's beliefs and fears. Just before Kennedy's inauguration the Soviet leader had forecast the ultimate triumph of Communism through wars of national liberation in Third World countries such as Vietnam, for which he promised Soviet aid. Convinced that Khrushchev meant to intimidate the United States, Kennedy made the text of that speech compulsory reading for all in his administration (Khrushchev's speech was actually aimed at China, the USSR's rival for the leadership of world Communism). The outgoing President Eisenhower had warned Kennedy that the Republican Party would attack 'any retreat in Southeast Asia', so if Kennedy was to make a stand in the Third World it would probably be somewhere in that region. The nature of that stand was likely to be shaped by Kennedy's fascination with counter-insurgency. Kennedy's specially trained American counter-insurgency force wore and became known as 'Green Berets'. Kennedy kept a green beret on his Oval Office desk.

iv) Advisers

Kennedy's eagerness to get things moving made him impatient with the State Department, so when he sought advice on foreign affairs he looked to those in his close circle whom he trusted, such as Secretary of Defence Robert McNamara. Kennedy was thus influenced by the Defence Department rather than the State Department. The interests and emphases of the former were naturally very different from those of the professional diplomats of the latter. The Defence Department was naturally inclined to see problems in terms of military solutions. There was something about Kennedy's methods of seeking advice that made even his own brother, the Attorney-General Robert (Bobby) Kennedy, uneasy and critical:

> The best minds in government should be utilised in finding solutions to … any problems. They should be available in times other than deep crises and emergencies as is now the case. You talk to McNamara but mostly on Defence matters, you talk to [Treasury Secretary] Dillon but primarily on financial questions … These men should be sitting down and thinking of some of the problems facing us in a broader [con]text. I think you could get a good deal more out of what is available in Government than we are at the present time.

b) Secretary of Defence Robert McNamara – the statistics man

i) Background

The son of a shoe salesman, McNamara attended two top American universities, Berkeley and Harvard. He taught accountancy at the Harvard Business School and the army utilised his statistical expertise in the Second World War. Medical bills for his wife's polio forced him to give up Harvard and seek greater financial rewards. He joined Henry Ford II's 'Whiz Kids' and had risen to the presidency of the Ford Motor Company when Kennedy offered him the Defence Department.

ii) Personality

At Defence, McNamara's enormous energy amazed one colleague, who described him as a man who never walked but ran – even up escalators! The dynamic, tough-talking, fluent, competent and down-to-earth McNamara was the only cabinet member to become part of the charmed social circle around the president. Although McNamara was meticulous in his relations with Secretary of State Dean Rusk, taking care to give him due deference, McNamara's powerful personality coupled with Rusk's deliberately colourless public persona meant that his power within the cabinet was inevitably greater. Enormous influence and judgemental lapses on the part of McNamara proved unfortunate with regard to Vietnam. Like Rusk, McNamara was a great believer in the US commitment to Vietnam, but the Secretary of Defence's solutions to the problems in that faraway land were always military – an emphasis which proved unhelpful.

Profile: Robert McNamara 1916–

1916		– Born in San Francisco, California
1937		– Graduated from University of California, Berkeley
1939		– Master's degree from Harvard Business School. Joined Harvard faculty
1941–5		– Disqualified by poor vision from active service; developed logistical systems for bomber raids and statistical systems for monitoring ground troops and supplies during the Second World War
1940s–50s		– One of the Ford Motor Company's dynamic young 'Whiz Kids' hired to revitalise the company. Successful cost-accounting methods
1960		– President of Ford
1961		– Secretary of Defence in Kennedy administration. Advocated 'flexible response', including counter-insurgency techniques
1962		– Visited South Vietnam; optimistic about US success there. Staunch advocate of increased involvement
1963		– Remained Secretary of Defence in Johnson administration
1964		– Visited South Vietnam, publicly optimistic about US success there
1966		– Visited South Vietnam, publicly optimistic, but privately questioned US involvement
1967		– Openly tried for peace negotiations with Hanoi; publicly opposed bombing of North Vietnam
1968	February	– Left Defence to become President of the World Bank
1968–73		– As President of the World Bank, sympathetic to Third World nations
1995		– Wrote *In Retrospect: The Tragedy and Lessons of Vietnam*, in which he described mistaken assumptions of US foreign policy but managed to avoid putting too much blame on himself personally

McNamara is vitally important in the history of US involvement in Vietnam. As Secretary of Defence, he greatly encouraged first President Kennedy then President Johnson to send US ground troops to Vietnam, and also advocated large-scale bombing. Having played perhaps the major role in getting thousands of US troops into the war, he then changed his mind, and declared that the US had got it all wrong.

iii) Beliefs

Behind his cool and rational exterior, McNamara was emotional and passionate in his beliefs. His good friend Bobby Kennedy thought him 'the most dangerous man in the Cabinet, because he is so persuasive and articulate'. A *New York Times* reporter commended his efficiency but found cause for concern in his total conviction that he was always right, his lack of historical knowledge and his tendency to try to reduce problems to statistics by eliminating the human factor. With regard to Vietnam, as McNamara subsequently admitted, these weaknesses were to prove disastrous. Trained in the importance of statistics, McNamara tended to look at numbers of weapons and men, while forgetting that poorly armed people will sometimes fight to the death for their independence. 'We were kidding ourselves into thinking that we were making well-informed decisions', said one McNamara deputy years later. Unfortunately, President Lyndon Johnson retained McNamara as Secretary of Defence until 1967.

c) Secretary of State Dean Rusk – the quiet professional

i) Background

Born to a middle-class family that fell upon hard times, the poverty-stricken young Rusk was fascinated by politics and international relations. After spending three years at Oxford University on a scholarship, he returned to America and became a lecturer. Second World War desk service led him into the Truman State Department.

Rusk believed that the appeasement of aggressors had led to the outbreak of war in Europe in 1939 and in the Pacific in 1941. His determination to oppose what he considered to be Communist aggression made him a hard-line Cold Warrior. He had had a considerable influence on America's Vietnam policy since the late 1940s.

ii) Relationship with Kennedy

While discussing choices for Secretary of State, Kennedy confessed that he wanted to dominate foreign policy personally, so the self-effacing Rusk seemed a good choice. After their first meeting Rusk told a friend, 'Kennedy and I simply found it impossible to communicate. He didn't understand me and I didn't understand him.' Although in 1987 Rusk could not recall saying that, it seems to have been an accurate summary of their working relationship. Subsequently, and frequently, Rusk almost boasted that he had never been one of the 'in' crowd, saying with sarcastic undertones that he had never been pushed into Ethel Kennedy's swimming pool or played touch football at the Kennedy compound in Hyannis Port. Bobby Kennedy particularly disliked him, claiming that Rusk had had a near mental and physical 'breakdown' during the Cuban Missile Crisis – a 'breakdown' that appears to have escaped the notice of everyone else!

Profile: Dean Rusk 1909–94

1909 – Born in Georgia
1931–4 – Won prestigious Rhodes scholarship to Oxford University
1934–40 – Taught political science at a Californian college
1941–5 – In the Second World War, deputy chief of staff to General 'Vinegar Joe' Stilwell in China–Burma–India theatre
1945–50 – Served in State Department
1950 – Became Assistant Secretary of State for Far Eastern affairs during the Korean War
1952–60 – President of Rockefeller Foundation
1961 – President Kennedy's Secretary of State; let McNamara's Defence Department dominate national policy-making
1963 – After Kennedy's assassination, President Johnson retained Rusk as Secretary of State
1964–8 – Consistently and publicly defended US military intervention in Vietnam
1969 – Professor of International Law at University of Georgia until 1984
1984 – Retired
1994 – Died

Rusk played a vital part in the first three decades of the Cold War. Militantly anti-Communist (he always rejected diplomatic recognition of the People's Republic of China), he encouraged ever-increasing US involvement in Vietnam and, with his self-effacing personality, let State Department influence decline during that increased involvement, 1961–9.

iii) Style and beliefs

As Secretary of State, Rusk was irritated by the theatricality and amateurism of his boss, who listened to brother Bobby rather than the State Department experts. The president complained (to Rusk's underlings among others) that the methodical Rusk was frustrating, slow and indecisive. Rusk felt it his duty to put all the options before the president so that Kennedy could make an informed judgement. Kennedy preferred more decisive recommendations and scathingly referred to Rusk as 'a good errand boy'! Like McNamara, Rusk believed in American involvement in Vietnam, but as the fighting continued there, he felt it was the preserve of the Defence Department rather than the State Department. Unlike McNamara, Rusk never visited Vietnam, confirming the view that he saw it as a Defence Department operation.

Here then was an explosive situation: a crusading president keen to be assertive and to make a name for himself, who felt that the Third World and probably Southeast Asia was the next great Cold War arena; a president who listened to those more likely to put the emphasis upon the military battles than upon the battles for the hearts and minds of the people. It is easy to see how all this would lead to increasing US military involvement in Vietnam.

Summary diagram: The president and his advisers

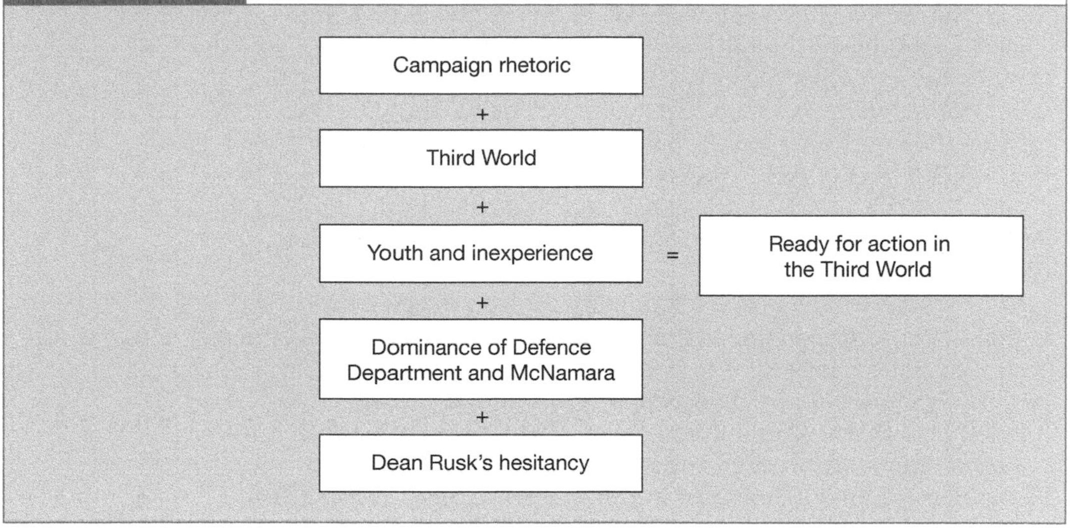

4 | Kennedy's Actions in the Third World

a) Cuba – an early failure

Key question
How do problems in Cuba and Laos help us to understand why Kennedy continued and increased the American involvement in Vietnam?

In his first week in office Kennedy privately declared that the major problem areas of the Third World were the Congo, Cuba, Laos and Vietnam, the last being 'the worst we've got'. Despite a few warning voices within the administration, the US sponsored an unsuccessful anti-Communist invasion at the Bay of Pigs in Cuba in 1961. This Bay of Pigs fiasco bore many of the characteristics of the subsequent Vietnam experience. In Cuba, as in Vietnam, Kennedy felt bound to support an enterprise to which his predecessor had committed America and which took the form of military opposition to a popular nationalist leader who was also a Communist. Fidel Castro, like Ho, had a radical reform programme which many considered appropriate for a Third World country and it was by no means inevitable that he would be the tool of Moscow or Beijing.

Key date
Kennedy humiliated by failure to overthrow Castro in Cuba (Bay of Pigs): April 1961

There was dissent within the Kennedy administration over Cuba as over Vietnam. Some talked of 'adventurism' in Cuba and said intervention would 'compromise our moral position in the world', but what social psychologists call '**group-think**' proved triumphant. In both Cuba and Vietnam the Kennedy administration's policy and actions were neither systematically thought out nor exhaustively discussed by all who might have contributed valuable ideas.

Key term
'Group-think'
When the herd instinct halts independent thought or disagreement.

This Bay of Pigs failure naturally had an impact on US policy towards other Third World countries, including Laos.

b) Laos – neither winning nor losing

Of the three countries (Vietnam, Cambodia and Laos) that had emerged from French Indochina, it was Laos that occupied Kennedy most in the early days of his presidency.

Despite a friend's observation that Laos was not exactly 'a dagger pointed at the heart of Kansas', Kennedy feared a Soviet-backed Communist triumph there. In a March 1961 news conference he implied that the US might intervene militarily – an option favoured by the State Department, the CIA, the JCS, and his close advisers. However, as Bobby Kennedy subsequently recalled, President Kennedy was held back by the Bay of Pigs failure. Also, there were too few soldiers and aircraft available, and Congress feared that intervention might lead to a clash with China.

Kennedy nevertheless sent US military advisers to assist the Laotian leader, an unpopular general whom he described as a 'total shit'. Then, between September 1961 and summer 1962, Kennedy's representative managed to 'neutralise' Laos: the superpowers agreed that it would be governed by a coalition. However, Laotian Communists proved uncooperative and Ho's Vietcong continued to use Laotian trails to get to South Vietnam, confirming Kennedy's feeling that the Communists must be stopped somewhere in Southeast Asia. Events in Laos thus contributed to the increased commitment to Vietnam, although it was not until the final year of Kennedy's presidency that Vietnam overtook Laos in his order of priorities.

c) How Cuba and Laos helped to lead to Vietnam

Key date: Cuban Missiles Crisis: October 1962

The failure of the Bay of Pigs and the 'draw' consequent upon the supposed neutralisation of Laos meant that outright victories had to be won elsewhere. Partly because of the Bay of Pigs failure, Kennedy rejected the option of an early privately negotiated solution to the Cuban Missiles Crisis, preferring a confrontational stance. Similarly, the backing down in Laos was countered by a firm commitment to Diem and South Vietnam. 'There are just so many concessions that one can make to the Communists in one year and survive politically', Kennedy told a friend after the Bay of Pigs. 'We just can't have another defeat in Vietnam.' One insider has suggested that **hawks** within the administration would only accept neutrality in Laos in return for an activist policy in Vietnam.

Key term: **Hawks** Militant Cold Warriors in the USA; those at the other end of the spectrum were known as doves.

Vietnam was more suitable for US intervention than Laos in several ways. It had a long coastline where US naval supremacy could be brought to bear. Diem seemed to many Americans to have South Vietnam under control and democracy seemed to have a good chance of working there. Given that the US was already committed to help South Vietnam before Kennedy's presidency, and given that he had continued that commitment as president, a US departure would result in a loss of face and would 'undermine the credibility of American commitments everywhere', as Rusk and McNamara told Kennedy. They pointed out that there would be 'bitter' divisions amongst the American public if

Kennedy got out of Vietnam, and that 'extreme elements' would make political capital out of the retreat. Kennedy did not want to be accused of 'losing' Vietnam in the way that Truman had 'lost' China.

Summary diagram: Kennedy's actions in the Third World

Cuba Total failure + **Laos** Partial failure = Need to try to win in Vietnam

5 | Kennedy and Diem

It was not really until the summer of 1963 that Kennedy paid much attention to Vietnam. Until then he was preoccupied with other crises. Back in 1961 the journalist Stanley Karnow told the Kennedys that what he had seen in Vietnam was really ominous, but Bobby was impatient: 'Vietnam, Vietnam … we have thirty Vietnams a day here'. Dean Rusk and his State Department were more interested in the Soviet threat in Germany and seemed content to leave Vietnam to Robert McNamara's Defence Department. Tragically, that meant that Kennedy tended to see the Vietnam problem in terms of a military solution, especially as McNamara's team included several generals.

Key question
Did Kennedy's military solution to the Vietnam problem work?

a) Military solutions

i) 1961 – decisions

At Kennedy's accession, there were 800 American military advisers in South Vietnam. Within days of becoming president, Kennedy stepped up the financial aid to Diem to enable him to increase his army. The fact that Diem's quarter of a million soldiers could not wipe out roughly 12,000 Vietcong ought perhaps to have rung louder American alarm bells. The JCS and the **National Security Council** (NSC) recommended putting US ground troops in, but Kennedy preferred to increase the number of advisers there.

Key term

National Security Council
The 1947 Act that established the CIA also established the National Security Council, to co-ordinate US government work on internal and external security; members included the president, vice-president, secretary of state, secretary of defence, and the chiefs of the CIA and JCS.

Convinced that the Eisenhower administration had encouraged the South Vietnamese army (ARVN) to fight the wrong kind of (conventional) war, the Kennedy administration emphasised counter-insurgency. His Green Berets co-operated with the ARVN in counter-insurgency efforts. Diem's soldiers nevertheless continued to lose ground, so in October 1961 Kennedy sent Second World War hero General Maxwell Taylor to evaluate the military situation.

The cultured Taylor was the president's favourite general and a great advocate of flexible response. Like Kennedy, Taylor felt that counter-insurgency would be effective against Communist guerrillas in the Third World. By now there were over 2000 American military advisers in Vietnam. Taylor recommended sending 8000–10,000 American ground troops, while McNamara wanted to send 40,000 and even 200,000 if North Vietnam and China openly intervened.

ii) Increased military involvement

In the first two years of Kennedy's presidency, the number of American military advisers rose alarmingly (3000 in December 1961 to nearly 12,000 by 1962). At the same time, increasing quantities of American weaponry flooded into South Vietnam.

Information about the increased involvement in South Vietnam was mostly kept from the American public. In December 1961 American journalist Stanley Karnow saw a US aircraft carrier bringing 47 American helicopters to Saigon. Shocked, he pointed the carrier out to a US officer who said, 'I don't see nothing'. The US not only provided helicopters, but also pilot 'advisers'. Although Kennedy publicly denied it, these pilot 'advisers' were actively involved in the war. They transported troops, undertook reconnaissance missions and provided fire support for ARVN units. Kennedy authorised the use of defoliants. Sprayed from American helicopters, the defoliants stripped the trees and enabled better aerial observation. Meanwhile, on the ground, more and more American advisers accompanied ARVN units.

In order to co-ordinate this increased US military involvement, the Kennedy administration created the **Military Assistance Command, Vietnam** (MACV), which replaced MAAG (see page 20).

Initially, the greater input of US aid seemed successful. Helicopters dramatically increased the mobility of Diem's troops, while MACV Chief General Paul Harkins boasted that napalm 'really puts the fear of God into the VC … and that's what counts'. However, the military situation soon deteriorated again. The helicopters soon lost their shock value. The VC fired on them and even brought some down. Disloyal and/or cowardly ARVN men warned the VC away from certain areas. ARVN weakness was exposed in the battle of Ap Bac in January 1963.

iii) The battle of Ap Bac (January 1963)

Course of events

In January 1963, a Vietcong force was located in **Ap Bac**, not too far from Saigon. Two thousand ARVN troops, accompanied by 113 American armoured personnel carriers, American-operated helicopters and bombers, and American advisers, went to surround Ap Bac. They did not know that there were as many as 350 guerrillas there. The guerrillas were keen to show that they could counter American firepower and they wanted a victory to boost morale.

The ARVN troops refused to attack the VC at Ap Bac. Five US helicopters and three pilots were lost and the ARVN troops refused to mount a rescue mission.

Key terms

Military Assistance Command, Vietnam
Created by Kennedy to co-ordinate US efforts in South Vietnam in February 1962.

Ap Bac
An important battle, the first major clash between the Vietcong and ARVN, in which American advisers and materials played a big part.

Reasons for the US/ARVN failure

The US/ARVN effort had failed because:

- The strength and preparedness of the Vietcong had been unexpected.
- According to the Americans, the ARVN's General Cao was unwilling to fight.
- Diem was unwilling to listen to American advice on the deployment of his troops: he feared losing too many men and preferred to use his best CIA-trained soldiers to keep himself in power.
- The Americans had not helped in that they had delayed the attack by a day to enable American helicopter pilots to sleep off the excesses of New Year's Eve.

The results/significance of the battle of Ap Bac

The battle was significant because it drew unprecedented attention in the US, where the South Vietnamese performance was unfavourably reviewed. Also, it showed that Diem was probably militarily incapable of winning the war.

Thus, by early 1963, it was clear that, despite ever-increasing US military aid, Diem was not winning the war against the Communists. American officials estimated that Saigon controlled 49 per cent of the population, the VC 9 per cent, with the rest in dispute.

Key dates

Vietcong defeated ARVN and Americans at Battle of Ap Bac: 1963

de Gaulle warned Kennedy of Vietnamese quagmire: May 1961

McNamara said US winning the war: May 1962

iv) Differing viewpoints

When Kennedy visited France in May 1961, President de Gaulle had warned him:

> the more you become involved out there against Communism, the more the Communists will appear as the champions of national independence … You will sink step by step into a bottomless military and political quagmire, however much you spend in men and money.

In November 1961, Kennedy sent a trusted friend, Kenneth Galbraith, to Saigon to assess the situation. Galbraith criticised the administration's diagnosis that this was a military rather than a political problem and said Diem was a loser. Galbraith asked the president what difference there was between French colonialism and American activities in South Vietnam. Galbraith expressed incredulity that anyone in Kennedy's administration could claim that Vietnam was strategically important. He feared that increased US involvement could only end in defeat and humiliation.

When McNamara visited Vietnam in May 1962 he declared that 'every quantitative measurement we have shows we are winning the war', but this was a very dubious assertion. The military solution attempted by Kennedy and Diem was not working. There were many differing viewpoints within the Kennedy administration. Some wondered whether the solution was to send in American ground troops, but Under-Secretary of State George Ball warned that 'we'll have 300,000 men in the paddies and jungles' within five years. 'George, you're crazier than hell', said the president. 'That just isn't going to happen.'

In November 1962 Kennedy sent Senator Mike Mansfield to report on Vietnam. Mansfield's report was critical of Diem and the increasing American involvement. Kennedy was displeased. 'You expect me to believe this?' 'Yes. You sent me', replied Mansfield. 'This isn't what my people are telling me', said Kennedy. Subsequent reports were a mixture of pessimistic references to Diem and the optimistic belief that American firepower must win eventually and that the VC could not afford to continue the struggle in the face of it. Rusk meanwhile warned that US involvement could provoke Hanoi and Beijing and destabilise Laos.

These warnings and uncertainties made Kennedy cautious. He worried that American power might become over-extended. He felt that the Vietnamese situation was very complex, that this was not a clear-cut case of Communist aggression as Korea had been (see page 19). He doubted that Congress and America's SEATO allies (see page 41) would be tempted to intervene in an obscure war so far away with so many guerrilla opponents, where millions had been spent for years without success. While he accepted that Diem needed a great deal more aid and advisers, Kennedy was as yet unwilling to send in US ground troops:

> The troops will march in, the bands will play; the crowds will cheer, and in four days everyone will have forgotten. Then we will be told we have to send in more troops. It's like taking a drink. The effect wears off, and you have to take another.

v) Alternative solutions

Were there alternatives to the military solution? Although some of Kennedy's advisers, such as Averell Harriman, suggested negotiating the US out of Vietnam, none was of Kennedy's inner circle. The negotiation option was never really seriously considered and/or pursued.

In the contemporary Cold War climate, few dared suggest that the US should just get out, especially after one liberal who did so was virtually accused of Communism by Rusk. Kennedy sanctioned unofficial peace talks in the summer of 1962 but Hanoi's position was that America must get out before any meaningful negotiations could take place, so that was the end of that.

Key date

Unsuccessful unofficial peace talks with Hanoi: Summer 1962

One State Department expert suggested to Kennedy that it would be better to concentrate upon giving economic and social assistance to Vietnam. There were others in the State Department, the White House and Congress who felt that the emphasis should be not on military solutions but on internal political, social and economic reform by Diem. It was, however, difficult to persuade Diem to reform.

Key question
Was reform a feasible option?

b) The reform option

i) Vice-President Johnson and Diem

Key dates
Vice-President Johnson visited Diem, urging reform: May 1961
Strategic hamlets programme: 1962

Kennedy was not convinced that Diem and the South Vietnamese really cared about the Cold War, democracy or freedom. Nevertheless in May 1961 he sent Vice-President Johnson to try to persuade Diem that one of the best ways to defeat the Communists was to introduce greater political, social and economic equality to South Vietnam. Johnson urged Diem to reform and also tried flattery. On the advice of the State Department, Johnson proclaimed Diem to be another Churchill! Karnow asked Johnson if he really meant it. 'Diem's the only boy we got out there', said Johnson. While recognising that Diem needed to introduce reforms, Johnson believed that it was a question of national honour to continue supporting 'friends' like Diem. Diem listened to the advice with conflicting emotions: nationalistic fears that Vietnam might become a US protectorate struggled with the realisation that his repressive regime was in trouble and that America might desert him altogether if he was too awkward.

ii) Strategic hamlets

Key term
Strategic hamlets
Fortified villages in South Vietnam, similar to agrovilles.

From early 1962, Diem adopted the policy of '**strategic hamlets**', fortified villages in which the Vietnamese peasants would hopefully be isolated from the Vietcong. Unfortunately the Vietcong frequently joined the other residents and played upon their discontent at having to pay for and to build the stockades.

An American observer noted that the Saigon regime's officials, 'haven't the faintest idea what makes peasants tick – how can they? They are city boys who earned promotion by kissing the asses of their bosses.' The strategic hamlets scheme was run by Diem's brother Ngo Dinh Nhu, who ignored US advice when establishing them, so that within a year the Vietcong captured thousands of US weapons from hamlets foolishly set up too far from Saigon.

Karnow felt that Nhu was 'approaching madness' by this time. Concerned only with increasing his own power, Nhu ignored the social, economic and political reforms that the US suggested he introduce in the hamlets. This led to increased opposition to the Diem/US regime. Many years later it was revealed that Nhu's deputy in this business was a Communist who did his best to sabotage the scheme. The unpopular policies and personalities of Diem and his family and their reluctance to introduce reforms helped to ensure continued Communist successes. Diem's brother Nhu and his wife Madame Nhu were particularly unpopular.

Key question
Why did Americans turn against Diem?

c) Debate and division in Diem's Vietnam

i) 1962

During 1962 there was slowly increasing criticism of Diem's military and political ineptitude in the American press. This was led by Neil Sheehan of United Press International and David Halberstam of the *New York Times*. The latter was warned that he was on Diem's assassination list. Madame Nhu told reporters,

THE MOST IMPORTANT WOMAN IN THE VIETNAM WAR: THE 'DRAGON LADY'

The Kennedy administration spent over two years helping the unpopular Diem, vainly trying to make him reform his government. Diem stubbornly persisted in repressive policies, relying upon his equally unpopular relations. One American diplomat likened Diem and his brother Nhu to Siamese twins, but Diem was not keen on Nhu's wife (nor indeed on any woman). However, Diem patiently suffered his formidable sister-in-law out of family loyalty.

Nhu had been his future mother-in-law's lover but in 1943 he had switched his attentions to the daughter, whom he married. In the absence of any alternative candidate, she became the first lady of her bachelor brother-in-law, Diem, in 1955. Madame Nhu's family were very French in their outlook and her French-style low-necked dresses shocked some of the more old-fashioned Vietnamese. Although her first language was French and she could never write in Vietnamese, Madame Nhu made it clear that she considered herself to be like the patriotic and heroic sisters who had led the Vietnamese struggle against China 2000 years before. As first lady she promoted conservative legislation, including the banning of beauty contests, boxing matches and night-clubs. Cafés were allowed to remain open, provided that the prostitutes who frequented them wore white tunics like nurses! Many southern Vietnamese were traditionally tolerant in matters such as this and they developed an intense dislike of Madame Nhu and her decrees. When US Ambassador Lodge (see page 71) first met Diem he told him that many Americans thought Madame Nhu must be the leader of South Vietnam as they had seen her picture so often. In a rare moment of humour, Diem joked that he frequently threatened his sister-in-law that he would marry, thus depriving her of her supremacy.

Madame Nhu played an important role in the war in that her behaviour, policies and public statements (see page 70) helped to make Diem even more unpopular in South Vietnam and in Washington. Americans were keen to be rid of her and her husband – 'no Nhus is good news', joked one American official.

'Halberstam should be barbecued and I would be glad to supply the fluid and the match.' The Kennedy administration attempted to pressurise the *New York Times* into a change of viewpoint but failed, and then attacked the reporters as unpatriotic and tried to discredit them. On one occasion, Diem's police cornered several American reporters in a back alley in Saigon. They tried to kick one in the kidneys, retreating when the massive Halberstam charged, crying, 'Get back, get back, you sons of bitches, or I'll beat the shit out of you'.

The glamorous Madame Nhu photographed in 1963.

As yet the American press was not questioning the wisdom of involvement in Vietnam, just the tactics pursued and the results attained. Even so, Halberstam had a hard time persuading his editors to print what he wrote.

ii) Early 1963

By the spring of 1963 relations between Diem and the US were very tense. Diem's refusal to work with the French had been a major cause of his rise to power, but it had become increasingly clear that he was incapable of working with anyone. Diem resented US 'advice' and seemed to be considering a settlement with Hanoi which would get the Americans out, while Kennedy told a journalist friend that:

> we don't have a prayer of staying in Vietnam ... These people hate us. They are going to throw our asses out ... But I can't give up a piece of territory like that to the Communists and then get the American people to re-elect me.

iii) Catholics versus Buddhists

It is possible that their mutual Catholicism had played a part in Kennedy's support of Diem. However, Catholics were a minority in South Vietnam and in spring 1963 there was trouble.

The Diem regime allowed the flying of Catholic flags in honour of Diem's brother (an archbishop in the Catholic church), but banned flags for the celebration of Buddha's birthday. When 10,000 Buddhists protested, Diem sent in soldiers. Seven Buddhists were killed.

In June, a 73-year-old Buddhist priest set himself alight in protest. His flesh burned away leaving only his heart, which became an object of worship to the Buddhist majority. This dramatic protest made headlines in America. Other such deaths followed and Madame Nhu made things worse by flippant references to barbecued martyrs. 'Let them burn and we shall clap our hands', she told the press. She and Diem remembered how hundreds of their ancestors had been murdered by Buddhists in the nineteenth century.

Key date

Anti-Diem protests by Buddhists: 1963

Kennedy was shocked at the front-page newspaper pictures of the Buddhist martyrs. 'How could this have happened?' he asked. 'Who are these people? Why didn't we know about them before?' If Kennedy really did not know of the Catholic–Buddhist tension, he had been lax in doing his homework on a country to which he had sent several thousand Americans. If he did know, he was indulging in one of his favourite tactics for deflecting blame from himself (he had blamed faulty intelligence for the Bay of Pigs fiasco) (see page 61).

By August, Diem appeared to be waging religious war on the Buddhist majority, and the administration felt it was time for a new American ambassador. Ambassador Frederick Nolting, who knew little about Asia, was replaced by Henry Cabot Lodge II, who knew a little more.

A Buddhist burns himself to death in protest against Diem's religious policies.

d) Ambassador Lodge

i) 'A single, strong executive ... is needed'

A January 1963 State Department report had summarised America's problems in Vietnam:

> There is no overall planning effort that effectively ties together the civilian and the military efforts. There is little or no long-range thinking about the kind of country that should come out of victory and about what we do now to contribute to this longer-range goal ... The real trouble, however, is that the rather large US effort in South Vietnam is managed by a multitude of independent US agencies and people with little or no overall direction. No one man is in charge ... What is needed, ideally, is to give authority to a single, strong executive, a man perhaps with a military background but who understands that this war is essentially a struggle to build a nation out of the chaos of revolution. One possibility would be to appoint the right kind of general as Ambassador. An alternative would be to appoint a civilian public figure whose character and reputation would permit him to dominate the representatives of all the other departments and agencies.

ii) The right man for the job?

The State Department clearly felt the need for a new ambassador to Vietnam. Was Lodge the right man for the job? In some ways he was. Lodge was a patriot, Second World War military hero, and an experienced and ambitious Republican politician with a particular interest in foreign affairs. When Kennedy offered the post to Lodge he was worried about the photos of the burning monks and said that one of Lodge's main tasks would be to improve relations with the American press, sections of which were attacking US support of Diem. From this point of view Kennedy had chosen the right man, for Lodge's relations with the press were good and he was well aware of its importance. Talking of the Diem regime in August 1963, Lodge said:

> The United States can get along with corrupt dictators who manage to stay out of the newspapers. But an inefficient Hitlerism, the leaders of which make fantastic statements to the press, is the hardest thing on earth for the US Government to support.

iii) The wrong man?

On the other hand, as Nolting said, Lodge was simply 'a piece of Republican asbestos to keep the heat off Kennedy'. Some of those close to Kennedy were shocked at the appointment, knowing Kennedy's low opinion of Lodge's political talents. As so often with Kennedy, personal feelings played a role in his policies: one White House insider said the president was keen to deflate a pompous old rival and therefore approved the appointment 'because the idea of getting Lodge mixed up in such a hopeless mess as Vietnam was irresistible'. Lodge was not ideal for the co-ordinating role envisaged by the State Department. He lacked practice in team work and administration. In some ways he was like Kennedy himself, preferring to use his own sources of information rather than utilise the collective wisdom of the American military and civilian aid agencies in Vietnam.

Rusk told Lodge in June 1963 that Vietnam had become a great burden to the president. It was now taking up more of the president's time than any other issue. Rusk sent Lodge on his way with the comment that:

> We need an ambassador out there who is tough; who can act as a catalyst; who will take responsibility and make decisions and not refer many detailed questions to Washington. We want to make the political side of things go as well as the military side has been going.

Lodge was indeed 'tough' and he certainly did 'act as a catalyst'.

e) Washington, Lodge and the overthrow of Diem

i) Lodge's arrival

Key question
What was the US role in Diem's overthrow?

Lodge believed that 'our help to the [South Vietnamese] regime in past years inescapably gives us a responsibility that we cannot avoid', and that victory was impossible if Diem remained in power. Lodge arrived in Vietnam on 22 August 1963 and was happy to learn of an ARVN plot against Nhu. An anti-Diem group in the Kennedy administration got a preoccupied president to agree that Diem must be got rid of unless he instituted dramatic changes, especially with regard to Nhu and his wife. There had been no real discussion about this, to the anger of McNamara and other influential men. Kennedy had been relaxing on Cape Cod and absorbed by the forthcoming civil rights march on Washington. One member of the administration said that the whole confused episode taught them 'never do business on the weekend'. The administration grew ever more divided over the Diem issue. 'My God', said the president, 'my government's coming apart'.

ii) Paul Kattenburg

On 31 August 1963 an NSC meeting reviewed the prospects of working with Diem. Paul Kattenburg, a State Department expert on Vietnam, was unimpressed by those present – Rusk, McNamara, Maxwell Taylor, Johnson and Bobby Kennedy:

> I listened for about an hour or an hour and a half, before I was asked to say anything at the meeting and they looked to me absolutely hopeless, the whole group of them. There was not a single person there who knew what he was talking about. They were all great men. It was appalling to watch. They did not know Vietnam. They did not know the past. They had forgotten the history. They simply did not understand the identification of nationalism and Communism, and the more this meeting went on, the more I sat there and I thought, 'God, we're walking into a major disaster'.

Kattenburg gave the others his opinions on Vietnam but Rusk snapped, 'That's just your speculation. We will not pull out of Vietnam until the war is won', while McNamara intoned, 'We are winning the war'.

iii) Lodge vs Diem

Meanwhile, in the absence of firm leadership from Washington, Ambassador Lodge acquired an unusual amount of control of US policy in Vietnam. In his first meeting with Diem, aware of Diem's interview tactics ('merciless monologues', according to one historian), Lodge took the initiative and began to criticise Madame Nhu. Lodge then made the common mistake of letting the 'merciless monologist' talk, which Diem did without pause for two hours. Lodge could not get another word in and therefore decided to try to avoid further encounters. He proceeded to turn Congress and American public opinion against Diem and Nhu, through press 'leaks' on their activities and by establishing highly publicised shelters for persecuted Buddhists in the US embassy. Meanwhile, the ARVN plotters were unconvinced of total US support and they began to falter while the Washington search for a meaningful policy continued.

iv) Administration disunity

Kennedy's disunited administration rejected both the option of using US combat troops and the idea of a total withdrawal. In a September interview with TV journalist Walter Cronkite, Kennedy criticised the Saigon regime and said:

> We can help them, we can give them equipment, we can send our men ... as advisers, but they have to win it – the people of Vietnam – against the Communists.

He acknowledged that Diem needed to change his policies and personnel. However, he said it would be a mistake for the United States to get out of Vietnam. 'That only makes it easy for the Communists', said Kennedy. 'I think we should stay.' In another interview three days later Kennedy reiterated the domino theory and warned of the influence of expansionist China in Vietnam.

In early September, Kennedy sent two more observers to Vietnam. The Defence Department representative concentrated upon US military activity and was optimistic; the State Department representative concentrated upon the Diem regime and was pessimistic. 'You two did visit the same country, didn't you?' queried the exasperated president. 'This is impossible. We can't run a policy when there are such divergent views on the same set of facts.'

Kennedy then sent McNamara and the chairman of the JCS, General Maxwell Taylor, to report. Encouraged by Lodge, McNamara and Taylor were critical of Diem. However, their itinerary was dictated by the military in Vietnam and this, coupled with their own unwillingness to admit that their earlier optimism had been unjustified, led them to say that all was going well militarily and that the 16,000 US forces could be withdrawn by

1965. Kennedy publicly announced that 1000 would leave in late 1963.

By this time Nhu was negotiating with Hanoi, confirming the American conviction that he and Diem had to go. President Kennedy said there needed to be a change in the Saigon government, because of the:

> harm which Diem's political actions are causing to the effort against Vietcong rather than … [because of] our moral opposition to the kind of government Diem is running.

Key date: Kennedy said the South Vietnamese had to win the war themselves, but that it would be wrong for the USA to exit: September 1963

Bobby Kennedy floated the idea that perhaps 'now was the time to get out of Vietnam entirely', but there was no one in the administration willing to take up the challenge to look at the problem afresh.

v) The coup

The ARVN plotters now knew that they would have America's tacit support in their **coup**. The White House said it did not wish to 'stimulate' a coup but that it would not 'thwart' one and would help any new regime. The debate about the wisdom of dumping Diem continued until the army generals' coup occurred on 2 November 1963. Lodge had given vital encouragement but publicly he denied any US involvement.

Key term: **Coup**
A *coup d'état* is the illegal overthrow of a government, usually by violent and/or revolutionary means.

It was perhaps naive to think there could be a coup but no assassinations. After the generals' coup, Diem and Nhu fled the government buildings. They were found dead the next day. 'Every Vietnamese has a grin on his face today', said Lodge triumphantly, but Kennedy heard the news of the assassination of Diem and Nhu 'with a look of shock and dismay'. During 1970s' investigations of CIA complicity in plots to assassinate Castro, Kennedy's speech writer said the idea of assassination was 'totally foreign' to Kennedy's 'reverence for human life and his respect for his adversaries' and his 'insistence upon a moral dimension in US foreign policy'. In November 1961 Kennedy himself had told the *New York Times* that 'morally' the US must not be a party to assassination. 'If we get into that kind of thing, we'll all be targets.' We might never know for certain whether Kennedy tacitly approved the idea of assassinating his Cuban enemy Castro or his Vietnamese friend Diem, but it seems possible that he did.

Ironically Kennedy himself would meet the same fate as Diem within three weeks. 'The chickens have come home to roost', said Madame Nhu with grim satisfaction.

Key date: Diem assassinated; Kennedy assassinated: November 1963

vi) The situation at Kennedy's death

At the moment of Kennedy's death there were nearly 17,000 American 'advisers' in Vietnam. The increase in the number of American advisers in Vietnam during Kennedy's presidency is the most convincing argument that Kennedy would not have 'got the United States out of Vietnam'. Historians disagree over what Kennedy's Vietnam policy would have been, had he lived. He was talking of a thorough review of America's Vietnam policy just before he died. Some of his intimates insist he would have got America out of Vietnam. Kennedy told one senator friend, 'I can't [get out] until 1965 – after I'm re-elected'.

However, Rusk, Johnson and Bobby Kennedy were among those who said he had no plans to get out. Indeed, Bobby, who knew him best, said that, effectively, his brother had no plans at all! Kennedy's biographer James Giglio describes Kennedy's Vietnam policy as a shambles at the time of his death. The formulation of that policy raises many questions about the leadership qualities of John Fitzgerald Kennedy, and about the way he selected and listened to advisers. It also raises disturbing questions about the difficulties of conducting foreign policy in a democracy (see page 48).

Summary diagram: Kennedy and Diem

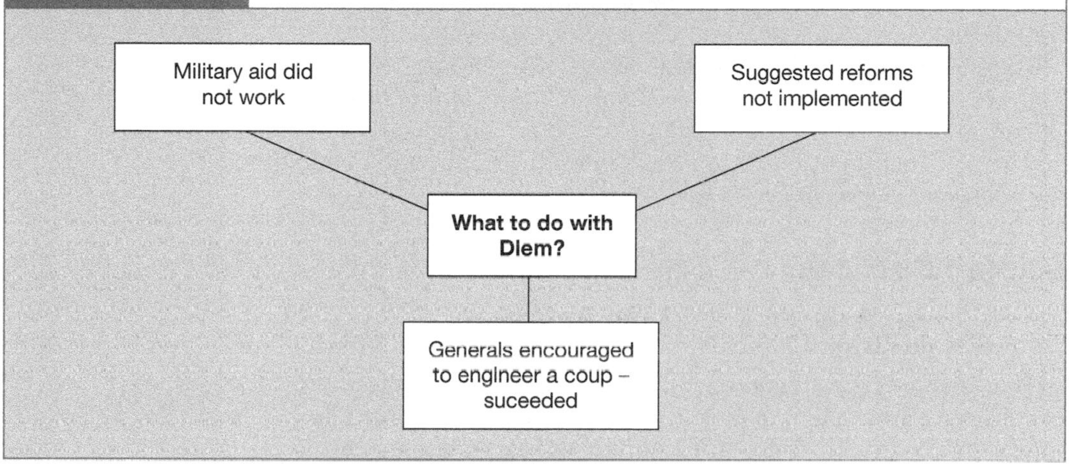

6 | Conclusions

Key question
Were Kennedy's Vietnam policies wise?

Kennedy's belief that little Vietnam was so important seems ludicrous to us, but it must be said that in the contemporary Cold War context many other Americans agreed with him. Early setbacks in his presidency (the Bay of Pigs and the Vienna summit with Khrushchev, see page 55) caused Kennedy to confide to a *New York Times* reporter, 'Now we have a problem in making our power credible, and Vietnam is the place'. The JCS warned Kennedy that, 'any reversal of US policy could have disastrous effects, not only on our relationship with South Vietnam, but with the rest of our Asian and other allies as well'. Particular events confirmed and shaped Kennedy's Cold War mentality, leading him into increased commitment to Vietnam.

That country's internal politics and Diem's failings in particular led to confusion as, having decided that 'Vietnam is the place' and having continued the commitment to Diem, it was then difficult for Kennedy to admit that this was all a mistake. Getting rid of Diem did not improve the situation and served to confirm the tendency to believe that in the absence of any other constructive ideas, increased force would somehow do the trick. General Westmoreland subsequently attributed enormous significance to the American role in the demise of Diem. It 'morally locked us in Vietnam'. By encouraging a change of government in South Vietnam, Kennedy greatly increased America's obligation to subsequent Saigon governments. Kennedy recognised this in a cable to Lodge on 6 November 1963.

Following the route sketched out by his predecessors, Kennedy had interpreted events in Vietnam within a Cold War context which did not really apply. Ho Chi Minh was neither a Moscow nor a Beijing puppet and it could be argued that Kennedy had invested Vietnam with a Cold War importance that it did not really merit. Despite his frequent uncertainty about the wisdom of US involvement, he had increased his country's commitment to an unpopular regime which he then helped to overthrow in the last weeks of his life. The Kennedy administration claimed to be promoting democracy in South Vietnam but had supported a dictator and then a military clique. The nature of that US support was primarily military and financial and the reforming efforts of the non-military American personnel were handicapped by the unpleasant nature of the South Vietnamese regimes. Kennedy had passed a poisoned chalice to his successor.

7 | Key Debates

a) Why Kennedy increased the American commitment

Historians differ in trying to explain why Kennedy increased the American commitment to South Vietnam. Orthodox historians (for example, Smith, 1984–90) argue that Moscow/Beijing support of Hanoi gave Kennedy little choice. In the Cold War era, he simply had to resist Communism.

Revisionists are critical of Kennedy's motives. For example, McCormick (1989) and Hearden (1991) claim that he was sustaining America's overseas empire. Duiker (1994) and Berman (1982) accused Kennedy of exaggerating the strategic importance of Vietnam and emphasised domestic political calculations. Kaiser (2000) is generally sympathetic to Kennedy, emphasising how he long resisted great pressure from his military and civilian advisers to get involved in a war in Southeast Asia, whether Vietnam or Laos. That great pressure naturally contributed greatly to the increased American commitment.

b) The commitment trap

Many historians believe that as Truman and Eisenhower had committed the US to involvement in Vietnam, Kennedy was caught in the '**commitment trap**'.

Kennedy himself told General de Gaulle that he had inherited the possibly unwisely created SEATO from Eisenhower and that it would look bad if the United States dumped SEATO. In 1976, Jonathan Schell pointed out that a crucial change from the Eisenhower administration to the Kennedy administration was

Key term

Commitment trap The theory that each president after Truman was bound to continue the US involvement in Vietnam.

that the 'territorial domino theory' became the 'psychological domino theory' or the 'doctrine of credibility'. It was not so much the territorial loss as the psychological loss that would be crucial if Vietnam fell – not so much that other territories would become Communist, but that the world would see that the United States lacked the determination to prevail.

c) The assassination of Diem

Historians differ over the significance of the assassination of Diem. Some historians (for example, Hammer, 1987) and contemporaries (for example, Lyndon Johnson and Richard Nixon) cite US collusion in the coup against Diem as the US government's greatest mistake and probably the single most important cause of the full-scale American involvement in the war. On the other hand, Kaiser (2000) claims that the greatest responsibility for the overthrow of Diem lay with Diem himself, as he had managed to alienate all his supporters, whether South Vietnamese or American. Kaiser also emphasised how Rusk and in particular McNamara urged continued support of Diem to the very end.

d) What if Kennedy had lived?

Counterfactual history asks 'what if' a particular event had not happened. It is currently highly fashionable and much debated. Because Kennedy's assassination cut short his presidency, there is inevitably much counterfactual speculation on 'what might have happened if Kennedy had lived'.

History as written by Kennedy's old friends and associates, such as Arthur Schlesinger Jr, claims that Kennedy would have got out of Vietnam. This exonerates Kennedy (and his friends and associates) from any blame for what turned out to be a highly unpopular and unsuccessful war. Much depends upon which Kennedy pronouncements and/or actions one concentrates upon. Persuaded by Kennedy's expressed doubts about involvement, William Rust and John Newman contend that, had he lived, Kennedy would have withdrawn American military advisers. Freedman (2000) studies Kennedy's Vietnam policies in the context of Kennedy's response to crises in Berlin, Cuba and Laos, and concludes that Kennedy would not have escalated the US involvement in Vietnam. Freedman's well-substantiated arguments are in themselves quite persuasive, although, significantly, Freedman makes little mention of Kennedy's dramatic increase in the number of advisers sent to Vietnam.

On the other hand, concentrating upon the scale of Kennedy's escalation of the involvement, Bassett and Pelz doubt that Kennedy intended to withdraw. 'There had been no official American reassessment of the strategic value of Vietnam. The commitment, in fact, was stronger than ever', said Anderson (2005); thousands more advisers had been sent in and Kennedy had 'embraced the war both in private and in public, making it more difficult for his successor to walk away from it'. Fredrik Logevall (2001) emphasises that 'public outrage' in the US at

Diem's refusal to reform and mistreatment of Buddhists gave Kennedy 'a plausible excuse for disengaging the United States from Vietnam' – had he wanted to do so.

Some key books in the debates

L.J. Bassett and S.E. Pelz, in T.G. Paterson, editor, *Kennedy's Quest for Victory* (New York, 1989).
W.J. Duiker, *US Containment Policy and the Conflict in Indochina* (Stanford, 1994).
E.J. Hammer, *A Death in November: America in Vietnam, 1963* (New York, 1987).
L. Freedman, *Kennedy's Wars* (Oxford, 2000).
P.J. Hearden, *The Tragedy of Vietnam* (New York, 1991).
D. Kaiser, *American Tragedy: Kennedy, Johnson, and the Origins of the Vietnam War* (Harvard, 2000).
F. Logevall, *The Origins of the Vietnam War* (Longman, 2001).
T.J. McCormick, *America's Half-Century: US Foreign Policy in the Cold War* (Baltimore, 1989).
J.M. Newman, *JFK in Vietnam* (New York, 1992).
W.J. Rust, *Kennedy in Vietnam* (New York, 1985).
R.B. Smith, *An International History of the Vietnam War*, 3 vols (New York, 1984–90).
J. Schell, *Time of Illusion* (New York, 1976).

Summary diagram: 'Vietnam is the place' – the Kennedy crusade 1961–3

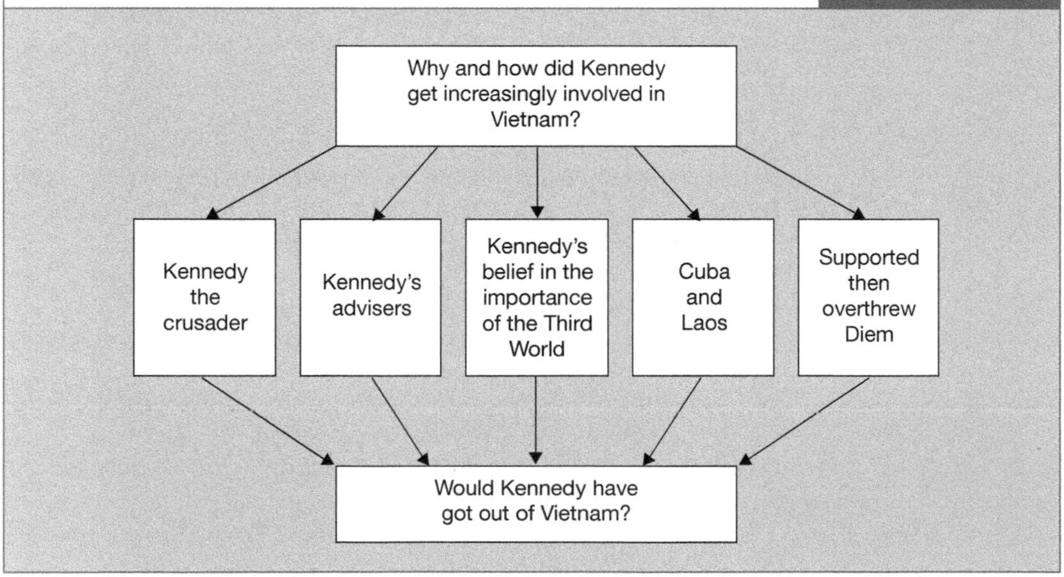

Study Guide: AS Questions

In the style of AQA

(a) Explain why the Vietcong were able to win popular support in South Vietnam between 1956 and 1963. (12 marks)

(b) 'Kennedy chose to increase American commitment to South Vietnam because he wanted to maintain the USA's status as a super-power.' Explain why you agree or disagree with this statement. (24 marks)

Exam tips

The cross-references are intended to take you straight to the material that will help you to answer the questions.

(a) To answer this question you will need to provide a range of factors and prioritise between these. There are a number of reasons to assess:

- The appeal of Communism (page 13).
- Ho Chi Minh's nationalism and patriotism (pages 11–12).
- The military effectiveness of the Communists, and the ineffectiveness of ARVN (pages 25–7 and 64).
- The refusal of Diem to introduce meaningful political and economic reform (pages 67–8).
- The corruption and unpopular policies and personnel in Diem's government (for example, the Nhus, agrovilles, strategic hamlets, the persecution of Buddhists and the favouring of Catholics; pages 67–70).
- The association of the Diem regime with the United States, which offended Vietnamese nationalism (page 43).

Structure your answer carefully and try to offer a logical and well-supported conclusion that emphasises what you consider to be the main factor or factors.

(b) Clearly it would be wrong to suggest there was only one reason for the increase in US involvement in Vietnam under Kennedy and this question is effectively asking you to evaluate a range of reasons and to assess whether the desire for superpower status was the most important or overriding factor. Historians are divided on the issue (see pages 76–7), so there is really no right or wrong answer. Your response should be as convincing as you can make it, given the evidence available to you, but do try to offer some sort of judgement. You will probably want to consider Kennedy's early ideas about Vietnam (summarised on page 54); his own character and youth when he became president; his personal advisers; the influence of Cuba; and his relationship with Diem. As well as the broad internal and external pressures on Kennedy, you should assess the importance of ideological (the domino theory, page 52), economic (Southeast Asia contained minerals and other important economic resources), and strategic considerations (referring, for example, to the debate over Laos). Your answer should be analytical, leading to a balanced and convincing conclusion.

5 'Johnson's War'?

POINTS TO CONSIDER

President Johnson's real preoccupation was social reform in United States, where he wanted a 'Great Society'. Yet he sent nearly a million American soldiers to Vietnam and became the president most associated with and hated for what he called 'that bitch of a war'.

This chapter covers what is probably the major question facing anyone studying American involvement in Vietnam: was it Johnson's war? This question is investigated in sections on:

- Why Johnson continued US involvement in the war
- How Johnson was able to escalate the war
- Why did Johnson escalate the American involvement in Vietnam?
- Johnson's doubts – 'Where are we going?'
- Historians and 'Johnson's war'?

Key dates

1963	November	Kennedy assassinated; Johnson became president
	December	Increased numbers of PAVN regulars sent to South Vietnam
1964	March	South Vietnamese situation 'very disturbing' (Taylor and McNamara); Johnson publicly confident, privately uncertain
	August	Gulf of Tonkin incident and resolution
	November	US presidential election
		Working Group recommended escalation
	December	Vietcong attacked Saigon bar full of American officers
1965	February	Vietcong attacked huge US airbase near Pleiku
		Johnson authorised 'Rolling Thunder'
	March	'Rolling Thunder' began
		First American ground troops landed in Vietnam
		First anti-war protests in American universities

	May	Congress voted $700 million for war in Vietnam
	June	Ky became leader of South Vietnam
	July	Johnson announced he was sending 50,000 more troops to South Vietnam
	October	Americans beat North Vietnamese army at la Drang President Johnson asked 'Where are we going?'
	December	Over 200,000 US troops in Vietnam; polls showed most Americans pro-escalation
1968		535,000 US troops in South Vietnam

Key question
Did the US world-view in 1963, the circumstances of Johnson's accession to the presidency and the presidential advisers, make Johnson's continuation of the war inevitable?

1 | Why Johnson Continued US Involvement in the War

a) A man of his time

Johnson aroused much hostile criticism for 'his' war, but he was a typical American of his time in his patriotism, anti-Communism and misunderstanding of foreigners.

i) Patriotism

Johnson was intensely patriotic and proud of US military prowess. As a senator he always voted to build up the armed forces. America had always been victorious in wars. Defeat by what he called 'that damn little pissant country', 'that raggedy-ass little fourth-rate' Vietnam was inconceivable.

ii) Ideology, security and national honour

Like many Americans, Johnson genuinely believed his country fought for world freedom as well as American security in two world wars, in Korea and in Vietnam. Like many of his generation, he abhorred the idea of appeasing an enemy: 'If you let a bully come into your front yard one day, the next day he'll be up on your porch, and the day after that he'll rape your wife in your own bed'. As vice-president, Johnson firmly believed that America should fight Communist 'aggressors' in Southeast Asia whatever the cost. Like Kennedy and Eisenhower, Johnson believed that Vietnam was a 'domino': if it fell to Communism the countries around it would rapidly follow suit. He felt that it was a question of national honour for the United States to continue its commitment to its South Vietnamese ally.

iii) Misunderstanding foreigners

Like many Americans, Johnson found it quite difficult to understand foreign affairs and foreigners. 'The trouble with foreigners is that they're not like the folks you were reared with', he said, only half jokingly. Johnson read and travelled widely but it did not necessarily lead to greater understanding. On a

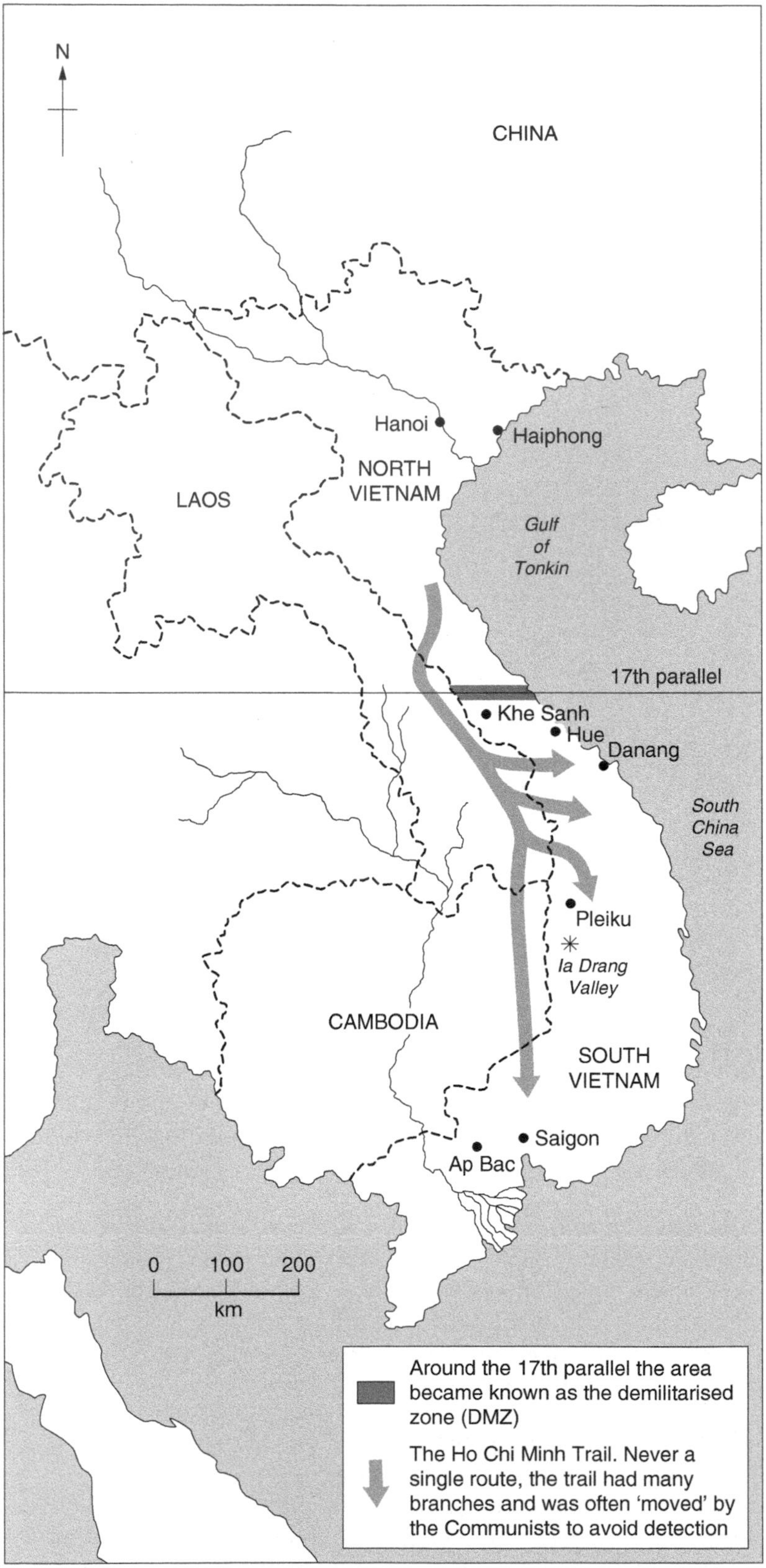

Important places in the American era in Vietnam (c. 1956–73).

Profile: Lyndon Baines Johnson 1908–73

1908		– Born into poor Texas ranching family
1920s		– Three years' teacher training at college; volunteer work in state politics
1932		– Went to Washington DC as legislative assistant to a congressman
1935–7		– Director of a New Deal agency (designed to help the poor) in Texas Ran successfully for seat in House of Representatives
1941		– Failed to get elected to Senate
1948		– Elected senator after vicious campaign that included vote fraud on both sides in the Democratic primary
1951		– Democratic whip
1955–61		– Majority leader in Senate
1960		– Joined Democratic ticket as Kennedy's vice-presidential candidate
1963	November	– Kennedy assassinated, Johnson became president
1964	November	– Elected president, with unprecedented majority
1965		– Sent first American ground troops to Vietnam, which made him increasingly unpopular
1968	March	– Said would not stand for presidency again, and would request peace talks
1969	January	– Returned to Texas ranch
1973		– Died

In the context of the Vietnam War, Johnson is usually considered to be the most important president. It was he who sent in tens of thousands of American ground troops, for which he became (and remains) exceptionally unpopular.

vice-presidential visit to Thailand he was furious when a fellow American advised him against shaking hands with the Thais, who dislike physical contact with strangers. 'Damn it', cried Johnson, 'I have shaken hands with people everywhere and they have all loved it!' He felt that Ho Chi Minh was another Hitler and should be treated accordingly.

b) The impact of Kennedy's assassination

Key date

Kennedy assassinated; Johnson became president: November 1963

Did Johnson's patriotism, anti-Communism and misunderstanding of foreigners make it inevitable that he would continue American involvement in Vietnam? Perhaps not. He knew that a long war would probably lose the support of Congress and the public. He knew the weaknesses of the Saigon government. In 1961 he said that Diem must reform and fight his own war. He knew that only China and the USSR would benefit if America got 'bogged down chasing guerrillas' over Asiatic rice fields and jungles. Nevertheless, he continued the American involvement. One major reason was the Kennedy legacy.

During Johnson's vice-presidency he fretted at the insignificance of vice-presidential tasks and it must have crossed his mind that Kennedy's death was all that stood between him and the world's greatest office. He resented the younger and less experienced man being president. Amidst the sorrow that Johnson felt at Kennedy's assassination in November 1963, there was also joy at attaining the presidency.

Guilt feelings contributed to his determination to stand by all Kennedy had done and those who had helped Kennedy to do it. 'I swore to myself that I would carry on', Johnson subsequently explained. 'I would continue for my partner who had gone down ahead of me … When I took over, I often felt as if President Kennedy were sitting there in the room looking at me.' Two days after Kennedy's assassination, the new president told Ambassador Lodge he was not going to 'lose Vietnam … Tell those generals in Saigon that Lyndon Johnson intends to stand by our word'. 'My first major decision on Vietnam had been to reaffirm President Kennedy's policies', Johnson said later.

The tragic circumstances of Johnson's accession to power thus caused him to make a vital decision with little apparent debate and discussion. Emotionally and constitutionally, the new president felt that he had to continue the policies of his properly elected predecessor.

There is a case for calling Vietnam 'Kennedy's war'. Kennedy had increased American involvement in Vietnam. As vice-president, Johnson had opposed American support for the coup against Diem, realising that it dramatically increased American obligation to subsequent Saigon regimes. However, Kennedy's death ensured that Johnson would not repudiate his predecessor's Vietnam policy. Knowing he had no real **popular mandate**, the new president hesitated to abandon any Kennedy commitment or Kennedy officials. The retention of Kennedy's advisers helped to ensure continued involvement in Vietnam.

Key term

Popular mandate
Clear evidence that a political leader has the majority of the people behind him and his policies.

c) Johnson and his advisers

In order to decide whether Vietnam was 'Johnson's war', his relationship with his advisers must be investigated. Did they share responsibility for the war?

i) Was Johnson in charge?

Johnson thought he was the boss. He told his advisers he wanted a 'kiss-my-ass-at-high-noon-in-Macy's-window and tell me it smells like roses' loyalty. He wanted every assistant's 'pecker in my pocket'. He made his aides work with him while he defecated in the bathroom. Johnson said he wanted honesty, good judgement and sound ideas from advisers but, understandably, they often just said what he wanted to hear. In 1966 an official told Stanley

Karnow that Johnson's friend Judge Abe Fortas was his most influential adviser on Vietnam. 'But Fortas doesn't know anything about Vietnam', exclaimed Karnow. 'True', said the official, 'but he knows a lot about Lyndon Johnson'. Some think Johnson had a closed mind, but others say he was poorly advised on Vietnam.

ii) Kennedy's men

Johnson's freedom of action and thought were inevitably circumscribed because in the circumstances of his accession to power he was tied to Kennedy's men. Johnson's retention of Kennedy men such as McNamara and Rusk meant that no fresh ideas emerged on the Vietnam problem. Rusk was obsessive about continuing the struggle in Southeast Asia. He believed that withdrawal would cause loss of faith in America's commitment to oppose Communist aggression and lead to a Third World War. McNamara was so important in making policy that some called Vietnam 'McNamara's war'. In his memoirs (1995) McNamara criticised both himself and Johnson's other civilian and military advisers for an inability to ask the searching and relevant questions that needed to be asked at every stage of US involvement in Vietnam. McNamara lamented the administration's lack of historical knowledge and understanding of matters such as Sino-Vietnamese rivalry (there was a scarcity of China experts in the State Department due to the McCarthy hysteria) (see page 19).

iii) Warning voices

There were some warning voices. In 1963 the influential Democratic Senate majority leader, Mike Mansfield, suggested a united and neutralised Vietnam. Johnson rejected this, correctly predicting that it would soon lead to the swift Communisation of the whole of Vietnam. Johnson, Rusk and McNamara assured Mansfield that if the South Vietnamese government adopted political, economic and social policies to win over their people there would be no need for major and direct US involvement. However, as Mansfield knew, the Saigon government was unlikely to reform. Mansfield never gave up. He kept asking Johnson pertinent questions:

- Why should a democracy like the US support military governments in Saigon?
- Did the people of South Vietnam really want a crusade against Communism?
- What US interest was at stake in little Vietnam?

Johnson did not want this kind of discussion. 'The president expects that all senior officers of the government will move energetically to insure the full unity of support for … US policy in Vietnam', said a secret memorandum of November 1963. Although the CIA was gloomy about the situation in Vietnam, many in the administration believed that America would somehow triumph. The Kennedy men remaining in the State and Defence Departments and the White House wanted to save face. No one wanted to admit past errors. No one seemed to want real debate.

iv) Advice from the military

In wartime the beliefs and advice of the military were inevitably influential. Like Kennedy, Johnson found some military men scary, especially Air Force chief Curtis LeMay. LeMay wanted to 'bomb Vietnam back into the Stone Age'. However, Johnson inherited involvement in a war and as commander-in-chief felt duty-bound to listen to the generals. As Vietnam was the only war the generals had, they wanted to continue with it and indeed intensify it in order to win.

v) The first president to lose a war

Johnson's personal political ambition reinforced what the generals were advising. He repeatedly said he did not want to be the first president to lose a war, especially to the Communists. Johnson's military and civilian advisers and his own beliefs and ambitions thus guided him towards the continuation of the commitment to Vietnam, even though the situation there was deteriorating.

d) Early debates, doubts and decisions

Key question
How was Vietnam being 'reassessed' by the Johnson administration in 1963–4?

i) The situation in Vietnam, 1963–4

From December 1963 Hanoi sent increasing numbers of People's Army of North Vietnam (PAVN) regulars south, which greatly strengthened the VC. Diem's successor, General 'Big' Minh, retreated to his tennis court and his garden where he raised orchids. He was soon deposed. Minh's successors were even less impressive. The strategic hamlets programme was clearly a failure and the VC impressively countered US air power with ever-increasing supplies of Soviet and Chinese weaponry. It was estimated that the Communists controlled around half of South Vietnam. General Maxwell Taylor and McNamara visited Saigon and in March 1964 described the situation as 'very disturbing'. The South Vietnamese were generally apathetic and unwilling to fight. Prime Minister Khanh begged for more US aid.

ii) The debate on what to do next

Taylor, McNamara and the JCS favoured direct action against North Vietnam. LeMay said North Vietnam should be bombed because 'we are swatting flies [in South Vietnam] when we should be going after the manure pile [North Vietnam]'. Johnson felt the war needed to be won quickly before Congress demanded American withdrawal. Early in the Johnson presidency Vietnam was supposedly being 'reassessed' every day, but what was being reassessed by the Johnson administration was not *whether* American involvement should continue but *how* it should continue.

Key dates

Increased numbers of PAVN regulars sent to South Vietnam: December 1963

South Vietnamese situation 'very disturbing' (Taylor and McNamara); Johnson publicly confident, privately uncertain: March 1964

iii) Public confidence, private doubts

On 20 April Johnson publicly declared that America was 'in this battle as long as South Vietnam wants our support' in its fight for freedom, but his private doubts were revealed in May 1964 conversations:

> I don't think the people of the country know much about Vietnam, and I think they care a hell of a lot less. We tell [Moscow, Beijing and Hanoi] ... that we'll get out of there [Vietnam] ... if they will just quit raiding their neighbours. And they say 'Screw you'. All the senators are all saying 'Let's move, let's go into the North.' They'd impeach a president that would run out, wouldn't they? ... I stayed awake last night thinking of this thing ... It looks to me like we're getting into another Korea ... I don't think that we can fight them 10,000 miles away from home ... I don't think it's worth fighting for. And I don't think that we can get out. It's just the biggest damned mess ... What the hell is Vietnam worth to me? ... What is it worth to this country? ... Of course if you start running from the Communists, they may just chase you into your own kitchen ... This is a terrible thing we're getting ready to do.

Summary diagram: Why Johnson continued US involvement in the war

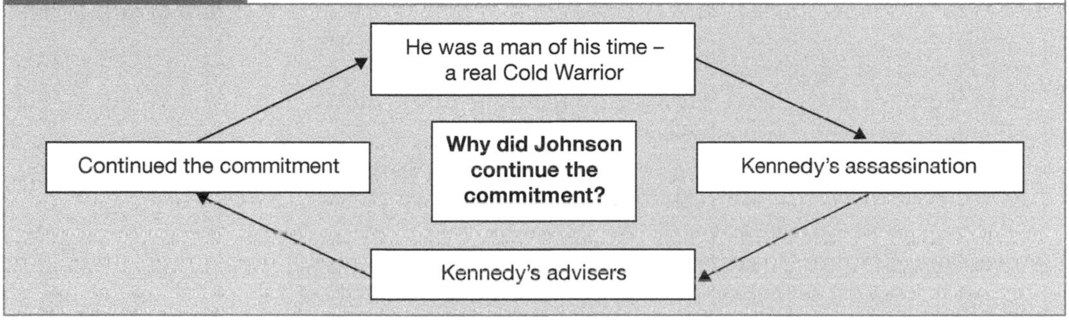

2 | How Johnson was Able to Escalate the War

Key question
How did the Gulf of Tonkin crisis and the 1964 presidential election impact upon US involvement in Vietnam?

By July 1964, 200 Americans had died in Vietnam, and Johnson had added 2500 men to the US forces there. South Vietnam's war against the Communists was not going well but debate in Washington centred on how to help Saigon to win it, not how to get out of it. Most of Johnson's advisers, led by Rusk and McNamara, now urged escalation. If it were necessary for success, they argued, America should even strike at North Vietnam itself.

Johnson thought that if the time came for escalation of American involvement in Vietnam, he would need congressional and public support. He believed that he obtained the former with the Gulf of Tonkin resolution, and the latter in the presidential election of November 1964.

a) August 1964 – the Gulf of Tonkin resolution

i) Sabotage and spying in the North

For a decade the CIA had been secretly sending South Vietnamese teams on sabotage missions to the North. In the first half of 1964 South Vietnamese gunboats raided North Vietnam's coast and Johnson approved covert American operations. American ships such as the *Maddox* went on espionage missions in the North's coastal waters.

Gulf of Tonkin incident and resolution: August 1964

Key date

ii) The Gulf of Tonkin incident

Johnson claimed that the North Vietnamese made two unprovoked attacks on the *Maddox* and the *Turner Joy* in the Gulf of Tonkin. On 4 August 1964 he asked for congressional support for avenging the attacks.

iii) The Gulf of Tonkin resolution

In June 1964, the administration had drawn up a resolution. The aim of that resolution was to raise Saigon's morale, but the administration had hesitated to introduce it into Congress. The Gulf of Tonkin incident now gave Johnson the opportunity to get this resolution passed.

Believing that the lives of innocent American sailors had been jeopardised by the North Vietnamese, Congress willingly passed the Gulf of Tonkin resolution. The resolution gave the president the power to wage war in Vietnam: as Johnson said, it was 'like grandma's night-shirt – it covered everything'. In its final form the resolution said North Vietnamese naval units:

> in violation of … international law, have deliberately and repeatedly attacked United States naval vessels lawfully present in international waters … The United States regards as vital to its national interest and to world peace the maintenance of international peace and security in Southeast Asia. Consonant [in accordance] with the Constitution of the United States and the Charter of the United Nations and in accordance with its obligations under the Southeast Asia Collective Defence Treaty [see page 41], the United States is, therefore, prepared, as the President determines, to take all necessary steps, including the use of armed force, to assist any member or protocol state of the Southeast Asia Collective Defence Treaty requesting assistance in defence of its freedom.

The resolution would expire when the president believed that the situation in Southeast Asia was safe or when Congress decided to terminate it.

A few senators led by Mansfield were unconvinced that America was acting correctly. One bitterly pointed out that they had no choice but to support the president when he said there was a crisis. Another said 'all Vietnam is not worth the life of a single American boy', but no one listened. The Senate had been two-thirds empty for the debate on the resolution, which it passed 88 to 2.

iv) Who was to blame for the escalation?

Should Congress be blamed for giving Johnson the power to escalate the war? Johnson and McNamara were not totally open with them about the covert raids, the incident or the implementation of the resolution. Did the administration wait for and even create the incident in order to get the resolution passed? The American naval missions were provocative and there are many doubts surrounding the second North Vietnamese 'attack'. 'Hell', the president admitted years later, 'for all I know, our navy was shooting at whales out there'.

During the summer of 1964, the Republican presidential candidate Barry Goldwater was accusing Johnson of being 'soft on Communism', so the president wanted to appear firm. Did Johnson exploit events both to intensify US military involvement in Vietnam and to win over the American public in an election year? While Johnson was trying to decide whether there had been a second attack, the press reported the supposed incident and Johnson felt trapped, fearing that if he did nothing his Republican opponent in the presidential election would call him a coward.

v) Results and significance of the Gulf of Tonkin resolution

The results and significance of the passage of the resolution were vitally important. With the resolution, Johnson appeared to have the nation behind him. Now the war could really be taken to the North: American aircraft bombed North Vietnam for the first time. This escalation made Johnson look tough. His public **approval rating** rose from 42 to 72 per cent, helping him to win the presidential election. Ominously, American prestige was even more firmly committed to defending South Vietnam. Should another escalatory step seem necessary it would be even easier. The resolution and the presidential election suggested a nation united behind its president in his Vietnam policy.

Key term

Approval rating
American pollsters continually check the public's opinion (approval) of the president's performance.

b) The 1964 presidential election

Key date

US presidential election: November 1964

During the election campaign the administration became aware that the voters were asking many questions about Vietnam:

- Why are we still there?
- Why are we there at all?
- Why haven't we trained the Vietnamese to do their own fighting?
- Why can't we win?
- Why can't it be a UN effort like Korea?
- Would it be so disastrous if we got out?

Foreign policy issues are rarely decisive in American presidential elections, but they were probably more important than usual in 1964. The Republican candidate Barry Goldwater was prone to verbal gaffes. When he said that America ought to use all its strength to win in Vietnam, he was seen as a trigger-happy hawk. He was widely if wrongly perceived as recommending the use of atomic weapons on Hanoi, while Johnson was perceived as the peace candidate. Privately, Goldwater said that as Vietnam was 'a national burden' and the people were divided over both the legitimacy of US involvement and the conduct of the war, it was not in America's best interests to make the war a campaign issue. Johnson was greatly relieved. This meant that there was no great open debate on Vietnam.

Johnson knew that if left-wingers accused him of being a war-monger or if right-wingers accused him of being 'soft on Communism' he might not get re-elected. He therefore reassured the left by saying that he did not intend to do anything rash or have a major war. He made a promise that might have been crucial to his re-election: 'We are not going to send American boys away from home to do what Asian boys ought to be doing for themselves'. On the other hand, he reassured the right by saying 'America keeps her word'. At Christmas 1963 he had told the JCS that he did not want to lose South Vietnam or get America into a war before the election: 'Just let me get elected and then you can have your war'. He also gained votes by appearing tough over the Gulf of Tonkin incident.

Did Johnson plan to escalate once elected? Like Kennedy, Johnson hoped that Saigon would be able to win its own war. During the election campaign neither he nor his advisers knew for sure exactly what to do about Vietnam, but most were reluctantly concluding that escalation was the only answer. He concentrated first on winning the election. Having won, he believed that he had a popular mandate to do as he saw fit.

Summary diagram: How Johnson was able to escalate the war

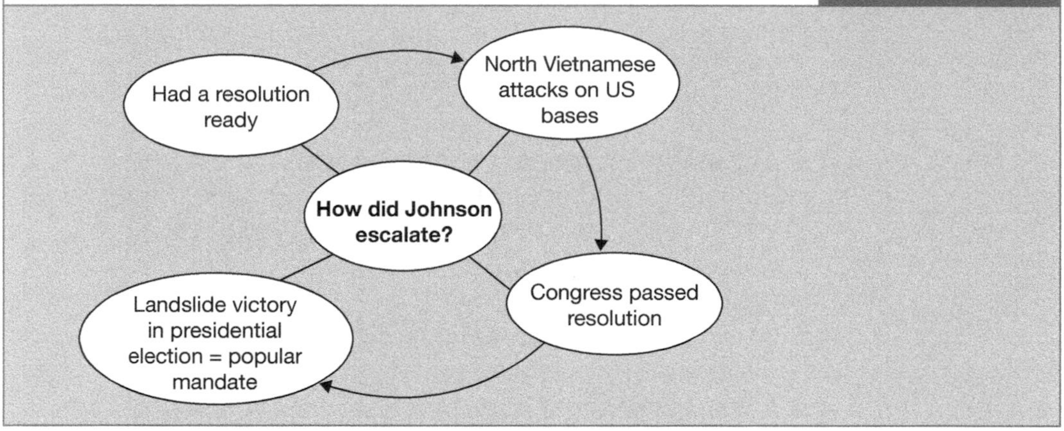

3 | Why Did Johnson Escalate the American Involvement in Vietnam?

Key question
How did the performance of the Saigon government lead Johnson to escalate?

Some people believe that Johnson's combative personality made escalation inevitable. Some make much of his macho Texas background, suggesting that such an aggressive man would seek military solutions to problems. Many consider him over-confident. Johnson could certainly be arrogant. When finally elected president in his own right in November 1964 he said, 'I've been kissing asses all my life and I don't have to kiss them any more. Tell those press bastards of yours that I'll see them when I want to and not before.' That kind of arrogance perhaps led, on some occasions, to an uncritical belief in his own rectitude.

However, generalisations about Johnson's character are probably unhelpful. Sometimes there was fear and uncertainty behind his confident bluster. Privately and frequently he admitted that he did not know what to do about Vietnam. More often than not, he responded to advice and the pressure of events.

a) The incompetence of the Saigon government

KEY DATES FOR SOUTH VIETNAMESE GOVERNMENTS

July 1954 to November 1963	– Diem
November 1963 to January 1964	– General Minh
January 1964 to February 1965	– General Khanh
February 1965 to June 1965	– Dr Quat
June 1965 to September 1967	– Air Vice-Marshal Ky
September 1967 to April 1975	– Thieu

One major cause of escalation was that the Saigon regime was obviously not winning the war.

The generals continued to squabble, exasperating the new American ambassador, General Maxwell Taylor. Ambassador Lodge (see page 71) had had enough by late 1964. All he could suggest was that America should be prepared to run South Vietnam! Despite Taylor's impeccable military pedigree and formidable intellect, he was a poor choice. Johnson picked him to please the JCS, but the situation demanded a real diplomat, not an impatient soldier. Taylor treated the Saigon generals like the cadets he once commanded at West Point, the US military academy. In December 1964 he summoned the generals to the US embassy: 'Do all of you understand English?' They nodded. 'I told you all clearly at General Westmoreland's dinner that we Americans were tired of coups. Apparently I wasted my words … Now you have made a real mess. We cannot carry you forever if you do things like this.'

Back in Washington, Dean Rusk was also tired of the South Vietnamese: 'Somehow we must change the pace at which these people move, and I suspect that this can only be done with a pervasive intrusion of Americans into their affairs.' The consensus among Johnson's advisers was that something must be done, especially when the Vietcong seemed able to strike at will at Americans in South Vietnam.

Key term

Working Group
A group of experts brought together by President Johnson to study Vietnam and make suggestions for future policies in Autumn 1964.

In November 1964, 100 Vietcong dressed in traditional black peasant pyjamas had attacked and greatly damaged a US airbase near Saigon. The JCS demanded retaliatory air strikes on North Vietnam. These Vietcong attacks, which the Saigon regime seemed powerless to halt, nudged the Johnson administration towards escalation. It seemed necessary for the safety of Americans in Vietnam.

Key question
How did the Working Group lead Johnson to escalate?

b) The Working Group recommendations

The presidential election made Johnson cautious about escalation, but he did order a **Working Group** from the Defence Department, the State Department, the CIA and the JCS to study Vietnam and suggest policy options.

Key date

Working Group recommended escalation: November 1964

The Working Group:

- said an independent and anti-Communist South Vietnam was vital to America
- reiterated the domino theory
- said that American 'national prestige, credibility, and honour' were at stake

- emphasised that escalation was necessary due to the weak Saigon government, which was 'close to a standstill' and 'plagued by confusion, apathy, and poor morale'
- suggested heavier bombing, to be halted only if North Vietnam would negotiate. US terms should be the continued existence of a non-Communist South Vietnamese government.

Thus, although Johnson is blamed for the escalation, most of those whom David Halberstam bitterly called 'the best and the brightest' were behind him. Johnson was **commander-in-chief** and his military and civilian experts were urging escalation in the interests of national security. Congress and the public seemed to be supportive.

Key term

Commander-in-chief
Under the US Constitution, the president is commander-in-chief of the US Armed Forces, giving him a great deal of control (sometimes contested by Congress) over making war.

c) Dissenting voices

Key question
Was there any opposition to Johnson's Vietnam policy?

An influential minority regretted that insignificant little Vietnam had taken on such disproportionate significance. George Ball (see page 65) wanted to concentrate on containing Communism in Europe. He warned Johnson that the more America got involved in Vietnam, the harder it would be to get out, and that the American public would not continue to support the war for long. Ball saw no point in bombing a country with a primarily agricultural economy, with industrial needs served by China and the USSR. Bombing the jungle in search of VC would be like seeking needles in a haystack. He felt that American soldiers were ineffective in Asiatic jungles and an increasing American presence was no substitute for good government in Saigon. He feared that while perseverance proved America's reliability as an ally, it also suggested lack of judgement. He worried about worldwide reaction to a superpower bombing a tiny Asiatic state. Both he and Mansfield (see page 66) feared Chinese involvement.

Johnson took the Working Group's recommendations far more seriously than those of the maverick Ball. In any case, whatever uncertainties existed about the wisdom of escalation were being dispelled by further VC successes, especially when the security of American bomber bases was at stake.

d) Defending American bomber bases with 'Rolling Thunder'

Key question
Why did Johnson take the first great escalatory step?

In early 1965 Johnson took the first great escalatory step, when he began large-scale and continuous bombing in Vietnam. Why did he do it?

The immediate trigger for the escalation in 1965 was concern over the security of US bomber bases and personnel. The VC moved freely around South Vietnam, even in the capital, where on Christmas Eve 1964 VC (wearing South Vietnamese army uniforms bought on the black market) planted a bomb in a bar frequented by American officers. Not wanting any dramatic escalation at Christmas, Johnson did nothing, but events conspired to invite American action. In February 1965, the VC attacked a huge American camp near Pleiku. Eight Americans were killed and 100 were wounded. Johnson was furious: 'I've had

Key dates

VC attacked Saigon bar full of American officers: 24 December 1964

VC attacked huge US airbase near Pleiku: February 1965

'Rolling Thunder' began: March 1965 (authorised in February 1965)

enough of this'. The pressure from his advisers was great. Even Ball urged retaliation.

Johnson ordered massively increased air attacks on North Vietnam, even though Soviet premier Kosygin was visiting Hanoi. America now moved beyond occasional air-raid reprisals to a limited air war against carefully selected parts of North Vietnam. Such was the intensity of the air strikes that by March they were known as **'Rolling Thunder'**. Sixty-seven per cent of Americans approved. Bombing the routes taking men and materials to the South would hopefully secure the position of Americans in South Vietnam, decrease infiltration from the North, demoralise Hanoi, and revitalise Saigon where there was some strong middle- and upper-class pressure for negotiations with Hanoi and an end to the bombing.

Key terms

'Rolling Thunder'
Heavy, often non-stop US bombing of Vietnam.

Ground troops
In March 1965, President Johnson sent the first few thousand regular soldiers (rather than just 'advisers') to Vietnam.

In February 1965 the *New York Times* said, 'It is time to call a spade a bloody shovel. This country is in an undeclared and unexplained war in Vietnam.' However, Johnson refused to declare war. Why? He feared pressure from his own extreme Cold Warriors. They wanted to go all out, which would jeopardise the financing of the Great Society and lead to increased Soviet or Chinese involvement. 'If one little general in shirtsleeves can take Saigon, think about 200 million Chinese coming down those trails', said Johnson. 'No sir! I don't want to fight them.' Johnson assured reporters there was no fear of Chinese intervention because he was seducing rather than raping the North: 'I'm going up her leg an inch at a time'. The next 'inch' would actually be a massive escalation: the commitment of thousands of American **ground troops** to Vietnam in order to protect the American bomber bases.

Key question
Why did Johnson take his second great escalatory step?

e) Defending American bomber bases with American troops

In spring 1965 Johnson made his second great escalatory step when he sent large numbers of American ground troops to Vietnam. Why did he send them?

i) The reasons for sending in ground troops

Johnson sent in ground troops in response to a request from General Westmoreland. William Westmoreland had commanded the 16,000 US 'advisers' in Vietnam since June 1964. In spring 1965 he requested US marines be brought in to protect the vital US bomber base at Danang.

Westmoreland's request represented the tip of the iceberg. It was one of the trigger events of the escalation. However, as has just been seen, there were many other reasons that help to explain Johnson's action.

Warnings against escalation

Like Lodge before him, Ambassador Taylor warned that once American forces were committed, more would have to be sent in to protect them. He rightly forecast that white Americans would fight no better than the French in Asian jungles and that

Americans would be unable to distinguish between a VC and a friendly Vietnamese farmer. He feared that Americans would look like colonialists and conquerors and discredit any nationalist credentials of the Saigon regime.

Mansfield foresaw thousands of US soldiers going to Vietnam, thereby alienating Congress and world opinion. He rightly pointed out that sending in American ground troops was the way to keep Moscow and Beijing involved. Soviet-designed anti-aircraft defences were already bringing down many American planes.

ii) Ground troops arrive in Vietnam

Johnson ignored the warnings of people such as Ambassador Taylor and Senator Mansfield and the first 3500 marines landed at Danang beach on 8 March 1965, cheered by pretty Vietnamese girls in a welcome arranged by the US navy. On 6 April 1965 Johnson approved an increase of over 18,000 American support forces to keep his soldiers supplied. He also sent in more marines. He said he wanted to avoid 'publicity' and 'minimise any appearance of sudden changes in policy'.

Key dates

First American ground troops landed in Vietnam: March 1965

Congress voted $700 million for war in Vietnam: May 1965

iii) Support for sending in ground troops

Many accuse Johnson of waging war without a declaration of war. Was it Johnson's undeclared war? Congress supportively granted $700 million for military operations in Vietnam in May 1965. Johnson told them that this was no routine grant: it was a vote to continue opposing Communism in Vietnam. The House of Representatives voted 408–7 and the Senate 88–3 in favour. As yet, the majority of American journalists were also hawks, even those like David Halberstam who later became bitterly anti-war. When Vietnam is called 'Johnson's war', this support from Congress and the press at the time of massive escalation should be remembered.

iv) Johnson's explanation of the escalation

In a speech in April 1965, Johnson summed up the reasons why the United States had to escalate its commitment to Vietnam:

- The US needed to fight if it wanted to live securely in a free world.
- North Vietnam, an aggressive nation that had attacked South Vietnam, needed to be opposed.
- North Vietnam was a puppet of the expansionist Communist powers, the USSR and China.
- The USSR and the People's Republic of China wanted to conquer all of Asia.
- Eisenhower and Kennedy had helped to build and defend South Vietnam: it would be dishonourable to abandon it.
- Abandonment of South Vietnam would cause all America's allies to doubt America's word and credibility.
- Appeasement could lead to a Third World War.

Summary diagram: Why did Johnson escalate the American involvement in Vietnam?

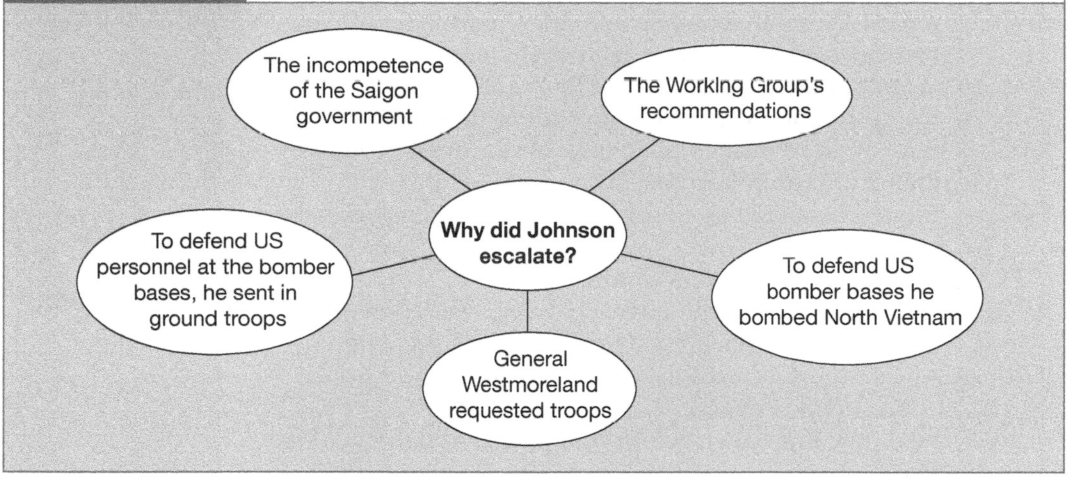

Key question
What was the immediate impact of the escalation?

Key date
Ky became leader of South Vietnam: June 1965

4 | 'Where Are We Going?'

a) Deterioration in Saigon

Johnson had hoped that the arrival of American troops would help to protect the bomber bases and improve the position of the Saigon regime. However, the situation in Vietnam continued to deteriorate.

In June 1965 the civilian government of Phan Huy Quat was overthrown by the military. General Thieu became head of state and Air Vice-Marshal Nguyen Cao Ky became prime minister – 'absolutely the bottom of the barrel', said one Johnson adviser.

Thieu was the son of a small landowner. He had served briefly as a village chief under the Vietminh, then decided he would do better in the French colonial army. He became an officer in 1949. Always ambitious, he married into a prominent Vietnamese Catholic family and became a convert. After the French left, the Americans were impressed by his military ability. He was given training in America. He was indecisive, cunning, stubborn, suspicious and corrupt. He often took advice from his personal astrologer. He would plot his way to the presidency in 1967.

Ky drank, gambled and womanised. He said Vietnam needed men like Hitler. Ky had been commander of South Vietnam's air force. He was a flamboyant figure, fond of purple jumpsuits, pearl-handled revolvers and dark sunglasses. At a meeting with McNamara in July 1965, Ky's tight white jacket, shiny black shoes and red socks shocked one American who pointed out that 'at least no one could confuse him with Uncle Ho'.

With these 'bottom of the barrel' individuals in power, it is not surprising that the Saigon government controlled less of South Vietnam and controlled it less effectively. Ky and Thieu were incompetent, corrupt and unpopular.

Profile: Nguyen Van Thieu 1923–2001

1923 – Born in Vietnam, son of a small landowner
1945 – Joined Vietminh, but switched sides and fought for the French colonialist regime against Vietminh
1956 – Served in Diem regime in South Vietnam
1963 – Played important part in successful coup against Diem
1965 – Became head of state in military government headed by Premier Nguyen Cao Ky
1967 – Elected president under a new constitution; supported by USA
1971 – Re-elected without opposition
1973 – Felt betrayed by US in peace settlement with North Vietnam, after which US troops left South Vietnam
1975 – As Communist forces took over Saigon, resigned, and attacked US in speech
Fled to Taiwan, then Surrey, England, and finally Massachusetts
2001 – Died

Thieu is perhaps as important as, and certainly similar to, Diem in the context of the US involvement in Vietnam. Like Diem, Thieu was supported by the US in his several-year rule in South Vietnam. Like Diem, Thieu was betrayed by the US when it suited the latter.

Profile: Nguyen Cao Ky 1930–

1930 – Born in northern Vietnam
1940s – Member of the French colonialist forces that opposed Vietnamese nationalists
1954 – Joined South Vietnamese air force; Americans liked his bravado and anti-Communist attitude
1963 – After Diem overthrown, became commander of South Vietnamese air force; with US help, built air force up to 10,000 men
1965 June – With Thieu and 'Big' Minh, led military coup against Premier Quat. Unpopular, due to authoritarianism
1967 – Military leaders agreed Thieu should be president and Ky his vice-president. Ky unhappy, so publicly criticised Thieu
1975 – When South Vietnam fell to Communism, fled to USA

Like Thieu, Ky was supported by the US when he was president of South Vietnam. Like Thieu, Ky lacked ability and was unpopular with his people.

Wearing matching flight suits and scarves, Nguyen Cao Ky strolls hand-in-hand with his wife as they make an inspection tour of a battlefield.

b) More American troops

In 1965 Ky's government was losing control of territory to the VC who, according to Thieu, had 75 per cent of the countryside. As Taylor had feared, the more American troops poured in, the less the ARVN wanted to fight. As usual, Westmoreland demanded more American troops to prevent South Vietnam's collapse and to protect the American troops already there. In cabinet meetings throughout July, Johnson expressed doubts about the usefulness of sending more American troops. Nevertheless, on 28 July 1965, at noon when TV audiences were minimal, he announced that Westmoreland had asked for more men to meet mounting Communist aggression and that his needs would be met: 'We will stand in Vietnam'. The 75,000 troops in Vietnam would be increased to 125,000. Congressional leaders had given their assent the day before.

Key dates

Johnson announced sending 50,000 more troops to South Vietnam: July 1965

Over 200,000 American troops in Vietnam: December 1965

During 1965, polls and White House mail showed that:

- 70 per cent of the nation was behind Johnson
- 80 per cent believed in the domino theory
- 80 per cent favoured sending American soldiers to stop South Vietnam falling
- 47 per cent wanted Johnson to send in even more troops.

Clearly, Johnson was supported by the majority of Americans in his Vietnam policy. By the end of 1965 nearly 200,000 American soldiers were in Vietnam.

On the rare occasions that American troops faced regular Communist soldiers (rather than guerrillas), the Americans gave a very good account of themselves. In October 1965, for example, American troops defeated North Vietnamese regulars at the Battle of Ia Drang.

Key dates

Americans beat North Vietnamese army at Ia Drang: October 1965

First anti-war protests in American universities: March 1965

President Johnson asked, 'Where are we going?': October 1965

c) Doubters

Not everyone was sure that this further escalation was the right answer. Protests had begun in the universities in March 1965 (see page 143). Vice-President Hubert Humphrey privately worried about two questions: why risk Chinese intervention and why support an unstable country?

Upon hearing that a plane had been shot down, Johnson himself cried, 'Where are we going?' He confessed that hawkish General Curtis LeMay 'scares the hell out of me'.

A December 1965 bombing halt failed to persuade Hanoi to negotiate and a cabinet meeting showed the lack of consensus within the administration. State Department official George Ball thought the situation hopeless. Ambassador Maxwell Taylor and the CIA opposed sending more US troops. McNamara felt that military victory was unlikely. The JCS were divided over tactics. 'Tell me this', said Johnson to the JCS chairman, 'what will happen if we put in 100,000 more men and then two, three years later, you tell me we need 500,000 more? … And what makes you think that Ho Chi Minh won't put in another 100, and match us every bit of the way?'

Johnson knew all the dangers. He was uncertain that America could win, but certain that it could not get out without irreparable damage to his own and his country's position. As American soldiers poured into Vietnam, the administration and military could not agree on what they should be doing there. Most, however, agreed that they *should* be there. This was not just Johnson's war.

d) Escalation, 1965–8

Despite their doubts about the competence of the Ky/Thieu regime, General Westmoreland, the JCS and McNamara all agreed that the number of American troops in South Vietnam should be increased in the second half of 1965. McNamara did not claim that this would bring victory, but it would 'stave off defeat in the short run and offer a good chance of producing a favourable settlement in the longer run'.

Key term

War of attrition
Westmoreland believed that US numerical and technological superiority would wear down the VC who must, after losing a certain number of men, finally decide to give up.

Thus, by the end of 1965, around 200,000 American soldiers bore the burden of the fighting in South Vietnam, while US planes bombed both North Vietnam and South Vietnam.
By the end of 1966, there were 385,000, and by early 1968, 535,000 American troops in South Vietnam. General Westmoreland had initially believed that he could end the Communist insurgency within six months, but his strategy of a **war of attrition**, using technology and firepower, failed to wear down the enemy.

Summary diagram: 'Where are we going?'

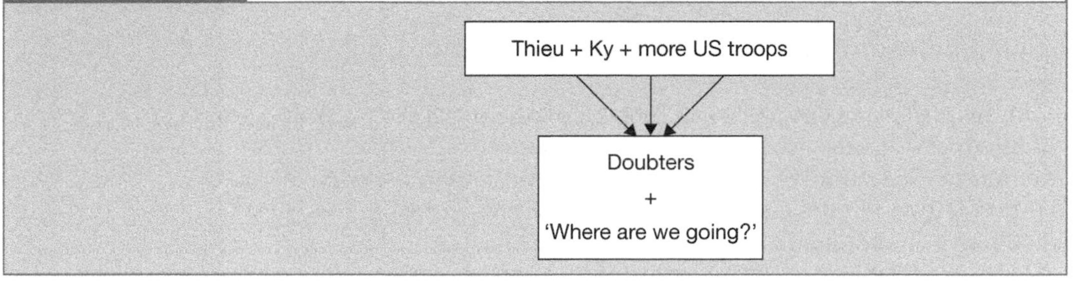

Key question
Who bore responsibility for the escalation of US involvement?

e) Was It Johnson's war?

In some ways it seemed as if it was Johnson's war. As president, he made the decision to continue Kennedy's commitment and then to escalate. He ordered each escalatory step, first 'Rolling Thunder', then the sending of increasing numbers of American troops.

On the other hand, many shared the responsibility for all this. He had inherited a strong commitment to South Vietnam from his predecessors with whose Cold War ideas he agreed. In the circumstances of his accession to the presidency, it would have been particularly difficult for him to disengage America from Vietnam, even had he been so inclined. He felt bound to continue Kennedy's policies and keep Kennedy's advisers.

When Johnson escalated American involvement in Vietnam dramatically, his military and civilian advisers shared responsibility for his policies. He always liked to claim that his responsibility had been shared with Congress and the public and there was a lot of truth in what he said: they *were* clearly supportive of his Vietnam policies early in his presidency. A December 1965 poll showed that a large majority of Americans favoured increasing American troops to 500,000 men. Johnson's biographer Vaughn Davis Bornet, while critical of the president's policies, reminds us that:

Key dates

535,000 US troops in South Vietnam: 1968

Poll showed most Americans were pro-escalation: December 1965

> If Vietnam did not ultimately go well, in a democratic republic like the United States one must look at the Congress and the people themselves, for three national elections were held during the Johnson years.

5 | Historians and 'Johnson's War'?

No historians dispute that Lyndon Johnson massively escalated the US commitment in Vietnam. However, there is great disagreement over the amount of control he had over the process, and why he escalated to such an extent.

a) How much control did Johnson have over the escalation process?

Some historians (for example, Burke and Greenstein, 1989) have contended that Lyndon Johnson dominated policy-making.

Herring (1979) admitted that Johnson's impatient character was not ideally suited to complex counter-insurgency warfare in Vietnam, but Herring warned against over-emphasis on the president's personality. Herring described Johnson as almost pathologically unable to make a decision, and cautious and reluctant in escalation. On that latter point, VanDeMark (1991) and Barrett (1993) agree.

Many historians are critical of Johnson's advisers and President Kennedy. McMaster accuses the JCS of dishonesty (1997). Kennard (1991) similarly accuses Kennedy and Maxwell Taylor. Di Leo (1991) blames George Ball's careerist ambitions for his ineffective challenges to Vietnam policy.

Yuen Foong Khong (1992) found Johnson and his advisers obsessed with lessons they thought they had learned from history, but Khong and others are convinced that the wrong lessons were learned: Ho Chi Minh was not Hitler. Universal ignorance of Vietnam was admitted by Robert McNamara in his memoirs (1995).

Historians agree that Johnson's domestic programme of social reform was his main interest, and Berman (1989) and Kearns (1976) emphasised that he felt he had to appear tough on foreign policy to stop conservatives defeating his domestic plans. There is considerable unanimity on this depiction of Lyndon Johnson as one who wanted to ensure the survival of South Vietnam, but who wanted to avoid a Third World War and the end of his Great Society dreams. Schmitz (2005) saw Johnson as a victim of the commitment trap: 'All the logic and rationale of the Cold War and containment called for escalation'.

b) Did Johnson lie about the Gulf of Tonkin incident?

Sometimes, historical research can alter interpretations, and Anderson (2005) cites the Gulf of Tonkin incident as an excellent example. Early studies (for example Windchy, 1971) based on congressional hearings and other public sources concluded that Johnson deceived Congress and the public about North Vietnamese attacks on US ships. However, Moise (1996) looks at declassified documents and found that the administration genuinely believed that there had been two attacks on American destroyers.

Key term

Neutralised Vietnam
Some contemporaries advocated taking Vietnam out of the Cold War context and allowing it to decide its own future, without influence or input from Moscow, Beijing or Washington, DC.

c) Are most historians' interpretations of Johnson's policies unsympathetic?

Many historians are highly unsympathetic to Johnson and his choices. Kahin (1986) criticised Eisenhower, Kennedy and Johnson for outright rejection of the idea of a **neutralised Vietnam**. Gelb and Betts (1979), like other 'stalemate theory' (see page 4) historians, say Johnson and his advisers knew the prospects were poor, but kept escalating lest they appeared weak. Logevall (1999) emphasised how Johnson rejected the idea of a negotiated settlement in 1964 and in 1965, and guessed that Kennedy would have chosen negotiation.

Some key books in the debate

D. Anderson, *The Vietnam War* (Palgrave Macmillan, 2003).
D. Barrett, *Uncertain Warriors: Lyndon Johnson and his Vietnam Advisers* (Kansas, 1993).
L. Berman, *Lyndon Johnson's War* (New York, 1989).
J.P. Burke and F.I. Greenstein, *How Presidents Test Reality* (New York, 1989).
D. Di Leo, *George Ball, Vietnam and the Rethinking of Containment* (North Carolina, 1991).
L. Gelb and R.K. Betts, *The Irony of Vietnam* (Washington DC, 1979).
G. Herring, *America's Longest War* (New York, 1979).
G.M. Kahin, *Intervention: How America Became Involved in Vietnam* (New York, 1986).
D. Kearns, *Lyndon Johnson and the American Dream* (1976).
D. Kennard, *The Certain Trumpet: Maxwell Taylor and the American Experience in Vietnam* (Washington DC, 1991).
Yuen Foong Khong, *Analogies at War* (Princeton, 1992).
F. Logevall, *Choosing War* (1999).
H.R. McMaster, *Dereliction of Duty* (New York, 1997).
R. McNamara, *In Retrospect* (New York, 1995).
E. Moise, *Tonkin Gulf and the Escalation of the Vietnam War* (North Carolina, 1996).
D. Schmitz, *The Tet Offensive* (Lanham, 2005).
R.D. Schulzinger, *A Companion to American Foreign Relations* (Oxford, 2003).
B. VanDeMark, *Into the Quagmire: Lyndon Johnson and the Escalation of the Vietnam War* (New York, 1991).
E. Windchy, *Tonkin Gulf* (New York, 1971).

Study Guide: AS Questions

In the style of AQA

(a) Explain why the American Congress passed the Gulf of Tonkin resolution in August 1964. (12 marks)

(b) 'Johnson alone bears the responsibility for the escalation of war in Vietnam in the years 1965–8.' Explain why you agree or disagree with this statement. (24 marks)

Exam tips

The cross-references are intended to take you straight to the material that will help you to answer the questions.

(a) You should re-read pages 88–9 before answering this question. You are required to provide a range of reasons here and it would be helpful to think of long- and short-term factors in your answer. In the short term, the resolution was passed because of attacks on American shipping in the Gulf. However, the longer-term reasons are connected with the USA's commitment to support South Vietnam against the Communist North Vietnamese and President Johnson's personal decision to increase US involvement so as not to be the first president to lose a war. It would also be helpful to refer to the public doubts that had to be appeased, and in your conclusion you might consider whether Johnson had merely been looking for an excuse. Try to offer some personal judgement on the relative importance of the factors you cite.

(b) The dates here direct you specifically to developments during Johnson's presidency, but to answer this question successfully you will need to consider other reasons for the escalation of war at this time and this would include some outline of the scale of US commitment before this date and consideration of whether the Americans could have ever avoided the increasing commitment of these years. You might like to begin with Johnson's own explanation of the escalation (page 94) and then move on to assessing Johnson's responsibility by evaluating:

- longer term and personal influences on Johnson (pages 81–3)
- the Kennedy inheritance (pages 83–4 and 85)
- Johnson and his advisers (pages 84–5) and the debates, doubts and opponents (pages 85–7)
- the importance of the Tonkin resolution and the presidential election (pages 87–90)
- the incompetence of the Saigon government and the Working Group recommendations (pages 90–2)
- concerns over the security of US bomber bases (pages 92–4).

Try to offer thoughtful and balanced comments and do remember that Johnson never had complete control and that others shared responsibility. The historiographical debate on this issue is provided on pages 100–1. Read this carefully before you begin so that you are able to offer a fair appraisal and appropriate conclusion.

In the style of Edexcel

How accurate is it to say that the USA increased its involvement in Vietnam in the period 1954–64 primarily for ideological reasons? (30 marks)

Exam tips

The cross-references are intended to take you straight to the material that will help you to answer the question.

Examiners frequently ask why the US got involved and escalated that involvement. Sometimes they simply ask 'why?'. Sometimes they suggest one reason why, and ask you to debate whether that specified factor is crucial. Perhaps most difficult to answer is the question where two factors are specified and you are asked to pick the one that you consider more important.

For all three types of question you need to know why the United States got increasingly involved. When preparing an essay on this you should think of it either in terms of topical paragraphs or in chronological paragraphs.

The chronological approach would cover the motives of Eisenhower, Kennedy and Johnson:

- Eisenhower: anti-Communism, domino theory, rollback, Asia-firsters, French exit (pages 30–2 and 42).
- Kennedy: as Eisenhower, adding commitment trap, memories of Republican attacks on Truman for his 'loss of China', youth and inexperience, Cuba and Laos, advisers (pages 52–62).
- Johnson: as Eisenhower and Kennedy, adding Kennedy legacy, 'first president to lose a war', stalemate theory (pages 81–7, 90–4, 98 and 100).

However, chronologically organised answers can degenerate into description. In order to show off your analytical skills, it is better to use thematic or topical paragraphs. Thematic paragraphs will certainly be needed for this question, where you are asked to weigh the significance of the stated factor 'ideological reasons' against other factors which drew the USA into the conflict. Your paragraph topics for both factors would probably be:

- anti-Communism (pages 30, 52 and 81)
- domino theory (pages 31, 52 and 81)
- French exit (page 42)
- domestic politics (pages 31, 52–4, 56, 62–3, 69, 86 and 89)
- president's personal position (pages 54, 56 and 83–4)
- commitment trap and stalemate theory (pages 4, 49, 76–7 and 100).

Although you will encounter many different questions essentially asking you to explain US involvement in Vietnam, it is important not to approach this sort of question thinking that you will always be able simply to write out exactly the same six paragraphs on why the USA became involved in the war. Essentially you will always be selecting from the same bank of material, but a good essay writing technique involves the organising of that material to meet a particular question. For this question you should devote about a third of your answer to 'ideological reasons' since they are your given stated factor. Note that the first two bullet points above relate to ideological reasons – be careful to make that clear.

In order to gain high marks you need to weigh up the relative importance of these factors against each other, and to decide on which is or which are the most important, giving persuasive arguments for your choice. But your reading of Chapters 3, 4 and 5 will have shown you that historians are themselves divided over the reasons for US involvement. There is not a 'right' answer here. It is a real opportunity for you to decide which factor seems more significant to you.

In the style of OCR

(a) Compare Sources A and B as evidence for the problems faced by South Vietnam. (30 marks)

(b) Using your own knowledge, assess how far the sources support the interpretation that the *main* reason America began and continued its involvement in Vietnam was to defend democracy. (70 marks)

Source A

From a letter from Dwight Eisenhower, 23 October 1954. The American president writes to Ngo Dinh Diem, the president of the Republic of South Vietnam, expressing his support for the new South Vietnamese government.

Dear Mr President: I have been following with great interest the developments in Vietnam, particularly since the conclusion of the Geneva conference. The implications of the agreement concerning Vietnam have caused grave concern regarding the future of a country temporarily divided by an artificial military grouping, weakened by a long, exhausting war and faced with external enemies and internal collaborators. We have fulfilled your recent requests for aid in the formidable task of moving several hundred thousand loyal Vietnamese citizens away from areas ruled by a Communist ideology they hate. I am glad that the United States is able to assist in this humanitarian effort.

Source B

From a programme of the National Liberation Front of South Vietnam, January 1962. A statement of the goals of the NLF, the united front that brought together Communists and non-Communists to liberate Vietnam from foreign control.

The present South Vietnamese regime is a camouflaged colonial regime dominated by the Yankees, and the South Vietnamese government is a servile government, implementing faithfully all the policies of the American imperialists. Therefore, this regime must be overthrown and a government of national and democratic union put in its place composed of representatives of all social classes, of all nationalities, of various political parties, of all religions; patriotic, eminent citizens must take over for the people the control of economic, political, social, and cultural interests and thus bring about independence, democracy, well-being, peace, neutrality, and efforts toward the peaceful unification of the country.

Source C

From a statement by President de Gaulle, 23 July 1964. At his tenth press conference in Paris the French president expresses his views on American policy in Vietnam.

Vietnam was shocked by the withdrawal of French administration and forces. The south was exposed to new perils by the existence of a Communist state in Tonkin, from where our troops withdrew. It tried to find, in itself, a solid national government. It was then that the Americans arrived, bringing their aid, their policy and their authority. The United States considered itself the worldwide defender against Communism. The regime established in the north aimed to impose itself also in South Vietnam, and America wanted to help this state to protect itself. Also, without intending to criticise, the American conviction of fulfilling a sort of vocation, their disapproval of other countries' colonialism, and the natural desire among such a powerful people to expand, made the Americans determined to take our place in Indochina.

Source D

From a speech by Lyndon Johnson in 1965. The US president explains why the USA continued to be involved in Vietnam.

We have a promise to keep. Since 1954 every American president has offered support to the people of South Vietnam. We have helped to build and defend its independence. To dishonour that promise and abandon this small, brave nation to its enemies, and the terror that must follow, would be an unforgivable wrong. We are also there to strengthen world order. Around the globe are people whose well-being rests partly on believing they can count on us if attacked. To leave Vietnam to its fate would shake these people's confidence in the value of America's word. Let no one think for a moment that retreat from Vietnam would bring an end to conflict. The battle would be renewed in one country and then another. The appetite of aggression is never satisfied. In Southeast Asia, as we did in Europe, we must follow the words of the Bible: 'Hitherto shalt thou come, but no further'.

Exam tips

The cross-references are intended to take you straight to the material that will help you to answer the questions.

(a) This question asks you to compare two sources as evidence by using their content and provenance to explain your answer to the question. Focus clearly on '*problems* faced by South Vietnam' and make it the heart of your answer. A true comparison needs sustained cross-reference of the two sources point by point, not one source after the other. Your answer should be balanced, and references to context are only valuable in helping you compare the sources.

Provenance:

- Authors and dates: subjective, national and ideological. Source A: Eisenhower, American attitudes in 1954 (pages 41–3); Source B: Vietnamese attitudes in 1962 in the Kennedy era (pages 43–6).
- Nature, purpose, style. Source A: official, impersonal, self-congratulatory in justifying American policy to solve problems (pages 29–41); Source B: secret war plans, summarising aims to solve a broader range of political, cultural and social problems (pages 67–9).

Textual content on problems faced by South Vietnam:

- Points of agreement on problems: disunity, external enemies and internal collaborators (of which the authors of Source B are an example), military activity.
- Points of disagreement: hatred of militant communism in Source A versus American imperialism in Source B; external enemies seen as North Vietnam (and implicitly foreign Communists) in Source A, versus the USA in Source B; subsidiary role of the USA in aiding Diem to solve problems in Source A versus servile Diem government and US intervention itself as key problems in Source B.

(b) This question asks you to use your own knowledge and *all four* sources to create a balanced argument evaluating the interpretation in the question. Focus clearly on '*reasons* why America began and continued its involvement in Vietnam' during the period covered by the sources.

The sources should drive your answer, and your factual knowledge should be used to support and exemplify the points in your argument.

There will be one reason given in the question, and your first task is to evaluate it. Group the sources by their side of the argument: Sources A and D support the interpretation, whereas Sources B and C refute it. Use factual knowledge to exemplify and discuss each point. Suggest a range of other reasons picking up the clues in the sources. Cross-reference phrases across the sources and use them to argue a case for and against the view that democracy was the main reason, using factual knowledge to develop and explain your points (Chapters 3, 4 and 5). Reach an evaluative judgement on the relative importance of each, at the end of each paragraph – remembering to link back to the question.

Other reasons might include:

- Imperialism (Sources B and C); humanitarian concerns (Sources A and D); domestic politics; presidents' personal stances (Sources A and D; pages 54, 56, 62–3, 69, 86 and 89).
- Anti-Communism (Sources A, C and D; pages 30, 52 and 81); domino theory; rollback (Source D; pages 31, 52 and 81); French exit (Source C; page 42).
- Economics and domestic politics, including defence and moral issues (Sources C and D; pages 31, 52–4, 62–3, 69, 86 and 89); commitment trap; 'loss of China'; and stalemate theory (Source D; pages 4, 48, 76–7 and 100).

In your conclusion, link together the reasons, weigh up their relative importance and reach a supported judgement to answer the question.

6 Why the USA Failed: I – The People in Vietnam

POINTS TO CONSIDER

The second great debate about Johnson and Vietnam concerns the reasons why Johnson's America (and its South Vietnamese ally) could not defeat the Communists. Despite Johnson's dramatic escalation of the American war effort, his advisers concluded that the war was unwinnable and Johnson began to retreat in 1968. This chapter looks at why he began the retreat, through sections on:

- The Vietnamese
- The Americans
- Key debates

Key dates

1965	November	Battle of Ia Drang
1967	January	Americans found Communist tunnel network near Saigon
1968		Operation Phoenix
	January	Battle of Khe Sanh
	March	My Lai massacre
1969		An American company refused to fight
		Fragging began
	May	Battle of Hamburger Hill
1971	February	ARVN retreated from Laos because of heavy losses

1 | The Vietnamese

Key question
How do the lives and beliefs of the ordinary Vietnamese help to explain why the Communists triumphed?

a) Winning the hearts and minds of the people

i) The decisive factor

One of the main reasons the Americans could not defeat the Communists was because they were unable to win the hearts and minds of the Vietnamese people. General Giap said that Hanoi won because it waged a people's war, a total war in which every man, woman and even child was mobilised, whether militarily or emotionally. He maintained that human beings were the decisive factor.

There were thousands of American civilian 'experts' in Vietnam during the war. By mid-1964 there were helpful Americans in the

An American soldier helping a South Vietnamese child in 1966.

provinces teaching the Vietnamese to breed pigs, dig wells and build houses. There were American doctors, school-teachers, accountants and mechanics. However, despite US social, medical and educational programmes, these civilian experts felt that too little was done to win the hearts and minds of the people. Understandably, the military men thought in terms of force. 'Grab 'em by the balls and their hearts and minds will follow', said the American military.

ii) Peasant life

Most Vietnamese were peasants, usually living in small villages, on the irrigated plains alongside the great northern Red River and the South's Mekong River. Their main crop was rice and whole families worked long hours in the rice fields. The villages lacked electricity. The houses had dirt or wooden floors. The dirt paths between the houses were piled with stinking human and animal ordure for fertilising the fields. The small homes were made of mud and bamboo with roofs of palm leaves or grass. The families slept on reed mattresses on the ground. There was no running water. American soldiers could not conceive of 'real' people living like this, and the resultant sense of an alien world goes a little way towards explaining why Americans sometimes treated the Vietnamese peasants as sub-human (see page 115) and were consequently unable to win many of them over to their side.

iii) Vietnamese peasants and Communism

The peasants had always been used to struggling to provide sufficient food for their families, and this had led to an emphasis upon collective discipline and endeavour. Harvesting was best approached communally. Within the family and the village individual interests were frequently subordinated to community interests. Many villages adapted with relative ease to the principles of Communism and to the fraternal leadership of **cadres**, who chivvied, inspired and monitored the people. The Communists worked hard to win over the peasantry, offering them a fairer distribution of land and urging Communist soldiers to avoid the rape and pillage characteristic of the ARVN.

Key term
Cadres
Group leaders within Communist societies.

iv) Carrot and stick

Although the Communists were generally better at winning the hearts and minds of the peasantry, they were ruthless when necessary. During the 1968 Tet offensive, the VC dragged 'unfriendly' people out of their houses in Hue and shot them, clubbed them to death, or buried them alive. Over 3000 bodies were found in the river or jungle. A judicious mixture of ruthlessness and frequent good behaviour gained the VC the sullen acquiescence or support of the peasants that was vital in guerrilla warfare. Giap's strategy was to use the Vietcong for incessant guerrilla warfare to wear down Saigon and its American allies, while the PAVN (see page 43) would only fight conventional set-piece battles at times and places when it was sufficiently strong. This emphasis upon guerrilla warfare meant that the Communists needed (and usually obtained) a great deal of support from South Vietnam's civilians. Villagers often gave them the food, shelter and hiding places necessary for survival. Greater success in winning peasant hearts and minds or simply peasant acquiescence helps to explain why the Communists defeated Washington and Saigon.

v) The unpopular policies of Washington and Saigon

The actions of both Washington and Saigon frequently antagonised the South Vietnamese peasants, which helps to explain America's failure. Life for the South Vietnamese peasantry deteriorated from bad to worse after the Americans arrived. Diem's strategic hamlets programme (see page 67) and then American bombing forced many peasants to move away from the homes, crops and ancestral graves which meant so much to them. One peasant recalled a day when:

> The bombing started at about eight o'clock in the morning and lasted for hours. When we first heard the explosions, we rushed into the tunnels, but not everyone made it. When there was a pause in the attack, some of us climbed out to see what we could do, and the scene was terrifying. Bodies had been torn to pieces –

> limbs were hanging from trees and scattered around the ground. The bombing began again, this time with napalm, and the village went up in flames. The napalm hit me. I felt as if I were burning all over, like a piece of coal. I lost consciousness. Friends took me to the hospital, and my wounds didn't begin to heal until six months later. Over 200 people died in the raid, including my mother, sister-in-law and three nephews. They were buried alive when their tunnel collapsed.

Ironically, American firepower was concentrated more on South than North Vietnam. The dependent Saigon regime was unlikely to complain. Johnson usually tried to avoid targeting non-combatants, saying 'if they [the US pilots] hit people I'll bust their asses'. However, in their search for VC the Americans killed and wounded tens of thousands of civilians who might or might not have been Communist sympathisers. Neither the American army nor the ARVN would take responsibility for wounded civilians, who were left to get what (if any) primitive medical care was available. Bombing obliterated five towns with populations over 10,000, and many villages. Some civilians lived like moles in caves and tunnels, emerging to work but ready to go back down when planes appeared. Children were kept down for days at a time.

From 1962 Agent Orange (see page 2) was used to defoliate 20 per cent of South Vietnam's jungles so that the enemy could be more easily seen, and to kill the rice crops that were partly used for feeding the VC. Bombs and chemicals best suited American technological superiority, wealth and reluctance to lose American

One of the most famous photos of the war: 10-year-old Kim Phuc (centre) ran away from her village, badly burned by napalm dropped from American bombers in 1972.

lives, but they were not the way to win this war: these methods alienated friendly and neutral Vietnamese and Americans themselves, contributing greatly to American failure in Vietnam. It was not surprising that the Communists controlled most of the countryside, as the JCS admitted in February 1968. In 1995 McNamara wrote that the administration was wrong to allow an arrogant American military to attempt a hi-tech war of attrition against a primarily guerrilla force willing to absorb massive casualties, in a state like South Vietnam which lacked the political stability and popularity necessary to conduct effective military and pacification operations.

vi) New weapons

American technology created formidable new fighting weapons. The Vietnamese called cluster bombs 'mother bombs' because after exploding in mid-air they released 350–600 baby bombs. Each one exploded on impact into thousands of metal pellets. Later, fibreglass replaced the metal; X-rays could not detect fibreglass, so it was harder and more painful to remove. Heat-sensitive and urine-sniffing devices were developed to pinpoint and destroy an enemy, but this often turned out to be a water buffalo or a child. An American pilot described the effectiveness of the new white phosphorus:

> We sure are pleased with those backroom boys at Dow [Chemical Company]. The original product wasn't so hot – if the gooks [Vietnamese] were quick they could scrape it off. So the boys started adding polystyrene – now it sticks like shit to a blanket. But then if the gooks jumped under water it stopped burning, so they started adding Willie Peter [WP – white phosphorus] so's to make it burn better. It'll even burn under water now. And one drop is enough, it'll keep on burning right down to the bone so they die anyway from phosphorus poisoning.

It was very difficult for the Americans to win the hearts and minds of the people and the war when their military tactics aroused such antagonism. One Vietnamese nun told an American relief worker that Vietnam was a beautiful country 'until *you* arrived'.

vii) 'They are all VC'

The circumstances of the war tended to make American soldiers dislike the people they were supposed to be helping, which then made it very difficult to win the war. In 1965 some marines were supposed to search hamlets for VC and dispense food and medical care, but one marine remembered differently:

> We would go through a village before dawn, rousting everybody out of bed and kicking down doors and dragging them out if they didn't move fast enough. They all had underground bunkers inside their huts to protect themselves against bombing and shelling. But to us the bunkers were Vietcong hiding places, and we'd blow

> them up with dynamite – and blow up their huts too. If we spotted extra rice lying around, we'd confiscate it to keep them from giving it to the Vietcong. [The peasants were] herded like cattle into a barbed wire compound, and left to sit there in the hot sun for the rest of the day, with no shade. [South Vietnamese policemen and an American interrogator would question some peasants about the VC presence in the area.] If they had the wrong identity card, or if the police held a grudge against them, they'd be beaten pretty badly, maybe tortured. Or they might be hauled off to jail, and God knows what happened to them. At the end of the day, the villagers would be turned loose. Their homes had been wrecked, their rice confiscated – and if they weren't pro-Vietcong before we got there, they sure as hell were by the time we left.

A marine recalled approaching a village which supported the VC:

> Our guys were falling everywhere … We were pinned down, all day and all night … we just lay there, waiting and waiting and hearing our partners dying, big guys dying and crying for their mothers, asking to be shot because they couldn't take it no more.

When the marine's unit finally entered the village only old men and women remained, denying any connection with the VC. The marine recalled:

> Our emotions were very low because we'd lost a lot of friends … So … we gave it to them … whatever was moving was going to move no more – especially after [our] three days of blood and guts in the mud.

Success could not be measured by territorial gain, so the emphasis was on enemy body counts. More bodies meant more promotions, medals, **R&R** and rations. You invented dead bodies or you created them: 'If it's dead and Vietnamese, it's VC'. The most famous, but by no means the only, example of American hatred of the Vietnamese was the massacre at apparently pro-Communist My Lai on 16 March 1968. Three hundred and forty-seven unarmed civilians were beaten and killed by American soldiers and their officers: old men, women, teenagers and even babies. Women were beaten with rifle butts, raped and shot. Water buffalo, pigs and chickens were shot then dropped in wells to poison the water.

Key term

R&R
Rest and recuperation for American soldiers in Vietnam.

Key dates

My Lai massacre: 16 March 1968

Operation Phoenix: 1968

viii) Operation Phoenix

War inevitably bred brutality. In 1968 the CIA introduced a system code-named 'Operation Phoenix', whereby tens of thousands of VC were sought out and interrogated. Few taken for interrogation came out alive. Torture was the norm. An American officer testified before Congress about the methods used:

> the insertion of the 6-inch dowel into the canal of one of my detainee's ears and the tapping through the brain until he died. The

Vietnamese villagers lie dead after the massacre at My Lai, 16 March 1968.

> starving to death [in a cage] of a Vietnamese woman who was suspected of being a … cadre … the use of electronic gear … attached to … both the women's vagina and the men's testicles [to] shock them into submission.

ix) Sub-humans

American attitudes to the Vietnamese made it difficult to win them over and thereby win the war. Many Americans considered the Vietnamese peasants in particular as less than human. When asked about civilian casualties Westmoreland agreed it was a problem, 'but it does deprive the enemy of the population, doesn't it? They are Asians who don't think about death the way we do'. Maxwell Taylor (see page 63) admitted years later that Americans never really knew or understood any of the Vietnamese. Helicopters and fire-power were no substitute for working amongst and winning over the people.

Key question
Why were the Communists so difficult to defeat?

b) Communist determination, heroism and ingenuity

i) Communist determination

Inspired by Communism and nationalism, the VC won admiration from their American foes. One American general was impressed by some besieged Communists in a bunker, who 'didn't even give up after their eardrums had burst from the concussion [from American fire-power] … and blood was pouring out of their noses'. Unable to afford replacement uniforms, the VC suffered from skin diseases because of the wet conditions in jungles, rice fields and tunnels. They picked up infections from insect bites, dirty water and dead bodies in the soil. Quinine was in short supply and all had malaria. The Vietnamese had always struggled for their existence against both nature and other, hostile peoples such as the Chinese. Continuous struggle ensured unusual patience in the face of adversity. This helps to explain Hanoi's refusal to be beaten. As Giap said:

> We were not strong enough to drive out a half million American troops, but that was not our aim. Our intention was to break the will of the American government to continue the war.

America did not understand that determination. American strategy never took it into account, and this was an important factor in the American inability to win.

ii) The Ho Chi Minh Trail

Most of Giap's men and women spent time on the **Ho Chi Minh Trail** (see map on page 82), which came southward via Cambodia and Laos.

Both sides knew that keeping the trail open was vital to the Communist war effort. Men and materials came south and the wounded were sent north on the trail. Giap's people used bulky pack bicycles with rag-stuffed tyres that did not burst. Many were full-time porters on the trail and an estimated 10 per cent of

Key term

Ho Chi Minh Trail North Vietnamese Communist supply route going south from North Vietnam through Cambodia and Laos to South Vietnam.

People power in action: Hanoi kept supplies moving south, on bikes if necessary.

them died, mostly from amoebic dysentery and malaria. A man could carry 55 pounds of rice or 40 pounds of other materials (the rice bags moulded themselves to the body and were easier to carry) over 15 miles by day or 12 by night. Human porterage lasted from 1959 to 1964, when the trail was widened and sometimes even covered with asphalt to accommodate big vehicles supplied by China and the USSR.

The trail was never a single route. There were several branches, along which were dotted repair workshops, stores depots, hospitals and rest camps. Around 50,000 women were employed at any one time to repair the road. If one part was damaged by American bombing, the traffic would be switched to other branches while repairs were done. Vehicles and parts of the trail were camouflaged with foliage. Giap's trails, troops and trucks melted into the landscape.

The Soviets and Chinese provided thousands of cheap trucks. While Hanoi lost many $6000 trucks, America lost many several million-dollar bombers, which were far harder and more expensive to replace. American bombers perpetually sought to obliterate the trail but failed. In 1967 the Americans dropped seismic sensors on the ground so that aircraft could target trail users. Vietnam's elephant population was badly depleted by the resultant bombing. When the VC saw the sensors they deliberately triggered them off by playing cassettes, then disappeared. The battle of the trail was a vital one, in which people could be said to have triumphed over technology.

iii) The battle of Ia Drang, 1965

Key date
The battle of Ia Drang: November 1965

In autumn 1965 the 66th regiment of the PAVN went south on the trail. Each soldier had a khaki uniform, a pair of sandals cut from old tyres and ankle-high green canvas Chinese boots. Each carried 22 pounds of food for the two-month walk from North Vietnam to the Ia Drang Valley. The weapons they carried were made in Albania, China, Czechoslovakia and the USSR. Each soldier took a daily malaria pill but most got the disease anyway. Several died on the trail each day, from disease, accidents, snake bites or American air raids. In November they clashed with the US army. In the 34-day battle of Ia Drang, 305 Americans and 3561 North Vietnamese died. Both sides thought they had won, that the other would not be able to sustain such losses. It was the North Vietnamese who were eventually proved right. Ia Drang is a good illustration of the Communist determination which helped to ensure their ultimate victory in 1975 (see page 188).

iv) Communist ingenuity

Communist ingenuity and preparedness was vitally important. In many areas supposedly controlled by the Saigon government there was a highly efficient Communist underground organisation. The Communist party had a web of informants and a multitude of social organisations which helped to comfort, control and motivate the people in uncertain times. The Communist network of tunnels in which VC could hide, shelter and regroup was literally underground. In January 1967 the Americans found a maze of tunnels north of Saigon. These were like an underground city, full of stoves, furniture, clothing and paperwork. An exploring American officer was killed by a booby trap so the Americans just pumped in tear gas, set off explosives, then got out. They had just missed the VC headquarters, several miles of tunnels away.

Key date

Americans found Communist tunnel network near Saigon: 1967

In Hanoi itself the government made excellent preparations against air raids. The ground was riddled with concrete bolt-holes, each with a thick concrete cover which could be pulled over the top. When the sirens sounded, most of Hanoi's population could vanish. Two million northerners, mostly women, were in the 'Shock Brigades' that repaired the effects of air-raid damage to roads and railways. Communist determination, heroism and ingenuity were all vital to the American failure to win.

c) Corruption, decay and Saigon

Key question

How did the Saigon regime contribute to the American failure in Vietnam?

Studying corruption and decay in the South (especially in Saigon) is important for understanding the outcome of the war.

i) Disruption and relocation

Incessant fighting and bombing drove millions of peasants out of the countryside into the towns and cities. By 1968 roughly one-third of South Vietnam's population had been relocated. Many were put up in camps where primitive sanitation bred disease. Many lived off Americans, particularly in Saigon. Saigon was where Americans and Vietnamese met and mixed most.

ii) Spoiling Saigon

Mid-twentieth-century Saigon was still a strange and lovely mixture of Southeast Asia and provincial France. Its tree-shaded streets were lined with quiet shops and sleepy pavement cafés. The beautiful villas of the residential districts had lush tropical gardens of yellow scented jasmine and mimosa and purple and red bougainvillaea.

Saigon became an unsavoury city in the American war years. Drugs were sold in its bars. Many hotels were brothels. The streets were awash with black-market goods, American soldiers, orphans, cripples, beggars and 56,000 registered prostitutes. The beggars targeted 'rich' Americans, tugging at them and making crying sounds. On the beautiful tiled terrace of the French colonial-style Continental Palace Hotel in Saigon, limbless Vietnamese victims of the war crawled crab-like along the floor seeking handouts from Americans.

The war had destroyed the social fabric of South Vietnam, uprooting peasants to the cities and dividing families. Poor peasant girls who turned to prostitution dismayed their families, despite earning more in a week than the whole family did in a year. American dollars distorted the economy. The salary of the lowest ranking American was gigantic by Vietnamese standards. Taxi drivers would not stop for other Vietnamese if it was possible

American GIs with their Vietnamese girlfriends.

to be hailed by an American. Vietnamese professionals lost status and influence in this new dollar-dominated world. A Vietnamese waiter serving big-tipping Americans would earn more than his doctor father. Garbage and sewage disposal suffered as municipal workers sought higher wages working for Americans. On one pavement pile of rat-covered garbage was a sign: 'this is the fruit of American aid'.

iii) 'The mysterious East'

Saigon was full of Vietnamese and American officials. There was much talk but little real communication. The Americans would put forward plans and, so long as America financed them, the Vietnamese would agree, although not necessarily co-operate. A cynical American official described how things worked:

> Say, for instance, that we hand them a plan to distribute 10,000 radios to villages so that peasants can listen to Saigon propaganda broadcasts. They respond enthusiastically, and we deliver the radios. A few months later, when we enquire, they tell us what we

> want to hear: peasants are being converted to the government cause, and we're winning the war. But what has really happened? Have all the radios reached the villages, or have half of them been sold on the black market? Are peasants listening to Saigon or to Hanoi? We don't know. We're in the mysterious East. We report progress to Washington because Washington demands progress.

iv) Aid and corruption

American aid rarely reached the peasants for whom it was primarily intended. Much of it found its way into the pockets of the military and urban elites. Even when American fertiliser got to the countryside, it was hoarded, and artificially created shortages caused the price to rise. Thieu's brother-in-law was a leading speculator. Thieu himself carried away millions of dollars in gold when he fled Vietnam in April 1975. Theft from the Americans was extensive. American products were stolen and sold on street corners, even rifles and ammunition. Whole consignments disappeared without trace. An investigation revealed that the amount of cement supposedly needed by and given to Vietnamese officials in one year could have paved over the whole country. The endemic corruption owed much to the Vietnamese emphasis on family duty. Poorly paid officials and even the highly paid president wanted to provide well for their relations. Thieu's cousin ran a wealthy province: for a fee he would let VC out of jail or keep ARVN men out of battle. One wonders whether the anti-Communist Vietnamese would have stood more of a chance of success had they not been distracted by the incredible temptations of American largesse or disoriented by the impact of the American presence.

d) The ARVN

i) ARVN weaknesses

Key question
How did the ARVN contribute to the American failure in Vietnam?

South Vietnam was never well governed under Diem and his successors. The corruption and mismanagement that characterised South Vietnam's government naturally permeated its armed forces.

Saigon wanted to avoid losses. In February 1971, 30,000 ARVN invaded Laos with orders to retreat if over 3000 died. They retreated, halfway to their objective. The Americans described their own tactics as 'Search and Destroy' but those of the ARVN as 'Search and Avoid'. Poor results damaged morale and led to further failure. Units were unwilling to engage the enemy if the astrological signs were against it or if great losses seemed likely.

Key date
ARVN retreated from Laos because of heavy losses: February 1971

Many military leaders were appointed for political rather than military reasons. Not surprisingly, they fought badly. The high command spent more time fighting among themselves than against the enemy. The urban middle-class officers did not get on well with the peasants in the lower ranks. Eighty per cent of South Vietnamese were Buddhist, but only five per cent of the ARVN leadership were.

ARVN wages were so low that by 1966 the soldiers depended on American surplus rice. Some ARVN officers sold American cigarettes, whiskey, rifles, ammunition, uniforms, boots and helmets on the black market. Others pocketed the pay of thousands of deserters, sick or dead men. Lower ranks bullied and robbed the population. Some deserted to the Communists.

On the other hand, because they were not always able to call on air support or helicopters to evacuate their wounded, the ARVN were often remarkably tenacious when cornered. Many ARVN fought often and bravely, and tens of thousands of them died.

ii) The American view of ARVN

The ARVN were compromised in the eyes of the Vietnamese people by their association with the Americans, while Americans such as Westmoreland were frequently unwilling to use ARVN assistance because they despised them and because any military leader is more at ease with his own men. In Westmoreland's headquarters in Saigon there were hidden nozzles to spray his 'elite' ARVN guards with tear gas if they defected. Relations between the American forces and the ARVN were never very good. After the disastrous battle of Ap Bac (see pages 64–5) American pilots sang new words to the tune 'On Top of Old Smokey':

> We were supporting the ARVNs,
> A group without guts,
> Attacking a village
> Of straw-covered huts.
> The VCs start shooting,
> They fire a big blast,
> We off-load the ARVNs
> They sit on their ass.
> An armoured battalion
> Just stayed in a trance,
> One captain died trying
> To make them advance.
> When the news was reported
> The ARVNs had won,
> The VCs are laughing
> Over their captured guns.

The morale and performance of the ARVN is a major factor in explaining the defeat of the Washington–Saigon alliance.

Summary diagram: The Vietnamese

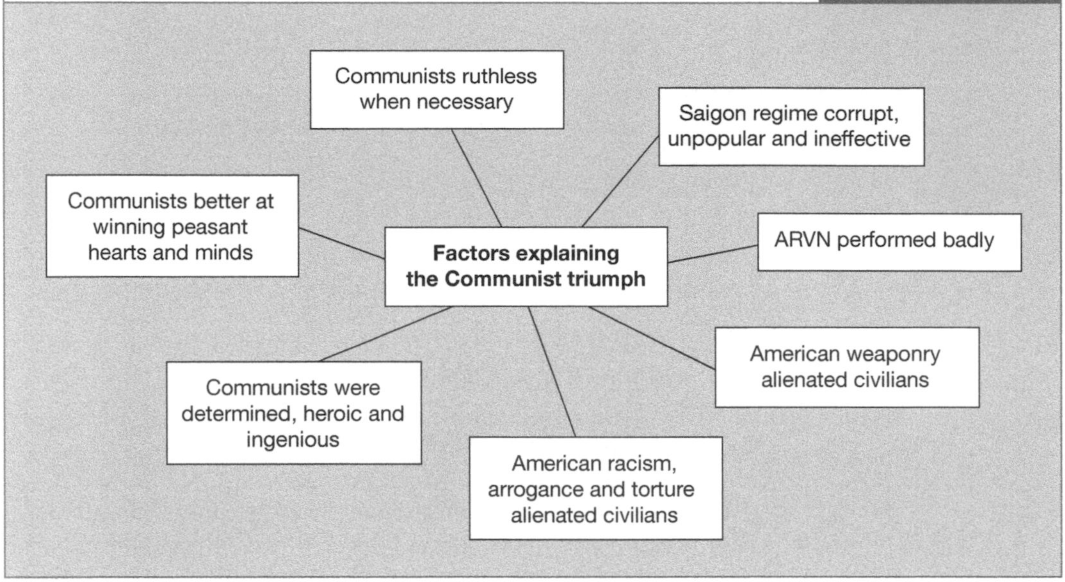

2 | The Americans

a) What motivated American soldiers?

Key question
Why did so many Americans volunteer to fight?

Of the 26.8 million American men of fighting age in the 1960s, 10.93 million served in the military; 2.2 million were drafted, but 8.7 million were volunteers, many inspired by a sense of duty, patriotism, family tradition or a belief in the rectitude of America's cause. This is well illustrated in *Born on the Fourth of July*, the autobiography of Ron Kovic. The book was made into an impressive film starring Tom Cruise as Kovic. Raised on a diet of Second World War movies, playing boyhood war games, believing Communists to be ungodly and evil, Kovic joined up when marine recruiters came to his high school. They reminded him of John Wayne, whose name frequently recurs in the history of the Vietnam War (President Johnson hoped Wayne would play him in any film of his life). When interviewed, many said that they were inspired by Hollywood movies. One said that he was influenced by the 'John Wayne syndrome'. Another thought he would be 'a soldier like John Wayne … who feared nothing and either emerged with the medals and the girl, or died heroically'.

Others joined for different reasons. Robert Mason's *Chickenhawk* is the well-written memoir of a helicopter pilot in Vietnam who says he joined up just because he wanted to fly. Mason claims he knew nothing then of what the war was about. A platoon leader suggested another motive: 'It turned out that most of us liked to kill other men'. Looking back, a high proportion of **veterans** said they were glad to have fought in Vietnam, and enjoyed their time there.

Key term
Veterans
Those who fought in the Vietnam War (as any other war) were afterwards known as veterans.

Factors such as duty, patriotism and even enjoyment of war help to explain why many American men fought in Vietnam.

THE PRESS

Journalists and photographers from all over the world flocked to and fed upon Vietnam. War makes good news: the public are interested in the drama of death. War images are a gift to writers and photographers. Some of the best war photographs were taken in Vietnam. Helicopters whirring over peasants in fields, shell-shocked faces or wounded bodies are very dramatic.

There is no doubt that many members of the press corps got 'high' on the war. The British photographer Tim Page was wounded twice in Vietnam. He left but could not resist returning for the Tet offensive (see pages 137–9). In 1969 an American sergeant in front of him stepped on a mine. A long piece of shrapnel blew away brain tissue the size of an orange: Page tried to take more photos then collapsed. A British publisher asked him to write a book to 'take the glamour out of war'. Page said no one could: it was fun, like sex and the Rolling Stones. He thought the pressmen liked the brush with that which was most evil, most dear, most profane. They liked the camaraderie and the sheer adventure of it all. Page felt sorry for the Vietnamese, 'whose country had become our adventure sandbox'. Page helps us to understand the attraction of war to some of the military and why so many Americans volunteered to fight in Vietnam.

Michael Herr was a journalist. His book *Dispatches* is an eloquent, dramatic, novelistic, self-consciously well-written account of his time reporting in Vietnam. He felt that he and the soldiers had watched too many war films all their lives, so that seeing real war and real death did not have the full impact. Everything seemed unreal, like a scene from a movie. Herr felt that the press were probably 'glorified war-profiteers', 'thrill freaks, death-wishers, wound-seekers, ghouls'. Perhaps some of us who write and read about war are similar.

In the work of the world's press on Vietnam we can see one of the great causes of the war, the romance and heroism that attracts many civilians and soldiers. We can also see one of the main reasons why America lost the war: the press coverage upset many Americans. Their writings and photographs showed up the horrors and truths about the war which are covered in this chapter.

American disunity, the insistence upon a 'comfortable' war and problems particular to fighting in Vietnam help to explain why these men were unable to defeat the Communists.

Key question
How did American disunity contribute to failure?

b) American disunity

Although many Americans fought with conviction and bravery, the American and allied forces were frequently disunited. The marines were traditionally linked with the navy and were not keen to obey orders from Westmoreland's army. The unconventional

Green Berets aroused antagonism. Americans distrusted the ARVN. At Khe Sanh (see page 139) in 1968, Westmoreland sent for ARVN representation as an afterthought, and then deployed them somewhere unimportant.

Ordinary soldiers served 365 days, marines 13 months. Many stencilled the return dates on their helmets. This short term of service meant that units never attained the feeling of unity vital to morale and performance.

Of Americans in Vietnam, 13 per cent were black but a disproportionate 28 per cent were in combat units (rather than desk jobs). This naturally led to resentment.

Many American soldiers did not like their country's manner of waging war. Others felt that America had no right to intervene in Vietnam. In 1966 an ex-Green Beret said he doubted that Vietnam would be better off under Ho's Communism, 'but it is not for me or my government to decide. That decision is for the Vietnamese'. Some disapproved of the mistreatment of civilians on humanitarian or military grounds.

Disagreement with the war or tactics led to indiscipline. An underground newspaper offered a $10,000 bounty for the death of the officer responsible for Hamburger Hill (see page 127). Things got much worse under Johnson's successor. In 1969 an entire company sat down on the battlefield, while in full view of TV cameras another company refused to go down a dangerous trail.

In the late 1960s anti-war feeling grew in America. Many American soldiers became confused about what they were fighting for. Many returned home to find themselves ostracised, jeered and spat on if they wore their uniform. Some found the families they had left at home had been victimised by opponents of the war. Homes belonging to soldiers might have broken glass spread across their lawns, or objects thrown at their windows.

> In the Second World War the folks back home cheered you as you worked your way towards Berlin or Japan. In Vietnam you fought for ground, won it, and left knowing the VC would move in again. Meanwhile, the folks back home called you 'baby-killer'.

The collapse of the home front (see pages 143–7) was a crucial factor in America's failure in Vietnam. It damaged troop morale and hamstrung the government in Washington.

Key dates

Battle of Khe Sanh: January 1968

An American company refused to fight: 1969

c) Trying to fight a 'comfortable' war

Key question
How did trying to fight a 'comfortable war' contribute to failure?

Ironically, the American desire to keep their soldiers as comfortable as possible in Vietnam helps to explain their defeat there. President Nixon said:

> If we fail it will be because the American way simply isn't as effective as the Communist way … I have an uneasy feeling that this may be the case. We give them the most modern arms, we emphasise the material to the exclusion of the spiritual and the Spartan life, and it may be that we soften them up rather than harden them up for the battle.

Many soldiers never actually fought. They had to organise the American lifestyle for everyone else – running clubs, cinemas and PXs (post exchanges). The main PX in Saigon was larger than a New York department store and contained almost as much – jewellery, perfume, alcohol, sports clothes, cameras, tape recorders, radios, soap, shampoo, deodorant, condoms.

Every week, several thousand combat soldiers were sent for R&R to Saigon or Japan. All this led to an air of unreality and disorientation. A soldier could be airlifted from the horrors of the jungle to a luxurious base where the air-conditioning was so cold there were homely fireplaces. He could have steak, French fries, ice-cream and Coca-Cola. Sometimes cigarettes and iced beer were dropped by helicopters in mid-siege, and hot meals were landed at remote jungle camps. One colonel got a Silver Star bravery award for delivering turkeys by helicopter for Thanksgiving.

When the last American soldier left Vietnam, there were 357 American libraries, 159 basketball courts, 90 service clubs, 85 volleyball fields, 71 swimming pools, 55 softball fields, 40 ice-cream plants, 30 tennis courts and two bowling alleys. The American soldier was fighting a different war from his enemy. Every soldier suffers great personal hardship in the field, but while many North Vietnamese and VC spent years away from their families, existed on a basic diet and lacked decent medical treatment, the typical American soldier served a short term in Vietnam, and had good food and medical treatment. One PAVN soldier thought this was the difference between the two sides:

> You ask me what I thought of the Americans. We thought the Americans were handsome soldiers but looked as if they were made with flour … it was difficult for them to suffer all the hardships of the Vietnamese battlefront. When we had no water to drink, they had water for showers! We could suffer the hardships much better than they could. That probably was the main reason we won.

Westmoreland said this was the only way you could get Americans to fight.

Frustration with the war led many American soldiers to seek comfort elsewhere. In 1966 there were around 30,000 war-orphaned child prostitutes, but they could not cope with the American demand. Around a quarter of American soldiers caught sexually transmitted diseases. Drug abuse became common. In 1970 an estimated 58 per cent of Americans in Vietnam smoked 'pot' (marijuana), and 22 per cent shot up heroin. One colonel was **court-martialled** for leading his squadron in pot parties. In 1971 5000 needed treatment for combat wounds, 20,529 for serious drug abuse. It was hard to take action over the drug market as so many prominent government officials in Saigon were involved, including Ky. It was hard to win a war when army discipline deteriorated: the process began under Johnson, then accelerated under his successor.

Key term

Court-martialled
Tried by an army court for breaking army regulations.

d) Problems for the officers

Key question
What problems faced officers?

Americans of different ranks had different experiences. An American army officer did five months in the front line. He would probably be less experienced than some of the soldiers he commanded. Five months was too little to get to know his men properly. He would then be moved on to a training, organisation or desk job.

Unpopular officers were shot in the back in action or had fragmentation grenades thrown at them. Under Johnson's successor, between 1969 and 1971, there were 730 '**fraggings**', killing 83 officers. Often they were simply trying to get their men to fight.

It was hard to win a war with so many inexperienced and increasingly unpopular officers.

e) Problems for the 'grunts'

Key question
What problems faced the 'grunts'?

The young foot soldier or '**grunt**', like Ron Kovic, was often horrified by what he saw in 'Nam' and was keen to get out. Many hoped for a small wound and some shot themselves in the foot. What was particularly awful about this war?

The average age of the grunt in Vietnam was 19, compared to a less vulnerable 26 in the Second World War. To make matters worse, there seemed to be no progress being made, as is illustrated in another evocative film, *Hamburger Hill*. The film told the true story of the bloody May 1969 attempt to gain a hill that was quickly retaken by the VC. Any time the Americans or ARVN moved out of an area, the Communists would move in.

Key dates
Fragging began: 1969
Battle of Hamburger Hill: May 1969

The grunt never felt safe. Twenty per cent of American wounded were victims of **booby traps** rather than direct enemy fire. There were booby traps all around, including the 'Bouncing Betty', which shot out of the earth and exploded after being stepped on. Explosions blew away limbs. The VC wired up dead bodies with mines in the hope that Americans would trigger them off. They camouflaged holes on trails so Americans would fall in and be impaled on sharpened bamboo stakes. These were positioned so the victim could not get out without tearing off flesh. The patrolling infantryman was thus in almost continuous danger, with enemy mines, booby traps or snipers likely to get him at any time. Sweat-drenched grunts hated the physical problems of patrolling the ground. They carried 50–70 pounds of equipment, and were plagued by heat, rain and insects:

Key terms
Fragging
When enlisted men tried to kill officers by throwing fragmentation grenades at them.
Grunt
Ordinary ground trooper or footsoldier.
Booby traps
Disguised traps.
DDT
An insecticide.

> We were covered with inch-long fire ants. They bit everything they landed on, and by the time we had sprayed **DDT** down each other's backs and finally killed them, we were all burning from the bites and the DDT.

The heat was often suffocating, making breathing difficult. Salt tablets were chewed to counter sweat loss. In the paddy fields metal gun parts burned in the sun. In the jungle thick foliage blotted out the sun and moving air, and thorn scratches bled. Uniforms rotted because of the dampness.

Not knowing which Vietnamese were the enemy was the worse thing. That was one of the biggest and most demoralising differences from the Second World War. One admiral said:

> We should have fought in the north, where everyone was the enemy, where you didn't have to worry whether or not you were shooting friendly civilians. In the south, we had to cope with women concealing grenades in their brassieres, or in their baby's diapers. I remember two of our marines being killed by a youngster who they were teaching to play volleyball.

A soldier recalled:

> You never knew who was the enemy and who was the friend. They all looked alike. They all dressed alike. They were all Vietnamese. Some of them were Vietcong. Here's a [young] woman ... She is pregnant, and she tells an interrogator that her husband works in Danang and isn't a Vietcong. But she watches your men walk down a trail and get killed or wounded by a booby trap. She knows the booby trap is there, but she doesn't warn them. Maybe she planted it herself ... The enemy was all around you.

It was hard to win the war when many of the grunts were terrified and demoralised.

Key question
Did the US adopt the wrong military strategy?

f) American military strategy

The American conventional forces, like the French before them, struggled to defeat Giap's army and guerrillas.

i) Search and destroy

Under Johnson, US troops engaged in 'search and destroy' missions, in which they would try to clear an area of VC. However, it was very hard to find the guerrillas. In 1967 the CIA reported that:

> less than one percent of nearly two million Allied small unit operations conducted in the last two years resulted in contact with the enemy.

It is notoriously difficult to try to wipe out a guerrilla movement, particularly when the guerrillas are sent in from another 'state' (North Vietnam) and when the guerrillas have a sympathetic, supportive or simply apathetic reaction from the local community. Frequently, US troops would 'clear' an area of VC. However, as soon as the Americans moved out, the Communists would move back in. A famous example of this is the bloody battle for 'Hamburger Hill' (so-called because of the bloody carnage) in 1969. The Americans 'won', but the ground was quickly retaken by the VC when the Americans left.

ii) Reliance upon superior technology

Bombing was a favourite tactic during Johnson's presidency. North Vietnam, the Ho Chi Minh Trail and South Vietnamese villages suspected of harbouring Communist sympathisers were all heavily bombed. From 1966 to 1968, an average 800 tons of bombs fell on North Vietnam daily. However, the bombing failed both to damage North Vietnamese morale and to stop the flow of men and materials coming down the trail from North Vietnam to South Vietnam. The Johnson administration ignored warnings (for example, from the CIA in 1966) about that lack of impact. Furthermore, the bombing alienated many people in South Vietnam and in America.

iii) The wrong strategy

Years later, McNamara admitted that US tactics were wrong, that it was unwise to use a high-tech war of attrition against a primarily guerrilla force that never considered giving up their war for independence. McNamara's successor Clark Clifford (Secretary of Defence, 1968–9) said that it 'was startling to me that we had no military plan to win the war'.

General Westmoreland hoped to be able to meet the VC in conventional set-piece battles in which US firepower would be decisive. However, his 'search and destroy' missions usually failed to find VC and the ratio of destruction was usually six South Vietnamese civilians for every VC soldier. The large-scale use of helicopters and the blasting of the zones where they were to land was not conducive to searching out guerrillas, who simply went elsewhere upon hearing all the noise. In Operation Cedar Falls in 1967, 20 American battalions entered an area north of Saigon. Defoliants, bombing and bulldozers cleared the land. Six thousand people were evacuated and their homes and lands destroyed. Thus 'friendly' civilians were made hostile to Saigon and its American ally. Only a few VC were found. During 1967–8 fewer than one per cent of the two million small unit operations undertaken by the Americans or ARVN led to any contact with the enemy.

iv) What if ...

Americans, particularly ex-soldiers, frequently debate what might have happened if the United States had done things differently in the Vietnam war.

What if President Johnson had gone beyond limited war and declared war on North Vietnam? Could the United States have won?

The war might have become even more unpopular. The USSR and China might have entered the war, something Johnson was determined to avoid. He clearly did not think South Vietnam was worth a Third World War, and the American public certainly would not have thought so. Congress would probably not have declared war for South Vietnam.

What if, as General Bruce Palmer contended in 1986, the United States had cut South Vietnam off from Communist infiltration, thereby giving South Vietnam time to build itself up into a viable state?

That 'cutting off' might have been possible in flatter terrain, as in Korea. However, to 'cut off' the jungles and mountains on the Cambodian and Laotian borders would have been impossible. Furthermore, the PLAF (see page 45) would have been 'trapped' inside South Vietnam, and would have continued guerrilla warfare. The strategic hamlets had been infiltrated by Communists, which proved that it was impossible to isolate the South Vietnamese population from South Vietnamese (or North Vietnamese) Communists. In 1967 the CIA established that most of the supplies used by the Communists originated in the South, so 'cutting off' supplies would have been difficult.

What if the United States Army had worked harder to win the hearts and minds of the people, as the historian Andrew Krepinevich suggested in 1986?

The historian Richard Hunt pointed out in 1995 that this would have taken too many American soldiers too long, and that the American public would have run out of patience. One commander pointed out that if he and his men became 'mayors and sociologists worrying about hearts and minds', they would not be much use if they had to fight the Soviets!

Americans still argue today about the Communist victory in Vietnam. Was it inevitable? Are guerrillas impossible to beat when much of the population is sympathetic to them? Or was it just that the Americans were not the people to win this war? Were American tactics wrong? Was Westmoreland's war of attrition the way to defeat determined nationalists and guerrillas? Should America have concentrated upon winning the hearts and minds of the people? Were bombing and 'search [for Communists] and destroy' tactics wise? Did the American public lose the war for America? Or the American media? Or American politicians? This chapter will probably have made up your mind about the answer to those questions which centre upon events in Vietnam. The next chapter will give you more ideas about the 'home front' and the loss of the war.

Summary diagram: The Americans

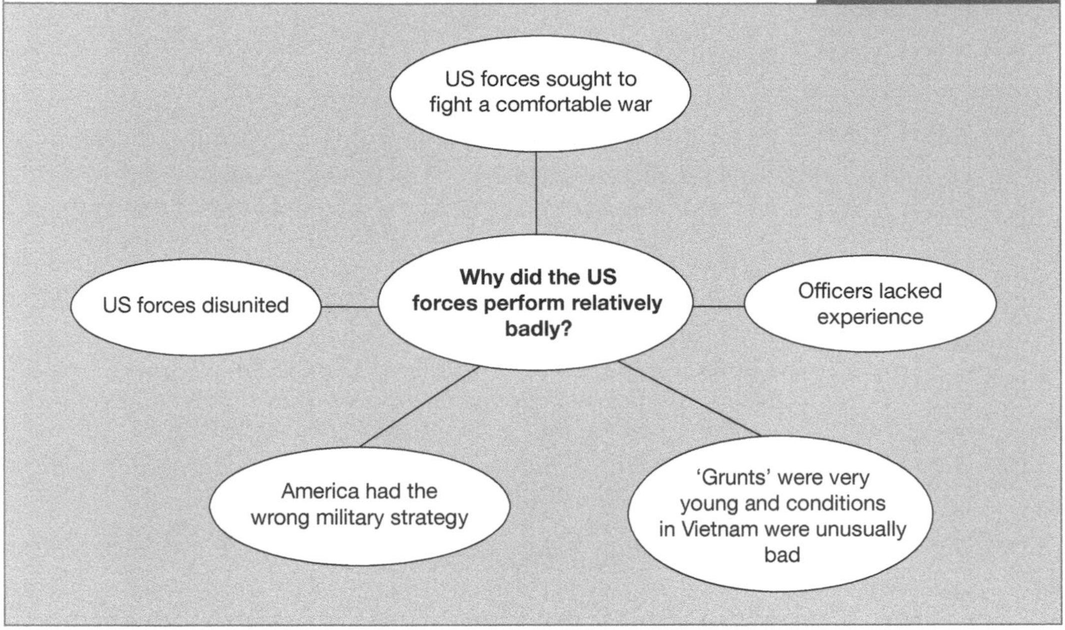

3 | Key Debates

a) Was the war unwinnable?

Some historians think that the war was unwinnable. They contend that America was fighting in the wrong place, against the wrong enemy, and that Americans never understood Vietnam or the Vietnamese.

On the other hand, those who fought in Vietnam and subsequently wrote about it often disagree. Orthodox historians generally accept that US intervention was morally justifiable in the struggle against Communism and that greater use of force would have been acceptable. In his memoirs, Westmoreland (1976) claimed that he was too restricted by orders from Washington, DC, and that more ground troops and air power would have defeated Hanoi. Colonel Harry Summers (1982) blamed civilian officials for dispersing US military power in the search for guerrillas. Summers advocated greater use of greater force.

b) Could military solutions solve Saigon's problems?

Historians such as Herring (1996) point out that military historians, rather like McNamara at the Department of Defence, err in imagining that military solutions could have solved the political problems of the unpopular Saigon regime. Some historians actually blame over-use of American military power for the US failure, for example, Thomson (1980). They point out that the bombing in particular served to alienate the South Vietnamese people. Others criticise US confidence in high-tech warfare and managerial techniques, for example, Gibson (1986).

Key terms

Pacification
Paying greater attention to the security and government of the South Vietnamese people.

Reunification
Vietnam was reunited in 1975 when the North took over the South.

c) Did Westmoreland use the correct strategy?

Some (such as Cable in 1991) contend that Westmoreland should have concentrated more on **pacification** and counter-insurgency, rather than on the war of attrition. However, Bergerud (1990) studied Hau Nghia province, where American troops worked closely with villagers on pacification, but nevertheless failed to win greater support for the Saigon regime.

d) Did America lose the war, or did the Communists win it?

Bergerud contends that the outcome of the Vietnam war is not so much an American failure, but rather a Vietnamese success. Several American historians, such as Duiker (2000), emphasise the Communist advantages: their undoubted patriotism, superb organisation, ruthlessness when necessary and effective military strategy.

e) Which was the villain: Saigon or Hanoi?

Some historians point out the frequently unpleasant nature of the Communist government in Vietnam after **reunification**, while others suggest that the Saigon regime was not as bad as is often thought (Hatcher, 1990).

Some key books in the debates

E. Bergerud, *The Dynamics of Defeat* (Boulder, 1990).
L. Cable, *Unholy Grail* (New York, 1991).
W. Duiker, *Ho Chi Minh* (New York, 2000).
J.W. Gibson, *The Perfect War* (New York, 1986).
P. Hatcher, *The Suicide of an Elite* (Stanford, 1990).
G. Herring, *America's Longest War* (New York, 1996).
H. Summers, *On Strategy* (California, 1982).
J.C. Thomson, *Rolling Thunder* (North Carolina, 1980).
W. Westmoreland, *A Soldier Reports* (New York, 1976).

7 Why the USA Failed: II – US Politicians and People

POINTS TO CONSIDER

When Johnson became president in 1963 he and his advisers were confident that America could 'win' in Vietnam. 'Winning' required the defeat of the Communists in South Vietnam and the sustaining of a strong and independent state there. However, by the time Johnson's presidency drew to an end, most of his advisers believed that the war was unwinnable and/or that America would have to dramatically change its approach, and maybe even get out of Vietnam altogether. Like Chapter 6, this chapter concentrates upon the second of the great debates about Johnson's presidency. Why could he not win the war in Vietnam?

This chapter looks at:

- Problems with Johnson's aims and methods
- Why and how Johnson was forced to retreat
- Johnson's last months
- Conclusions about Johnson and the war

Key dates

1965	March	First American combat troops landed in South Vietnam
	August	'Poisonous reporting' from Vietnam
1966		Increased domestic opposition to US involvement in Vietnam
	February	Senate Foreign Relations Committee hearings on war dominated by anti-war feeling
	November	Democrats did badly in the congressional mid-term elections
	December	Nearly 400,000 US soldiers in South Vietnam
1967	January	Martin Luther King publicly criticised US involvement in the war
	August	Unpopular tax rises to help to finance the war
		Senate hearings on the war dominated by hawks
	November	McNamara resigned

1968	January	Clark Clifford selected as Secretary of Defence
	Jan–Feb	Tet Offensive shook Americans' confidence Battle of Khe Sanh
	March	'Wise Men' advised Johnson against further escalation Johnson sought peace talks not re-election
	August	Riots during Democratic Convention in Chicago

Key question
Were Johnson's aims and methods conducive to victory?

1 | Problems with Johnson's Aims and Methods

a) Johnson's aims

It is not always easy to discover Johnson's aims. Nearly half of Americans polled in 1967 did not know for sure what the war was all about. McNamara's assistant privately quantified American aims as:

> seventy per cent to avoid a humiliating US defeat (to our reputation as a guarantor). Twenty per cent to keep South Vietnamese (and the adjacent) territory from Chinese hands. Ten per cent to permit the people of South Vietnam to enjoy a better, freer way of life.

Johnson publicly said that he aimed to defeat Communist aggression, build a nation in South Vietnam and search for peace there. His other aims were best kept private. He wanted to save American face, which he believed necessitated continuing and winning the war. He also wanted to ensure that his conduct of the war did not adversely affect the electoral prospects of any Democrat (especially himself). The problem was that the publicly stated American aims were probably impossible to achieve – certainly with the methods Johnson used and the criticism they aroused.

Johnson's methods were political and military. His administration advised, supported and tried to strengthen the Saigon governments, both politically and militarily. From 1965 he dramatically increased the numbers of US troops in South Vietnam and changed their role from an advisory to a participatory one. He bombed the North and the Ho Chi Minh Trail. He hoped this would convince Hanoi that it could not win, and must therefore accept a peace settlement. As has been seen in Chapter 6, these military methods did not bring an American victory.

b) Johnson's methods – political

The Kennedy and Johnson administrations considered the problem in Vietnam to be the weakness in the Saigon government and in its military performance. They recognised that the South

Vietnamese state needed large-scale reforms and massive US support. However, they failed to see that any state that needed this much support and change was clearly not viable.

Washington talked of bringing democracy to Vietnam but the concept was meaningless to the Vietnamese who had no tradition of American-style political democracy. The strongest Vietnamese political tradition was the hatred of foreigners. What Americans insisted on seeing as a South Vietnamese state went against that most powerful tradition, for the South Vietnamese regimes were all too clearly bound up with and dependent upon the American foreigners.

The Vietnamese peasants were often politically apathetic. Their concern was their day-to-day struggle for existence. When a leader offered ideas that might ease that struggle, many were attracted. Ho and the Communists offered another vision of freedom and equality, one characterised by the fairer distribution of wealth. Although Ho was greatly aided by Moscow and Beijing, their help was not as visible as American help in the South. Ho thus combined the appeal of nationalism and equality in a way that the South Vietnamese regimes never managed.

The American-sponsored governments in Saigon were generally corrupt, uncaring and unattractive to the ordinary Vietnamese. Thieu told Johnson that the Communists would win any South Vietnamese elections. Johnson's response was significant: 'I don't believe that. Does anyone believe that?'

Johnson never really understood what motivated Ho and his armies. In April 1965 he promised Ho economic aid if he would stop the war: 'Old Ho can't turn that down'. Johnson did not seem to understand that Ho was fighting for a united Communist Vietnam and would not compromise. In Chapter 6 we saw that the North Vietnamese knew why they fought and were willing to wait, suffer and persevere to achieve their aims in a way that many Americans and South Vietnamese were not.

c) Johnson's methods – military

The commander-in-chief bears ultimate responsibility for the choice of weapons and tactics used by his subordinates, but naturally Johnson often deferred to his military experts. 'Bomb, bomb, bomb – that's all they know', he sighed. Johnson's military men used the wrong methods in Vietnam. They told Johnson they could destroy North Vietnam's industrial and economic base and morale, but there were relatively few North Vietnamese factories and roads to destroy. Supplies could come in from China and the USSR. If the Americans bombed one part of the Ho Chi Minh Trail the North Vietnamese could simply change route. The bombing only succeeded in increasing North Vietnamese determination and raising morale, as the CIA pointed out from 1965 onwards. The bombing also alienated many South Vietnamese. The bombing was designed to prevent the alienation of the American people, in that it was less expensive than troops and incurred fewer US casualties. However, some Americans disliked the policy.

Between 1965 and 1968 Johnson's administration slowly became convinced that their aims, methods and vision were inappropriate. It became clear that the escalation of US military involvement in support of the Saigon regime was not going to stop Hanoi and that the involvement was becoming increasingly unpopular amongst Americans and South Vietnamese. Johnson would be forced to retreat because his aims and methods in Vietnam were inappropriate and increasingly unpopular.

Summary diagram: Problems with Johnson's aims and methods

Aims

- Avoid US defeat (humiliation)
- Defeat Communist aggression
- Keep South Vietnam independent

Methods

Political	Military
• Support Saigon government	• Bomb • Chemicals • Hi-tech war

2 | Why and How Johnson was Forced to Retreat

Even as Johnson was building up American forces in Vietnam in 1965–7, the problems which would eventually defeat him were becoming obvious. The Saigon government remained ineffective and unpopular, and increasing numbers of Americans doubted the wisdom of continuing to support it.

Key question
How did problems in South Vietnam help to force Johnson to retreat?

a) Problems in South Vietnam in 1966–7

During 1966–7 Johnson poured more men into Vietnam but the situation there did not look promising. In February 1966 Johnson met Ky in Hawaii. Ky said he wanted a Great Society for Vietnam. 'Boy, you speak just like an American', said the delighted Johnson. That was not surprising. Ky's speech had been written by his American advisers.

Ky's government was in reality corrupt and averse to reform. Ky and his American allies were unpopular. Many South Vietnamese wanted negotiations with Hanoi.

There were many protests in Saigon. A Buddhist nun sat cross-legged, her hands clasped in prayer, in a temple in Hue. A friend doused her with gasoline. The nun lit a match to set herself alight while the friend poured peppermint oil on her to disguise the smell of burning flesh. The dead nun's letters were widely circulated; they blamed Johnson for her death because he helped the repressive Saigon regime.

'What are we doing here?' asked one American official when American marines helped Ky to attack Buddhist strongholds. 'We are fighting to save these people and they are fighting each other.' At Johnson's insistence Ky held democratic elections. The elections were observed by American politicians, one of whom kept calling the country 'South Vietcong'! Although Ky ran the election, his candidate for president, Thieu, still managed only 37 per cent of the vote.

The Johnson administration was publicly optimistic, claiming in 1967 that the '**cross-over point**' had been reached: American and ARVN troops were killing the enemy faster than they could be replaced. Westmoreland said that there were only 285,000 Communists left fighting in the south (the CIA said over 500,000, but the administration kept it quiet to preserve morale).

Key term

Cross-over point
Point at which Americans anticipated that Communists would give up because they were being killed faster than Hanoi could replace them.

Privately the administration was pessimistic. Its members disagreed over how the war should be prosecuted. 'Rolling Thunder' was causing tremendous divisions. Johnson railed against 'gutless' officials who leaked 'defeatist' stories to the press: 'It's gotten so you can't have intercourse with your wife without it being spread by traitors'. Things were clearly going badly in Vietnam and it was destroying confidence within the administration. Most worrying was Secretary of Defence McNamara's change of position.

b) The loss of McNamara

i) McNamara and the Kennedys

Key question
How did McNamara help to force Johnson to retreat?

Johnson had always thought very highly of McNamara. McNamara had been vital in the formulation of Kennedy and Johnson's Vietnam policies. However, Bobby Kennedy had become passionately anti-war and publicly opposed the war from January 1966. Johnson privately insulted 'nervous Nellies' who disagreed with him about Vietnam, calling one senator a 'prick', Senator Fulbright 'Senator Halfbright' and Bobby Kennedy 'spineless'. Johnson considered the Kennedy–McNamara friendship dangerous.

ii) McNamara's doubts

McNamara's health and family life had suffered because of the war. His daughter and son had told him that what America was doing in Vietnam was immoral. They participated in the anti-war protests. McNamara blamed himself for his wife's stomach ulcer. He seemed physically and mentally tortured, bursting into tears during discussions. He was losing his old certainty. McNamara told Johnson in early 1967:

> The picture of the world's greatest superpower killing or seriously injuring 1000 non-combatants a week, while trying to pound a tiny, backward nation into submission on an issue whose merits are hotly disputed, is not a pretty one.

Key dates

Senate hearings on the war dominated by hawks: August 1967

McNamara resigned: November 1967

Clark Clifford selected as Secretary of Defence (took office in March): January 1968

iii) Senate hearings, 1967

In August 1967 hawks organised Senate hearings designed to force Johnson into lifting restrictions on the bombing of North Vietnam. Public opinion polls in spring 1967 revealed that 45 per cent of Americans favoured increased military pressure in Vietnam (41 per cent favoured withdrawal). During the hearings the military blamed McNamara and Johnson for tying their hands behind their backs, by limiting the bombing. McNamara testified that the bombing was not worth risking a clash with the Soviets. He said bombing would only stop Hanoi if the bombing totally annihilated North Vietnam and all its people. He pointed out that bombing of the Ho Chi Minh Trail did not stop Communist troops and supplies moving south.

Johnson and the JCS were furious with McNamara's performance. The president thought that McNamara had degenerated into 'an emotional basket case'. The JCS said his doubts were undermining all the rationale for America's previous and present efforts.

iv) McNamara's resignation

Suffering from severe chest pains, McNamara was relieved to move to a job outside the government. In November 1967, in a last tearful White House conference, McNamara condemned:

> the goddamned Air Force and its goddamned bombing campaign that had dropped more bombs on Vietnam than on Europe in the whole of World War II and we hadn't gotten a goddamned thing for it.

He had not advocated getting out of Vietnam, but halting the escalation, which option his administration colleagues considered unacceptable.

v) Clark Clifford

In January 1968 Johnson selected Clark Clifford as Secretary of Defence. In July 1967 he had toured the countries helping the US in Vietnam. In exchange for enormous American aid, South Korea had contributed 45,000 troops, Australia 5000, Thailand 2000, the Philippines 2000 (non-combatants) and New Zealand under 500. Clifford told Johnson that 'more people turned out in New Zealand to demonstrate against our trip than the country had sent to Vietnam'. Like his predecessor, Clifford began to doubt the domino theory and the wisdom of US involvement. The Tet Offensive finally made Clifford conclude that he had to extricate America from this endless war.

Key question
How important was Tet in Johnson's decision to retreat?

c) The Tet Offensive, January 1968

i) Aims of the Tet Offensive

In January 1968 Hanoi launched an unprecedented offensive against South Vietnam. Tens of thousands of PAVN and VC attacked cities and military installations in the South. 'Uncle Ho was very old and we had to liberate the South before his death', explained one North Vietnamese officer. Hanoi dreamed that their great offensive would cause the Saigon government to collapse. At the very least Hanoi hoped to demonstrate such strength that America would give up.

Key term

Tet
The Tet Festival was the Vietnamese equivalent of Christmas, New Year and Easter combined. Americans use the word 'Tet' as shorthand for the 'Tet Offensive'.

ii) Course of events

The attack broke the traditional **Tet** holiday truce. The Americans and South Vietnamese were preoccupied with the Tet festival. Saigon, Washington and the US public were shocked that the Communists could move with such impunity and so effectively throughout the South. The American ambassador had to flee the embassy in Saigon in his pyjamas. It took 11,000 American and ARVN troops three weeks to clear Saigon of Communist forces. The attackers had even hit the US embassy and dramatic scenes there were headline news in America. The Tet Offensive cost a great many lives and caused incredible damage; 3895 Americans, 4954 South Vietnamese military, 14,300 South Vietnamese civilians, and 58,373 VC and PAVN died. Out of 17,134 houses in historic Hue, 9776 were totally destroyed and 3169 were seriously damaged.

Key date

Tet Offensive shook US confidence: January–February 1968

iii) Results and significance of Tet

- The Tet Offensive was the largest set of battles fought in the Vietnam War up to that point.
- It was the first set of battles to be fought in the cities of South Vietnam.
- It could be argued that the Tet Offensive was one of those rare battles lost by both sides (see below).
- The Communists had suffered grievous losses. It took Hanoi several years to get over this great effort.
- The South Vietnamese people had not risen *en masse* to help the Communists, which damaged the VC claim to be a liberation force, but also showed up the weakness of the Saigon regime.
- The Communist position in the South Vietnamese countryside was strengthened because of the Communist performance in Tet.
- The ordinary South Vietnamese had not rallied to the Saigon regime. Tet seemed to show that although the US could stop the overthrow of the Saigon government, it had failed to make it viable in the face of Communist determination.
- US intelligence officials had failed to notice clear warnings and their confidence was shaken. Had Americans and President Thieu known their Vietnamese history better, they would have remembered that during Tet in 1789 the Vietnamese defeated a Chinese occupation army distracted by the festival.
- One famous photo of a Saigon general shooting a bound captive in the head damaged Americans' faith in their side as the 'good guys' (see page 140). (Only later was it discovered that the captive was a VC death-squad member who had just shot a relation of the general.)

- An anti-war newsman repeated an unforgettable and telling soldier's phrase about one South Vietnamese village: 'We had to destroy the town to save it'. That phrase made many Americans question what was being done in Vietnam.
- Tet so shook Westmoreland that one American official considered him almost broken.
- The administration had been claiming that America was winning the war but the TV pictures suggested US failure: even the American embassy was unsafe.
- Tet increased the credibility gap between the Johnson administration's explanations of events in Vietnam and the public's understanding of those events.
- Some historians claim that US reporters presented a uniformly hostile and negative picture of the Tet offensive, so that Americans felt it was a great defeat. These historians say that it was a psychological rather than a military defeat.
- Johnson performed badly at the press conferences following Tet:

  > It may be that General Westmoreland makes some serious mistakes or that I make some. We don't know. We are just acting in the light of information we have ... There will be moments of encouragement and discouragement.

  Johnson is often criticised for dishonesty but it has to be said that on this occasion, when he was honest, he was so uninspiring as to seem guilty of lack of leadership. After Tet his approval ratings plummeted.
- Tet encouraged anti-war presidential candidates to oppose Johnson in the forthcoming presidential election.
- Tet forced Johnson to withdraw from the 1968 presidential race. He said that he would concentrate upon the pursuit of peace.
- Tet forced the Johnson administration into a re-evaluation of US policy.
- After Tet, Johnson rejected demands that 200,000 more US troops be sent to Vietnam.

iv) The battle of Khe Sanh

Key date
Battle of Khe Sanh: January 1968

Key term
Khe Sanh
Crucial battle in 1968 between PAVN and American forces.

At the same time as Tet, the battle of **Khe Sanh** was being fought. Successfully designed to distract the Americans from the Tet Offensive, Khe Sanh was the biggest and bloodiest battle of the war: 10,000 Communists and 500 Americans died. Westmoreland wrongly thought that Khe Sanh was the great prize. This was the kind of fight he wanted, against uniformed and easily identifiable PAVN troops. Westmoreland wanted to use tactical nuclear weapons but Washington said no, 'kicked him upstairs' to a desk job and replaced him.

Johnson had a model of the Khe Sanh battlefield in the White House, and spent many sleepless nights inspecting it. Clifford feared that the president and indeed the whole government of the United States was on the verge of coming apart. The JCS

One of the most famous and most misinterpreted photos of the war. South Vietnam's police chief executed a VC in Saigon during the Tet Offensive in 1968.

repeatedly requested more troops. Clifford questioned them about their plan for victory and concluded that they did not have one.

By March Clifford was totally against the war and even Rusk (see page 85) was wavering. Back in September 1967 the CIA director had said America could get out of Vietnam without suffering any great loss of international standing. The treasury said the nation could not afford to send more troops and even hawkish senators said 'no more men'. Tet had shaken the confidence of the American government and people. Pictures of destruction and death had turned many Americans against the war.

v) Key debates

Historians disagree about some aspects of Tet.

Was Tet an American military defeat?

Although most historians agree that the Tet Offensive marked the start of an American de-escalation process that eventually got the United States out of Vietnam, they disagree over whether or not it was a US defeat.

Some historians (for example, Davidson, 1988) argue that Tet was a military victory for the US, upon which feeble politicians failed to capitalise. On the other hand, Buzzanco (1996) pointed out that the US army chief of staff felt that the offensive showed the limits of US military power. Others (for example, Duiker, 1996) disagree, pointing out that Tet was a costly Communist miscalculation, as no popular rising occurred in South Vietnam, but lots of Communist men and material were lost.

Did the Tet Offensive change American opinion on the war?

Kolko (1985) stressed that Tet was exactly what Hanoi wanted – a psychological victory against the Americans.

Several journalists, for example, Braestrup (1997), claimed that:

> for the first time in modern history, the outcome of the war was determined, not on the battlefield but on the printed page and, above all, on the TV screen.

On the other hand, scholars such as Pach (1998) have found no evidence that TV reporting had a negative impact on public opinion and therefore consider that it did not affect the outcome of the war. However, Pach admitted that coverage of Tet exposed the credibility gap and exacerbated doubts about American policy that had begun to develop within the Johnson administration since the autumn and the resignation of McNamara.

Schmitz (2005) rejected claims of media bias in American reporting, and argued that it was not the impact of Tet on the public that was significant, but rather the impact of Tet on senior officials in the Johnson administration. Those officials brought about a dramatic change in Johnson's policies. Schmitz recorded that polls showed steadily declining popular support for the war throughout 1967 until the Johnson administration's public relations campaign of autumn 1967 stabilised the percentages. Then, at the time of Tet, after an initial patriotic rise in support for Johnson and his war policies, the decline in support continued once more.

Some key books in the debate

P. Braestrup, *Big Story* (Boulder, 1967).
R. Buzzanco, *Masters of War* (Cambridge, 1996).
P.B. Davidson, *Vietnam at War* (California, 1988).
W.J. Duiker, *Sacred War* (Stanford, 1994).
G. Kolko, *Anatomy of a War* (New York, 1986).
C. Pach, in C. Fink, editor, *1968: The World Transformed* (Cambridge, 1998).

---

d) Public opinion

Johnson and Congress naturally paid great attention to public opinion. It is generally agreed that opposition to the war from the public and in the press was probably the main reason why Johnson finally decided upon retreat. However, the objectors were probably a minority, and supporters of the war also put pressure on Johnson. The latter wanted him to continue the fighting.

Key question
Was the majority anti-war?

i) The conservative right-wing

Cold Warriors criticised Johnson for insufficient escalation. These hawks felt that American boys were being forced to fight the Communists with one hand tied behind their backs. They were angry that America never used more than half of its combat-ready divisions and tactical air power in Vietnam. 'Win or get out' was a popular bumper sticker. Many believed that American boys, who fought out there on the orders of an elected president and funded by an elected Congress, deserved more support from the folks back home. Those who wonder why Johnson continued to escalate for so long often forget this right-wing pressure upon him. On the other hand, not all conservatives approved of the war. Many considered developed areas such as Europe and Japan more important to America. One retired general argued that Asians did not want American ideas 'crammed down their throats'.

ii) Pacifist feeling

Many Americans hated the thought of themselves or their loved ones having to fight in Vietnam. Some were repelled by the sufferings of Vietnamese non-combatants. Some Americans felt that their international image was suffering. One said that:

> By any objective standard, the United States has become the most aggressive power in the world, the greatest threat to peace, to **national self-determination**, and to international co-operation.

iii) College students

College students were in the forefront of protest, especially after February 1968 when the **draft** boards stopped automatic exemption for students. As in all wars many draft dodgers were caught and convicted (952 in 1967). Many draft dodgers (some claim 50,000) slipped into Canada. College students used ingenious methods to avoid the draft: braces on your teeth meant one year's deferment if your teeth were really crooked, and six months if they seemed straight! Young men psyched themselves up to have apparent blood pressure problems when tested, or feigned mental instability. Claiming to have considered suicide usually did the trick. One interesting by-product of the war before February 1968 was a fall in academic standards as colleges swelled with students motivated only by a desire to avoid the war and distracted by protests against it! Some professors were reluctant to fail students as failed students might be drafted.

Key terms

National self-determination
The right of a people to choose their own form of government in their own country.

Draft
US equivalent of British conscription; when military service is compulsory.

iv) Debates about the protests

There are many debates about anti-war protesters on the streets and in the press. To what extent did they affect government policy in Washington and Hanoi? Were protesters just a vocal minority? In order to try to answer these questions we need to look at the home front, at the chronological history of public opinion through protests, polls and TV.

Key question
To what extent did anti-war protests affect Johnson's Vietnam policy?

e) The collapse of the home front

The anti-war protesters contended that there was no threat to US national interest in Vietnam, and that US policy there, whether by bombing or by support of the corrupt regime in Saigon, went against American values.

i) 1964

The protests began in 1964 when 1000 students from prestigious Yale University staged a protest march in New York and 5000 professors wrote in support. However, the Gulf of Tonkin resolution and the presidential election (see pages 88–90) suggest that at this stage Johnson had near unanimous support for his Vietnam policy from the public and most congressmen.

Key dates
First American combat troops landed in South Vietnam: March 1965
'Poisonous reporting' from Vietnam: August 1965

Key terms
Teach-in
Anti-war lectures and debates in American colleges.

Pentagon
Headquarters of the US Department of Defence.

ii) 1965

During 1965 many universities held a '**teach-in**', with anti-war lectures and debates; 20,000 participated in Berkeley, a leading Californian university. However, thousands of students signed pro-Johnson petitions, including one-quarter of Yale undergraduates. Thousands of other citizens participated in protests. In April 1965, 25,000 protesters marched on Washington. A young Quaker father of three, holding his baby daughter in his arms, set himself on fire outside McNamara's **Pentagon** window. There was frequent disorder, for example 8000 marchers in Oakland (many from Berkeley) clashed with the police and vandalised cars and buildings. Johnson insisted that the protests were financed by Communist governments, and that protesters encouraged the enemy.

During 1965, congressional unanimity developed cracks. One congressman reported 'widened unrest' among colleagues in January 1965. With the introduction of tens of thousands of additional American ground troops to Vietnam, the increasing number of casualties meant that in 1965 the press and TV networks went to Vietnam in full force. The war became America's first fully televised war. People talked of 'the living-room war' as Americans watched it on every evening news. In August 1965 Johnson was informed that increasing numbers of American reporters in Saigon were 'thoroughly sour and poisonous in their reporting'. However, as yet the opposition had little practical impact on American involvement, and fewer than 25 per cent of Americans believed that the US had erred in sending troops to Vietnam.

iii) 1966

During 1966 public support for the war dropped dramatically. Chairman of the **Senate Foreign Relations Committee** William Fulbright had steered the Gulf of Tonkin resolution through the Senate. He now decided that Johnson and McNamara had lied about the second North Vietnamese attack. During Fulbright's February 1966 Foreign Relations Committee hearings on the war, senators spoke against the bombing, and many said that Vietnam was not vital to America and withdrawal would do no great harm.

The Democratic Party suffered a sharp defeat in the **Congressional mid-term elections** of November 1966 and congressmen blamed Vietnam. They urged Johnson to end the war before it damaged the Great Society and the party. Congress nevertheless continued to fund the war, unwilling to face accusations of betraying the 400,000 American boys in the field.

There were relatively few marches and only one state governor refused to declare his support for government policy. However, Johnson felt bound to limit his public appearances to avoid chants of 'Hey, hey, LBJ, how many boys have you killed today?' He was infuriated by noisy demonstrators: 'How can I hit them in the nuts? Tell me how I can hit them in the nuts.'

Westmoreland complained that 'The enemy leaders were made to appear to be the good guys' by the media. Government propaganda was pedestrian and ineffective and (unlike the Second World War) Hollywood gave minimal assistance. Two ageing national institutions did their best. Veteran comedian Bob Hope sought to recapture the camaraderie of the Second World War, giving shows to servicemen in Vietnam. John Wayne made a poor film, *The Green Berets*. The film's idealisation of Americans in Vietnam aroused much hostile criticism but it drew large audiences. This might have reflected the enduring box-office magnetism of its star, the appeal of war films, the undiscriminating movie-going habits of the masses, support for the war from the 'silent majority', or a combination of all these factors.

iv) 1967

As yet, the criticism had not caused Johnson to alter his policies, but during 1967 opposition to the war grew. Tens of thousands protested in the great cities of America. Congressmen put ever more pressure on Johnson. The churches and black civil rights leader Martin Luther King led the opposition. Black people resented the disproportionate number of black casualties in Vietnam and felt kinship with the poor, non-white Vietnamese. When King saw a picture of Vietnamese children showing burn wounds from American napalm bombs in January 1967 he became publicly critical. He said that the poverty programme had raised hope for the inhabitants of the inner-city ghettos, but now the funds were being diverted to the war. Young black males, 'crippled by their own society', were being sent to:

> guarantee liberties in Southeast Asia which they had not found in Southwest Georgia and east Harlem … We have been repeatedly

Key dates

Senate Foreign Relations Committee hearings on war dominated by anti-war feeling: February 1966

Increased domestic opposition to US involvement in Vietnam: 1966

Democrats did badly in the congressional mid-term elections: November 1966

Nearly 400,000 American soldiers in South Vietnam: December 1966

Martin Luther King publicly criticised US involvement in the war: January 1967

Key terms

Senate Foreign Relations Committee
Highly influential body of recognised specialists in foreign policy in US Senate.

Congressional mid-term elections
The presidential term of office is four years; in the middle of that term, some congressional seats are contested.

> faced with the cruel irony of watching Negro and white boys on TV screens as they kill and die together for a nation that has been unable to seat them together in the same schools. I could never again raise my voice against the violence of the oppressed in the ghettos without having first spoken clearly to the greatest purveyor of violence in the world today – my own government.

Key date

Unpopular tax rises to help to finance the war: August 1967

Key terms

National Guard
US Armed Forces reservists, called up by the president in times of crisis.

Wise Men
A group of experienced politicians, generals and others who had previously held high office, frequently consulted by Johnson over the Vietnam War.

Tax rises turned more Americans against the war in August 1967. In October 1967 draft cards were publicly burned throughout the country. Berkeley radicals tried to close down the draft headquarters in Oakland. The police attacked 2500 demonstrators with clubs and the demonstrators retaliated with cans, bottles and smoke bombs. The demonstrators put thousands of ball bearings on the street to stop police on horseback. Between 4000 and 10,000 demonstrators brought the streets around the draft headquarters to a standstill. They escaped from 2000 police officers, then vandalised cars, parking meters, news-stands and trees. Many were high on drugs. The divisions between protesters were well illustrated in a Washington rally. Johnson had 2000 policemen, 17,000 **National Guard** troops and 6000 regular army men to meet 70,000 protesters. Most of the protesters just listened to speeches but some extremists were involved in violence outside the Pentagon. McNamara watched from his office window and found it 'terrifying. Christ, yes, I was scared'. The government's bill for the operations was just over $1 million. There were 625 arrests.

Abe Fortas (see page 85) believed that McNamara was one who had been over-influenced by the protesters. In some ways Fortas had a good point. During August 1967 hawkish senators had conducted hearings aimed at pressurising Johnson into lifting all restrictions on bombing in Vietnam. The respected and experienced group of elder statesmen nicknamed the '**Wise Men**' and including Acheson (see page 17) and Rusk, all assured Johnson that they supported his Vietnam policy. Such support for the war and escalation is too often forgotten because it is overshadowed by the drama of the protests. On the other hand, a growing number of Johnson's friends and supporters were changing their views on the war because of the loss of someone close to them, or because their children opposed the war. Those in the White House were increasingly unsettled. McNamara left and Rusk's son disagreed so intensely with his father over Vietnam that his psychiatrist told him, 'You had your father's nervous breakdown [for him].' In 1966 Rusk had visited an army hospital in Saigon where a nurse:

> stared long and hard at me with a look of undisguised hatred … from the look on her face she clearly held me responsible for what had happened to those men. I never forgot the look on that nurse's face.

v) Was 1967 a turning point?

Pinpointing turning points in support for the war is difficult, but it seems that 1967 was crucial. Some influential newspapers and TV stations shifted from support to opposition. Draft calls, deaths in Vietnam and taxes all increased, arousing more discontent, but it is difficult to know exactly how many opposed Johnson's policies. Polls can be misleading. In October 1967, 46 per cent of Americans felt that the Vietnam commitment was a mistake, yet a massive majority wanted to stay there and get tougher – so, one could say that this poll indicated both widespread support and widespread opposition to the war. 'I want to get out but I don't want to give up', said one housewife to a pollster. Even the White House was surprised by a poll which showed considerable support for the war in early 1968:

- 49 per cent to 29 per cent favoured invading North Vietnam.
- 42 per cent to 33 per cent favoured mining Haiphong (the main port in North Vietnam) even if Soviet ships were sunk as a result.
- 25 per cent did not oppose bombing China or using atomic weapons.

There were nearly half a million Americans in Vietnam and nearly 17,000 had died there, but Johnson's policies still had considerable support. As Westmoreland said, in the successful November public relations offensive by the Johnson administration, 'We are winning a war of attrition now'.

vi) 1968 – was Tet a turning point?

Perhaps the media coverage of the Tet Offensive in early 1968 was the crucial turning point. Walter Cronkite, the most respected TV journalist, had been strongly supportive of the war until a February 1968 visit to Vietnam. He concluded that the war could not be won. Some saw his defection as a great turning point: in the next few weeks Johnson's approval rating fell from 48 to 36 per cent. The Communists might have been defeated militarily, but Tet suggested that Johnson was losing the battle for the hearts and minds of an important percentage of his people. Some were against the war altogether, others wanted him to wage it differently. A minority were protesting vociferously.

It is difficult to trace the interrelationship between the protests and rising dissatisfaction in Congress and in the White House itself, but there is no doubt that politicians were sensitive to the wishes of the voters, and the protesters probably played a part disproportionate to their numbers in bringing the war towards an end. By the spring of 1968, Johnson had lost confidence if not in the rectitude of his policies then at least in his capacity to maintain continued support for them. The protesters and the media had suggested that his war and his way of conducting it were wrong and this played an important part in loss of confidence amongst White House officials and the troops in Vietnam.

The massive anti-war protest outside the Pentagon, October 1967. The 'war criminal' is President Johnson.

vii) Key debate

Historians disagree over the extensive press responsibility for the US inability to win in Vietnam.

Johnson criticised the American press for failing to support the war effort. Journalist Peter Braestrup (1997) argued that media coverage of Tet helped to convince Americans that what was actually a victory was instead a US defeat. In contrast, Hammond's 1998 study of the press found most reporters supportive of the war until the public and government members started questioning it. Hammond said that the press reflected rather than shaped public opinion.

Studies of the anti-war movement (for example, Wells, 1994) often suggest that the protests did not end the war but did restrain Johnson and his successor. Small (1988) found presidents more influenced by protests than they cared to admit. On the other hand, Garfinkle (1995) contended that the radicalism of some protesters alienated the majority of Americans, discredited the anti-war movement, and may even have helped to prolong the war.

Some key books in the debate

P. Braestrup, *Big Story* (Boulder, 1997).

A. Garfinkle, *Tell-tale Hearts* (New York, 1995).

W. Hammond, *Reporting Vietnam* (Kansas, 1998).

M. Small, *Johnson, Nixon and the Doves* (Rutgers, 1988).

---

f) Financial and economic problems

The war cost a great deal of money and distorted the economy. Johnson did not want to admit how much he was spending lest conservatives in Congress cut off payments for his Great Society programmes, so he was slow to ask for the necessary wartime tax rises. In 1965 the government deficit had been $1.6 billion. By 1968 it was $25.3 billion. Such deficits caused inflation and endangered America's economic well-being. The Treasury warned him that this should not go on and taxpayers grew resentful, increasing the pressure on him to change direction in Vietnam.

Key question
How did the cost of the war impact on Johnson?

g) Johnson's loss of confidence

i) Johnson's agony

Key question
Why did Johnson finally decide to halt escalation?

It is not surprising that Johnson was losing confidence by the spring of 1968. He frequently grabbed visitors to the White House, thrust his face into theirs and cried out, 'What would you do [about Vietnam]?' Johnson described how 'I lay awake picturing my boys flying around North Vietnam' bombing the targets he had picked for them. 'Suppose one of my boys misses his mark … [and] one of his bombs falls on one of those Russian ships in the harbour?' Johnson imagined he saw an American plane shot down: 'I saw it hit the ground, and as soon as it burst into flames, I couldn't stand it any more. I knew that one of my boys must have been killed.' He received conflicting advice, as he told his brother Sam in February:

> That's just the trouble … it's always my move. And, damn it, I sometimes can't tell whether I'm making the right move or not. Now take this Vietnam mess. How in the hell can anyone know for sure what's right and what's wrong, Sam? I got some of the finest brains in this country – people like Dean Rusk … and Dean Acheson – making some strong convincing arguments for us to stay in there and not pull out. Then I've got some people like George Ball and Fulbright – also intelligent men whose motives I can't rightly distrust – who keep telling me we've got to de-escalate or run the risk of a total war. And, Sam, I've got to listen to both sides … I've just got to choose between my opposing experts … But I sure as hell wish I could really know what's right.

Johnson's health was suffering. In her diary Lady Bird described 10 March as a 'day of deep gloom'. 14 March was 'one of those terrific, pummelling White House days that can stretch and grind and use you'. Her husband was 'bone weary', 'dead tired' and unable to sleep. 'Those sties are coming back on Lyndon's eyes. First one and then the other, red and swollen and painful.' On 31 March, 'his face was sagging and there was such pain in his eyes as I had not seen since his mother died'.

Key date

'Wise Men' advised Johnson against further escalation; Johnson sought peace talks not re-election: March 1968

ii) The 'Wise Men' change their minds

On 25 March 1968 the 'Wise Men' met. Back in November 1967, after optimistic briefings from the JCS and CIA, the 'Wise Men' had declared their support for the continuation of US efforts in Vietnam. Now, however, the majority of them were in the process of changing their minds, and most advocated some kind of retreat in Vietnam. One of them said that the US could not 'succeed in the time we have left' in Vietnam, because that time was 'limited by reactions in this country'.

Johnson could not believe that 'these establishment bastards have bailed out'. Congress was pressing hard for retreat, and the polls were discouraging: 78 per cent of Americans believed that America was not making any progress in the war, 74 per cent that Johnson was not handling it well. The war-induced **balance of payments deficit** had dramatically weakened the dollar on the international money market, causing a gold crisis which was the final straw for many Americans. From now on Johnson knew there would have to be some sort of a reversal in Vietnam.

Key term

Balance of payments deficit
When the value of a country's imports exceeds that of its exports.

iii) 'I've given up the presidency'

Johnson agonised over how to announce any change in US policy, unwilling to admit that his country had been in error and unwilling to betray those Americans who were fighting and dying in Vietnam. On 31 March 1968 he said, 'I am taking the first step to de-escalate the conflict'. He offered to stop bombing North Vietnam if Hanoi would agree to talks. He said that as Americans were so divided, he would keep out of partisan politics and would not be running for re-election. Some think Johnson's decision not to run was a reaction to the unpopularity of his Vietnam policies, but both he and Lady Bird were genuinely anxious about his poor health. He claimed that:

> I've given up the presidency, given up politics, to search for peace. No one worries more about this war than I do. It's broken my heart – in a way, broken my back. But I think I can get these people at the conference table.

Summary diagram: Why and how Johnson was forced to retreat

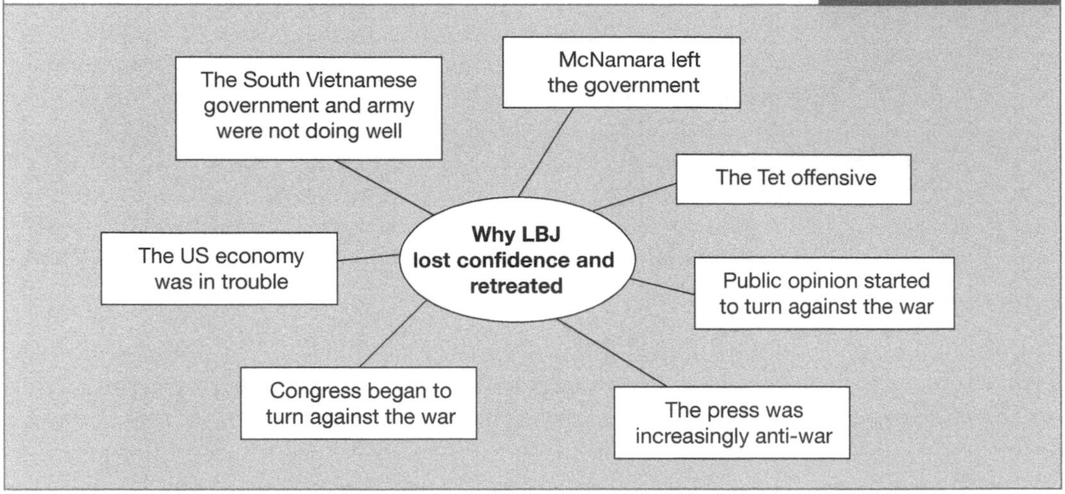

3 | Johnson's Last Months

Key question
Why could Johnson not end the war?

a) Peace talks

i) Lack of progress

Peace talks had been a recurring theme throughout Johnson's presidency. When he had introduced and continued 'Rolling Thunder' (see page 93) one of his great aims had been to 'persuade' Hanoi it could not win and therefore should negotiate. However, Ho rejected negotiations as long as the bombing continued, while Johnson said the bombing would only stop when Hanoi stopped waging war in the South. To show willing, Johnson ordered several bombing pauses, but according to David Halberstam (see page 67), he hated them. 'Oh yes, a bombing halt', he would say, 'I'll tell you what happens when there's a bombing halt: I halt and then Ho Chi Minh shoves trucks up my ass'. There were attempts at negotiation, usually by foreign intermediaries such as Poland in 1966 (this failed when Johnson ordered that Hanoi be bombed more heavily than usual) and Britain in 1967. Britain concluded that Washington was never serious about these peace initiatives. Senator Fulbright agreed:

> All you guys are committed to a military settlement. You don't want to negotiate; you're not going to negotiate. You are bombing that little pissant country up there, and you think you can blow them up. It's a bunch of crap about wanting to negotiate.

ii) A little progress

With Johnson's loss of confidence by spring 1968, the prospects improved. Hanoi was exhausted after Tet, anxious to divide Americans, and keen to negotiate. Talks began in Paris in May 1968. America demanded a North Vietnamese withdrawal from South Vietnam and rejected Communist participation in the

Saigon government, while North Vietnam demanded American withdrawal from South Vietnam and insisted on Communist participation in the Saigon government. These mutually exclusive demands explain why the talks continued intermittently for five years. Johnson recognised the need for some sort of retreat but was not the man to do it: he just could not bring himself to accept Hanoi's terms.

> If I left that war and let the Communists take over South Vietnam, then I would be seen as a coward and my nation would be seen as an appeaser, and we would both find it impossible to accomplish anything for anybody anywhere in the entire globe … Nothing was worse than that.

b) The disintegration of Johnson's presidency

i) Deaths in Vietnam

Events in the final few months of Johnson's presidency confirmed the need for a dramatic change in America's Vietnam policy. The fighting had reached maximum intensity in the first half of 1968. In two weeks in May alone, 1800 Americans were killed and 18,000 seriously wounded. US forces, now numbering over half a million, had began to suffer the severe morale problems that left the forces near to collapse.

Key date

Riots during Democratic convention in Chicago: August 1968

Key terms

Party convention
When delegates from all states meet to decide on their party's candidate for the presidency.

Hippies
Young Americans with long hair, casual clothing and anti-establishment attitude in the 1960s.

ii) Chicago 1968

The Democratic **Party convention** was held in Chicago in August 1968. Thousands of anti-war protesters turned out. Leading **hippies** calling themselves the Yippies (Youth International Party) nominated a live pig called Pigasus for president. A youth lowered the American flag and was beaten and arrested by police. With cries of 'Pigs!' the crowd threw stones and cans at the tense and combative police, who hit back with batons and tear gas, then began indiscriminate attacks on people. There were 668 arrests and 192 police injuries. Continuation of the war seemed to be leading to the disintegration of American society.

iii) Bombing North Vietnam

On 31 October 1968 Johnson ordered the cessation of the bombing of North Vietnam, partly, if not predominantly, to help ensure that his Vice-President, Hubert Humphrey, won the 1968 presidential election. However, the negotiations with Hanoi stalled. Despite many suggestions for the number and shape of tables, the negotiators could not even agree on where to sit: the South Vietnamese refused to sit at the same table as the North Vietnamese. The battle of the tables was the last battle of Johnson's administration.

iv) The 1968 presidential election

Humphrey lost the election, partly because of his inability to dissociate himself sufficiently from Johnson's Vietnam policy. However, like polls, elections are notorious for not telling the whole story. When the Democratic peace candidate Senator

Eugene McCarthy did so well against Johnson in the New Hampshire **primary**, it emerged that hawks greatly outnumbered **doves** amongst McCarthy 'supporters', which shows the difficulty of interpreting votes. McCarthy's 'victory' was seen as a vote for peace, when it could more accurately be seen as a vote to force Johnson to escalate.

The Republican candidate Richard Nixon pledged to bring an honourable end to the war in Vietnam, but a vote for him was not necessarily a vote against the war. Some voted according to habit or on domestic issues. The third candidate, the renegade Democrat George Wallace, was a pro-war candidate and he picked up many votes. It is therefore difficult to ascertain the role and unpopularity of the Vietnam War in the result. All we can conclude is that in 1968 the voters remained divided over Vietnam. Johnson's presidency and the war effort had disintegrated primarily because of these American divisions.

Key terms

Primary
When voters in an American state vote for one of several candidates to be their political party's presidential candidate.

Doves
Those who favoured a less aggressive foreign policy, including an early peace in the Vietnam War.

Summary diagram: Johnson's last months

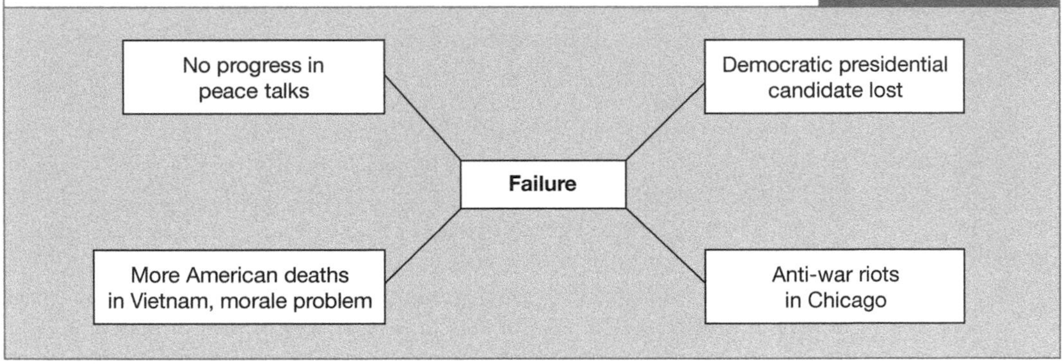

4 | Conclusions about Johnson and the War

a) Why had Johnson failed to win the war?

Perhaps the main reason why Johnson failed to win the war was that the establishment of a viable South Vietnamese state was beyond the powers of Johnson's America. Johnson considered real escalation an impossibility: it might bring the Soviets and Chinese in, and attacking 'little' North Vietnam would damage America's international image. So America just continued to fight a limited and ineffective war to support a series of unpopular Saigon regimes. The nature of the warfare and criticism back home led to the apparent collapse of the home front and the American forces in Vietnam.

b) Had Johnson's Vietnam policy been a total failure?

It could be argued that Johnson's Vietnam policy was not a total failure. He had restrained American hawks, whose policies might have led to full-scale war with China or the USSR. Perhaps Communist insurgents in other parts of Southeast Asia did badly in the 1960s because American actions in Vietnam encouraged anti-Communists and kept China busy.

c) Why did Johnson not get out?

Johnson did not get out because Hanoi was not going to give up, so neutralisation or peace would mean a coalition government containing Communists, which was unacceptable to Johnson and many other Americans. Johnson thought getting out of Vietnam on those terms would damage the credibility of himself, his party and his country, and be a betrayal of the Americans who had fought and died there.

d) What had the war done to America?

The war damaged America's armed forces, image, morale, national unity and economy. It also damaged the presidency and American society.

e) How did Johnson and the Vietnam War damage the presidency?

During 1965 the media became increasingly hostile, partly because of the Vietnam policies, partly because of Johnson and McNamara's lack of straightforwardness in describing them. When the marines landed in Danang in March 1965, the State Department readily admitted it, to Johnson's fury. He said there had been 'no change', which was untrue. The 'credibility gap' was the difference between what Johnson said and what actually was. One wit said that Johnson lost the most important battle of the Vietnam War, the 'Battle of Credibility Gap'! It had an adverse impact on the presidency; respect for the office decreased because of the increasingly unpopular and apparently dishonest person who held it.

f) How did the war damage American society?

'Vietnam took it all away', said Kennedy's brother-in-law, Sargent Shriver, 'every god-damned dollar. That's what killed the war on poverty.' Between 1965 and 1973 $15.5 billion was spent on the Great Society, compared to $120 billion on the war in Vietnam. During Johnson's presidency 222,351 US military were killed or wounded in Vietnam. Returning American veterans had physical and/or mental disabilities that for the most part would remain with them for the rest of their lives. Many veterans returned with drug problems and with sharpened class and racial antagonisms (see page 194). Ethnic minorities and poor whites knew that middle-class white males were under-represented in Vietnam, except in the officer class, which they dominated. The middle class had frequently used their money and intelligence to avoid combat whether by continuing education or convincing the draft board of their uselessness. The unpopularity of the war divided friends and families. Many of these social wounds and divisions remain. A Johnson aide said that the war was like a fungus or a contagion: it infected everything it touched and seemed to touch everything. He was right.

As Johnson left the presidency he admitted he had made mistakes. He said history would judge him after current passions had subsided. The passions have still not subsided, for the impact of the war remains with Americans. Johnson is still greatly blamed and frequently reviled.

Study Guide: AS Questions

In the style of AQA

Source A

From a speech by President Johnson in 1965 explaining why Americans must fight in Vietnam.

Why must this nation hazard its ease, its interest, and its power for the sake of a people so far away? We fight because we must fight if we are to live in a world where every country can shape its own destiny, and only in such a world will our own freedom be secure. This kind of world will never be built by bombs or bullets. Yet the infirmities of man are such that force must often precede reason and the waste of war, the works of peace.

Source B

Adapted from G.B. Tindall, America, *published in 1988.*

In May 1967 even Secretary of Defence McNamara was not convinced about Johnson's policies in Vietnam. 'The picture of the world's greatest superpower killing or injuring 1000 non-combatants a week, while trying to pound a tiny backward nation into submission on an issue whose merits are hotly disputed, is not a pretty one.' Then, a few months later Walter Cronkite, the most important of American television journalists, confided to his viewers that he no longer believed the Vietnam War was winnable. 'If I've lost Walter', Johnson was reported to say, 'then it's over. I've lost Mr Average Citizen.' Polls showed that Johnson's popularity declined to 35 per cent. Johnson was increasingly isolated over his failing policies. Clark Clifford, the new Secretary of Defence, reported to Johnson that a task force of prominent soldiers and citizens saw no prospects for military victory.

Source C

From Vivienne Sanders, The USA and Vietnam, *published in 2007.*

Perhaps the main reason why Johnson failed to win the war was that the establishment of a viable South Vietnamese state was beyond the powers of Johnson's America. Johnson considered real escalation an impossibility: it might bring the Soviets and Chinese in, and attaching 'little' North Vietnam would damage America's international image. So America just continued to fight a limited and ineffective war to support a series of unpopular Saigon regimes.

(a) **Use Sources A and B.**
Explain how far the views in Source B differ from those in Source A in relation to the US involvement in Vietnam.
(12 marks)

(b) **Use Sources A, B and C and your own knowledge.**
'President Johnson failed in Vietnam because he lacked support from "Mr Average Citizen".' Explain why you agree or disagree with this view. (24 marks)

Exam tips

(a) You should identify clearly what the views of each source are, providing direct comparisons where possible. Try to make a broad general statement, such as, according to Source B the fighting is unjustifiable – whereas in Source A it is justified on the grounds of helping transform the world to preserve freedom. Then define aspects of disagreement more closely, with reference to the text:

- Source B is hostile to US involvement: the image of killing non-combatants and pounding a tiny nation into submission 'is not a pretty one'.
- Source A is in favour of US involvement and believes that 'force must often precede reason' and war must precede peace.

Finally you should consider the extent of disagreement by looking at any similarities:

- both sources are hostile to war as such
- both appreciate that the Vietnam War involves 'hazarding' American interests.

You will need to decide on the extent of disagreement the sources show and provide an overall conclusion.

(b) In answering this question you need to construct a balanced argument that uses both evidence from the given sources and your own knowledge. Source A shows Johnson working hard to gain popular support, which suggests that his policies were not always popular. Source B indicates that by 1967, Johnson was losing support amongst his advisers, the press and 'Mr Average Citizen', but it could be argued that this loss of support was a slow process, and that the war was once a relatively popular war, for example, in the months following the death of Kennedy. Source C provides additional information that suggests other reasons for the failure of the war: the impossibility of establishing a viable South Vietnamese state and the fear of antagonising China and the USSR by attacking the North. According to this source the war was bound to be limited and unpopular because of the Saigon regimes. Another argument that disagrees with the quotation is the fact that support for Johnson actually increased in the early days of the Tet Offensive.

While you should make a clearly supported case for agreement or disagreement, you do need to balance such points for and against to provide a full and convincing answer.

In the style of Edexcel

1. How accurate is it to say that the US failure in Vietnam resulted primarily from losing the hearts and minds of the American people? (30 marks)
2. How important was the Tet Offensive of 1968 in changing US policy in Vietnam? (30 marks)

Source: Edexcel specimen paper 2007

Exam tips

The cross-references are intended to take you straight to the material that will help you to answer the questions.

These two questions will need very different plans, although they are dealing with much the same period.

Question 1 is asking you why the US failed. Question 2 is asking you to look at the way the US government decided to approach the conflict – its aims and plans – and to assess the significance of the Tet Offensive in bringing about a change.

1. Plan to devote about one-third of your answer to the role of public opinion in the USA, showing that the 'hearts and minds' of the American people had turned against the conflict (pages 143–7). You could cover: growing anti-war protests; resentment of war costs; the intensification of hostile press coverage after the Tet Offensive and the sharp decline in public support for the war. Resist the temptation simply to describe the growth of anti-war feelings. In order to show its significance, it will be important to link it directly to its impact on government policy: Johnson's loss of confidence (page 146).

   Next, plan to deal with other factors that played a part; factors which had a bearing on how the conflict was going in Vietnam itself:

   - The Washington/Saigon failure to win the hearts and minds of the South Vietnamese people (pages 64–5, 109–15 and 118–21).
   - Communist determination, heroism, ingenuity and popularity (pages 44–5, 111 and 115–18).
   - The performance of the ARVN and the disunited Americans, who tried to fight a comfortable war in awful conditions and with the wrong methods (pages 64–5, 113–15 and 120–1).

- The loss of confidence by the Johnson administration, especially after Tet (pages 136–9 and 148–9).
- Increased public hostility and protest in the United States (pages 143–7).
- American financial and economic problems (page 148).

You could then bring both groups of factors together, showing how they interacted by dealing with the impact of the failure of the Tet Offensive (pages 138–41). You might choose to argue that ultimately the lack of military success in Vietnam was significant in increasing the opposition in the USA and hence was directly and indirectly responsible for the US failure in Vietnam.

2. The key words to note when planning your answer to this question are: 'Tet Offensive' and 'changing US policy'. You need to be clear about the ways in which policy changed after Tet, and you also need to be able to make an assessment of how influential the Tet Offensive was in bringing about those changes.

You could plan to deal briefly with the change in policy from increasing involvement in 1966–7 prior to Tet, to de-escalation afterwards and Johnson's decision in 1968 to hold negotiations and halt bombing. It will be important not to overemphasise the change here, since attempted negotiations and temporary halts were not altogether new (pages 150–1), but you could use Johnson's attitude to these in 1968, combined with the election of a president in 1968 committed to American troop withdrawal (page 152) to show a policy change which was permanent.

In order to show that the Tet Offensive was significant in bringing about this change, you will need to show that Tet had an influence on public opinion, military thinking and government opinion (pages 138–9). Remember to focus your coverage on the impact of Tet on US policy. For example, you should resist the temptation to describe the impact of Tet on the media and public opinion. You need to make this directly relevant by showing that the pressure of media and public opinion influenced government policy (pages 146 and 149).

In order to assess the significance of the Tet Offensive you will also need to show that these trends were in place prior to Tet:

- The impact of protests and hostile media coverage prior to Tet (pages 143–4).
- Questioning of US policy by senior military and political figures prior to Tet (pages 136 and 144).

In coming to your overall assessment you can choose to see Tet as an accelerator of pre-existing trends or an event responsible for a decisive change in policy. If you feel that public attitudes were crucial in influencing government policy (page 142), the link between Tet and this might be a point to highlight in a conclusion which dealt with the interaction of a number of factors.

In the style of OCR

(a) Compare Sources A and C as evidence for military morale during the Vietnam War. (30 marks)

(b) Using your own knowledge, assess how far the sources support the interpretation that the *main* reason America failed to win the Vietnam War was the strength of their opponents. (70 marks)

Source A

From a letter by Le Duan, Thu Vao Nam, November 1965. The Hanoi Politburo writes to the Communist Party in the South, outlining the party's commitment to a protracted war strategy.

Dear brothers,
Militarily, destroying the puppet government's troops is easier than American troops who have not fought us much, so are optimistic, proud of their weapons and keep their nationalist pride. The puppet troops, after many defeats, have low morale and little enthusiasm to fight. Therefore, we must strengthen our resolve to wipe out the puppet troops as fast as possible. However, our propaganda must emphasise the slogan 'Find Americans to kill'. We must thoroughly research suitable methods to destroy American troops in particular battlegrounds. Our guerrilla forces encircle the American troops' bases. Brothers and sisters must be encouraged and praised, so as to heighten their resolve to kill American troops.

Source B

From a lecture by Robert F. Kennedy, 18 March 1968. Senator Kennedy expresses his opinion on the reasons why America was losing the Vietnam War in a lecture at Kansas State University.

Our control over the rural population has evaporated. The Saigon government is now less of an ally. Our victories come at the cost of destroying Vietnam. Its people are disintegrating under the blows of war. The war is weakening our position in Asia and the world, and eroding international co-operation that has directly supported our security for the past three decades. The war is costing us a quarter of our federal budget and tens of thousands of our young men's lives. Higher yet is the price we pay in our own innermost lives, and in the spirit of America.

Source C

From a speech by Clark Clifford, 1969. The US Secretary of Defence addresses the Council on Foreign Affairs concerning the impact of the 1968 Tet Offensive.

The enemy's Tet Offensive was beaten back at great cost. The confidence of the American people was badly shaken. We questioned whether the South Vietnamese government could restore order, morale and army discipline. President Johnson forbade the invasion of North Vietnam because this could trigger their mutual assistance pact with China. He forbade the mining of the principal port through which the North received military supplies, because a Soviet ship might be sunk. He forbade our forces pursuing the enemy into Laos and Cambodia, for this would spread the war. Given these circumstances, how could we win?

Source D

Adapted from Time *magazine, 5 December 1969. An American magazine article reports the impact of the My Lai Massacre a year after it occurred.*

The massacre at My Lai was an atrocity, barbaric in execution. Yet as chilling to the American mind was that the culprits were not obviously demented men, but were almost depressingly ordinary and decent in their daily lives. At home in Ohio or Vermont they would never maliciously strike a child, much less kill one. Yet men in American uniforms slaughtered the civilians of My Lai, and in so doing humiliated the US and called in question the US mission in Vietnam in a way that all the anti-war protesters could never have done.

Source E

From a statement by John Kerry of Vietnam Veterans Against the War, 23 April 1971. Kerry addresses the Senate Committee of Foreign Relations, recalling the observations of some American soldiers during the Vietnam War.

We found most people didn't even know the difference between Communism and democracy. They only wanted to work in rice paddies without helicopters strafing them and bombs with napalm burning their villages and tearing their country apart. They wanted America to leave them alone in peace. They survived by siding with whichever military force was present at a particular time, be it Viet Cong, North Vietnamese or American. We saw first hand how American taxes supported a corrupt dictatorial regime. We saw America lose its sense of morality as it accepted My Lai very coolly.

Exam tips

The cross-references are intended to take you straight to the material that will help you answer the questions.

(a) This question asks you to compare two sources as evidence by using their content and provenance to explain your answer to the question. Focus clearly on '*military morale* during the Vietnam War' and make it the heart of your answer. A true comparison needs sustained cross-reference of the two sources point by point, not one source after the other. Your answer should be balanced, and references to context are only valuable in helping you compare the sources.

Provenance:

- Authors and dates: subjective, national and ideological. Source A: the north Vietnamese Communists – military tactics and propaganda in the lead up to the Tet Offensive (pages 109–13); Source C: US Secretary of Defence – looking back on the impact of the Tet Offensive after Johnson had left office (pages 127–9 and 137–54).
- Nature, purpose, style: Source A – secret, official, ideological propaganda to raise morale (pages 109–13); Source C – public, with hindsight, excusing failures, recording loss of confidence (pages 148–53).

Textual content on problems faced by South Vietnam:

- Points of agreement on morale: weakness of the South Vietnamese government; the high cost in lives and damage to morale from military defeats.
- Points of disagreement: Source A refers to a time when US troops had not seen combat, whereas Source C refers to the impact of destructive battles fought in South Vietnamese territory; in Source A the positive tone contrasts with US defeatism in Source C. In Source A the target is becoming the US troops now that the South Vietnamese troops have lost morale, but the war effort seems internal, whereas in Source C the American government sees the enemy in international terms, banning any provocative military strategy which might extend the war to China or the USSR, so undermining morale and hindering US military tactics. The sense of Source C is that confidence in the US ability to win has been lost, with lack of order, morale and army discipline, in contrast to Source A, where American troops are seen as nationalist, optimistic and proud of their weapons.

(b) This question asks you to use your own knowledge and *all four* sources to create a balanced argument evaluating the interpretation in the question. Focus clearly on '*reasons* America failed to win the Vietnam War' during the period covered by the sources. The sources should drive your answer, and your factual knowledge should be used to support and exemplify the points in your argument.

There will be one reason given in the question, and your first task is to evaluate it. Group the sources by their side of the argument: Sources A, C and to some extent E support the interpretation, whereas Sources B, D and E refute it. Use factual knowledge to exemplify and discuss each point. Suggest a range of other reasons picking up the clues in the sources. Cross-reference phrases across the sources and use them to argue a case for and against the view that 'the strength of their opponents' was the main reason, using factual knowledge to develop and explain your points (Chapters 6 and 7). Reach an evaluative judgement on the relative importance of each, at the end of each paragraph – remembering to link back to the question.

The other side of the argument concerns the weaknesses of America and its allies:

- Loss of confidence and moral opposition from both American troops and public opinion (Sources B and C); loss of South Vietnamese support (Sources B, C, D and E); domestic politics; the president's personal loss of confidence and status (Sources B and C; pages 128–49).
- International attitudes (Sources B, C and D; pages 136–7); domino theory; rollback (Source D; pages 31, 52 and 81); French exit (Source C; page 42).
- Reliance on superior technology, brutalisation and indiscipline among American troops (Sources A, D and E; pages 111–16, 128–9 and 122–7).
- Economics (Sources C and D; pages 137 and 148).

In your conclusion, link together the reasons, weigh up their relative importance and reach a supported judgement to answer the question.

8 1969–73: Nixon – Diplomatic Genius or Mad Bomber?

POINTS TO CONSIDER

American involvement in Vietnam finally ended under President Richard Nixon. Historians debate several issues concerning Nixon and Vietnam. Why was it Nixon, the great Cold Warrior and supporter of escalation, who ended the war? Having decided from the outset of his presidency that the war had to be ended, why did Nixon take so long to do so? Did he delay peace until the eve of the 1972 presidential election in order to get re-elected? Why did he apparently escalate the war by bombing Cambodia?

This chapter covers the above issues through the following sections:

- The transformation of a Cold Warrior?
- President Nixon
- 1969–71
- 1972 – getting re-elected
- Assessment of Nixon's Vietnam policy
- Key debates

There is also another bigger question facing any student of Nixon. Was he, as some Americans believe, an evil man whose policies were characterised by 'secrecy, duplicity, and a ruthless attention to immediate political advantage regardless of larger moral issues', as the historian Marilyn Young, writing in 1991, considered?

Key dates

1969	February	Communists launched offensive on South Vietnam
	March	Nixon secretly bombed Cambodia
	April	Nixon suggested secret Washington–Hanoi negotiations
	May	Nixon offered Hanoi concessions for peace
	June	Troop withdrawals began
	September	Nixon announced the withdrawal of 60,000 American troops from Vietnam
		Nixon's 'great silent majority' speech
	October	Nixon started 'linkage'

	Oct–Nov	Widespread anti-war protests; My Lai massacre publicised
1970	January	Heavy US bombing of the Ho Chi Minh Trail in Laos and Cambodia, and of North Vietnamese anti-aircraft bases
	February	Massive North Vietnamese offensive in Laos; US/ARVN invasion of Cambodia
	April	Nixon's 'pitiful helpless giant' speech
	May	Large-scale protests throughout United States; students shot at Kent State University
1971	February	Lam Son Offensive by ARVN in Laos
	May	Nixon offered Hanoi more concessions
1972	March	PAVN offensive against South Vietnam
	April	Nixon bombed Hanoi and Haiphong
	August	Kissinger and Hanoi made concessions
	October	Kissinger said, 'Peace is at hand'; Thieu rejected Kissinger and Hanoi's agreement
	November	Nixon re-elected president, but running out of money; Washington and Hanoi increasingly inclined to compromise
	December	Nixon's 'Christmas bombing' of North Vietnam
1973	January	Paris Peace Accords ended US involvement in Vietnam War

Key question
Why was it the leading American anti-Communist who got the US out of Vietnam?

1 | The Transformation of a Cold Warrior?

Nixon first made his name as a politician as an extreme anti-Communist, yet he got America out of Vietnam and drew closer to the Soviets and Chinese than any previous Cold War president. How did this happen? Was there a genuine conversion or 'ruthless attention to immediate political advantage'?

After years of being the leading Republican Cold Warrior, a combination of events made Nixon change his traditional stance.

a) Vice-president and Cold Warrior (1953–61)

During his years as Eisenhower's vice-president (1953–61), Nixon had an exceptional apprenticeship in foreign affairs. He frequently travelled abroad and met leaders of many nations. He was present during the foreign policy debates within the Eisenhower administration and had a thorough education in the problem of Vietnam. His ideas sometimes differed from Eisenhower's. He wanted to help the French at Dienbienphu (see page 28) with an American air strike and was even willing to use (small) atomic bombs. He said that if sending American boys to fight in Vietnam was the only way to stop Communist expansion in Indochina, then the government should take the 'politically unpopular position' and do it.

b) Republican foreign policy expert (1961–8)

After Kennedy defeated Nixon in the 1960 presidential race, Nixon held no political office for eight years but kept himself in the political news by foreign policy pronouncements. On Vietnam, he said:

> Victory is essential to the survival of freedom. We have an unparalleled opportunity to roll back the Communist tide, not only in South Vietnam but in Southeast Asia generally and indeed the world as a whole.

As the recognised leader of the Republican opposition on foreign policy, Nixon spurred Johnson to greater involvement in Vietnam. Whatever Johnson did, Nixon urged him to do more. He approved the sending of American ground troops, while wishing for more. 'The United States cannot afford another defeat in Asia', he said. Nixon called for victory and nothing less. By victory he meant two independent Vietnamese states, one of which was not Communist.

From 1964 onwards, Nixon aimed at being the 1968 Republican presidential candidate. Although he agreed with President Johnson over the importance of South Vietnam, as a Republican he naturally accused the Democrat Johnson of getting everything wrong. He said that Johnson had got bogged down in a long, costly ground war. He criticised Johnson for lacking new ideas, but had none himself. He could only advocate more bombing. 'When [President] Nixon said, in 1969, that he had inherited a war not of his making, he was being too modest', said his biographer Stephen Ambrose.

c) Republican presidential candidate (1967–8)

i) 1967

In 1967, presidential hopeful Nixon seemed the last man likely to advocate withdrawal from Vietnam. He criticised the anti-war protesters as a traitorous minority. 'The last desperate hope of North Vietnam is that they can win politically in the United States what our fighting men are denying them militarily in Vietnam.'

ii) Tet and Vietnamisation

In early 1968 Nixon was as shocked as everyone else by the Tet Offensive (see page 137). This was a great turning point for him. He realised that there would have to be changes in American policy. He started to call for the increased use of South Vietnamese soldiers, a policy which would soon become known as **Vietnamisation**:

> The nation's objective should be to help the South Vietnamese fight the war and not fight it for them. If they do not assume the majority of the burden in their own defence, they cannot be saved.

Key term

Vietnamisation
A phrase/policy introduced by the Nixon administration; the policy said that the South Vietnamese government and forces should take the main responsibility for the war against Communism. Previous administrations had wanted and worked for this. They had failed and so did Nixon.

(Kennedy and Johnson had of course said the same, but Johnson had nevertheless assumed the 'majority of the burden'.) Nixon said that American forces should be withdrawn while the ARVN was built up. He stopped talking about escalation. There was no more talk of a 'victorious peace', only an 'honourable peace'. 'I pledge to you, new leadership will end the war and win the peace in the Pacific.'

iii) Could Thieu survive without US forces?

Did Nixon really believe that Thieu could maintain a strong South Vietnam without the ever-increasing American aid that Nixon had so strongly advocated until Tet? Or was he guilty of duplicity? He probably genuinely believed that Thieu could survive with the help of a change of emphasis in American aid (more American bombing and fewer American soldiers) and a radical change of diplomatic direction. He said that America needed to diversify its methods in Vietnam, for example, by using diplomatic leverage with the USSR. The old Cold Warrior emphasised that world Communism had changed. There was no longer a **monolithic Communist bloc**; therefore the next president should replace the era of confrontation with the era of negotiation.

Key terms

Monolithic Communist bloc
During the 1950s, many Americans believed that Moscow and Beijing were united in their foreign policies; by the 1960s, it was increasingly clear that with the Sino-Soviet split (in which other Communist nations took sides) there was no longer a united/monolithic Communist bloc.

Coalition
A government containing several political parties; in this case, the Saigon regime would have to include Communists.

Peace with honour
Nixon always claimed he would get 'peace with honour' in Vietnam, by which he meant that Thieu's government must stay in power in a viable South Vietnamese state.

iv) Johnson and peace talks in 1968

The final months of Johnson's presidency were dominated by the Paris peace talks. Doves said that a bombing halt would lead Hanoi to negotiate a **coalition** government in Saigon. Hawks rejected that as nonsense: 'If you give them [Communists] the bombing pause and a coalition government, you give them the whole goddam country', Nixon said.

Nixon's '**peace with honour**' necessitated the continuation of Thieu's Saigon regime. In October 1968 there was the possibility of a breakthrough in the Paris peace talks. Hanoi seemed to be offering Thieu an opportunity to remain in power with a coalition government. Nixon disliked the idea of a coalition and also feared that successful talks would jeopardise his chance of beating Hubert Humphrey, the Democratic presidential candidate. 'We don't want to play politics with peace', said Nixon, but, he subsequently admitted, 'that was inevitably what was happening'. Privately, Nixon encouraged Thieu not to go to Paris. Had Nixon thereby sabotaged the talks? Thieu probably would not have gone anyway. He had nothing to gain there. Thieu totally rejected the idea of a coalition containing Communists and so did Nixon.

d) Had the Cold Warrior changed?

Key question
Had the old Cold Warrior undergone something of a transformation on the eve of his victory in the presidential election?

i) Opportunist

While Nixon might have changed his position on the Cold War, there had been no transformation of the political opportunist. When he had advised Thieu against compromise in October, he had tried to ensure that it was not Johnson who won 'peace with honour' in Vietnam!

ii) Tet

Tet had proved conclusively to Nixon that the Vietnam War was not going well, so he decided that America needed to withdraw as soon as possible, leaving South Vietnam to fight and win its own battle.

iii) Nixon's aims and methods

'Peace with honour' required Thieu to be left in power, in a strong position. There had thus been no transformation of his ultimate aim for South Vietnam, which was that it should survive as an independent state like South Korea. The transformation was tactical. He now advocated Vietnamisation and an improvement in relations with the USSR and China in order to gain peace with honour.

iv) The Sino-Soviet split

The Sino-Soviet split had shattered the threat of a monolithic world Communist bloc. Nixon had decided that America could play off the two rival Communist giants against each other, by improving relations with both. The Cold War world had changed, so thoughtful Cold Warriors had to adapt. Both China and the USSR would be vital in pressing Hanoi to a 'peace with honour' settlement in Vietnam.

v) Peacemaker

The political and dramatic impact of being a world peacemaker appealed to Nixon: foreign policy success could help his re-election in 1972. Improved relations with China and the USSR and peace in Vietnam would reinvigorate America and ensure Nixon's place in the history books.

An intelligent pragmatism, political ambition and an element of idealism made the old Cold Warrior ready to end the Vietnam War.

Summary diagram: The transformation of a Cold Warrior?

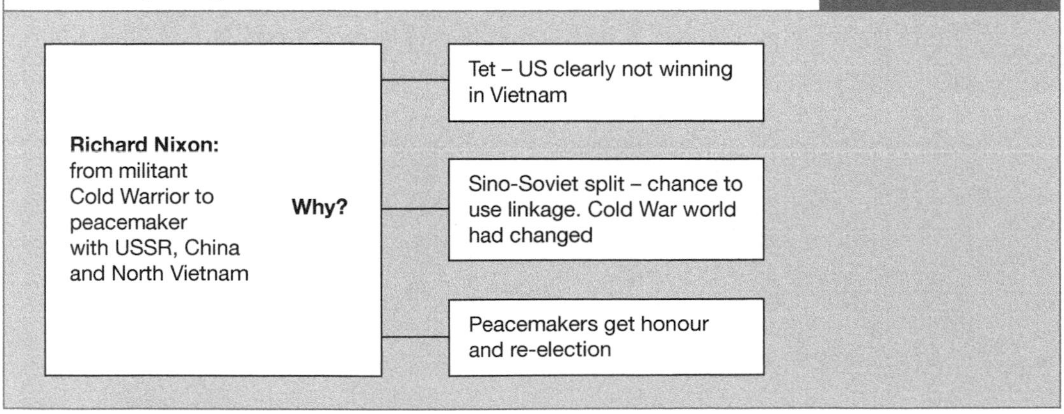

2 | President Nixon

a) The president and Henry Kissinger

Key question
What did President Nixon see as his great challenge and how did he plan to meet it?

Nixon thought that foreign policy was the most important and interesting task of any president, and he chose a national security adviser, Henry Kissinger, who agreed with him.

i) Kissinger's background

A Jewish refugee from Nazi Germany, Kissinger arrived in America as a teenager. He became a Harvard professor. He specialised in international relations and, like Nixon, travelled widely and learned quickly.

ii) Kissinger's political ambitions

Kissinger was politically ambitious. He had tried, but failed, to attach himself to the Kennedy family. During the presidential election campaign of 1968 he offered his services to several candidates. Until late 1968, Kissinger despised Nixon, 'the most dangerous' of the presidential candidates. He considered Nixon an anti-Communist fanatic, yet offered him information on Democratic election strategy. Kissinger's desire for power caused him to compromise.

iii) Kissinger and political power

Once in the Nixon administration, he liked to pretend he was an innocent academic in the vicious political jungle. If so, he learned quickly. 'Henry, you don't remember your old friends', said a minor civil servant whom he ignored. 'The secret of my success', said Kissinger, 'is to forget my old friends'. He told a journalist, 'What interests me is what you can do with power'. He enjoyed the company of glamorous Hollywood actresses, declaring that 'power is the ultimate aphrodisiac'.

Key terms

Realpolitik
A realistic, rather than moralistic or legalistic approach to foreign policy; a belief that foreign policy should be dictated by the national interest.

Conscientious objectors
Those whose religion (for example, Quakers) made them pacifists and therefore, they said, unable to fight if drafted. The US government allowed some conscientious objectors to avoid the draft.

iv) Kissinger and diplomacy

Kissinger was a great believer in personal and secret diplomacy. He distrusted bureaucrats and it was commonly said in Washington that he treated his staff as mushrooms: kept in the dark, stepped on, and frequently covered with manure. He felt that foreign policy for the most part was 'too complex' for 'the ordinary guy' to understand. Nixon shared those sentiments. This conviction proved to be a problem and a weakness. They did not always explain their diplomacy, and therefore did not always ensure popular support for their policies. Both thought in terms of American national interest with little apparent regard for moral considerations. That ***realpolitik*** can still arouse shock. Neither seemed to worry as Johnson had about the deaths of Vietnamese civilians or even of American soldiers. Kissinger's contempt for **conscientious objectors** led him to declare, 'Conscientious objection must be reserved only for the greatest moral issues, and Vietnam is not of this magnitude'.

Profile: Richard Nixon 1913–94

1913		– Born in California, son of a grocer
1934		– Graduated from local college
1937		– Graduated from prestigious Duke University Law School, North Carolina; practised law in California
1942		– Joined US Navy in the Second World War
1947–9		– Twice elected to House of Representatives; served on the subsequently notorious House Un-American Activities Committee; took a leading role (second only to Senator McCarthy) in hounding Communists
1950		– Elected to Senate; defeated Helen Douglas, partly by accusing her of Communist ('pink') sympathies – he said she was 'pink right down to her underwear'
1952–61		– Eisenhower's running mate in presidential election of 1952; served two terms as Eisenhower's vice-president
1954		– Advocated use of tactical (small) nuclear weapons to help France at Dienbienphu (see page 47)
1960		– Narrowly defeated by Democrat John Kennedy in presidential election; retired from politics
1962		– Defeated in Californian **gubernatorial** election; told the press he was retiring from politics, and they would not have Richard Nixon to kick around any more; practised law in New York City, but gained reputation as Republican Party senior statesman and foreign policy specialist
1967		– Published article that advised improved relations with Communist China, which would soon be a leading world power
1968	January–February	– Shaken by Tet Offensive, decided America must get out of Vietnam
	November	– Presidential election victory over Democrat Hubert Humphrey; said he would bring 'peace with honour' in Vietnam
1969–73		– First term as president. Began withdrawing American troops from Vietnam; emphasised Vietnamisation (see page 164)
1970		– Extended Vietnam War to Communist sanctuaries in neighbouring Cambodia; led to massive anti-war protests in US
1972	February	– Visited People's Republic of China, ending two decades of dangerous estrangement

Key term

Gubernatorial
Pertaining to being a state governor.

Key terms

Watergate affair
During Nixon's re-election campaign, Republicans authorised burglary and wiretapping of Democratic national headquarters at Watergate building in Washington, DC; the Nixon administration tried a 'cover-up'.

Detente
Relaxation of tension between the USA and the USSR in the Cold War in the 1970s.

	November	– Landslide victory in presidential election against peace candidate, Democrat George McGovern
1973–4		– Second term as president
1973	January	– Ended Vietnam War
	February	– Senate committee started investigation of **Watergate affair**
	May	– Made arms limitation treaty with the USSR, as part of his **detente** policy towards Communist nations
1974	July	– Congress considered impeachment of Nixon
	August	– Nixon announced resignation; succeeded by vice-president Gerald Ford
	September	– Nixon pardoned by Ford
1974–94		– Spent retirement years in California coastal home; wrote several books on international relations
1994		– Died

Richard Nixon is very important in the Vietnam War context as the president who finally got the United States out. Faced with the problem of getting out yet retaining US international credibility, his tactics included the promotion of detente and the massive bombing of Vietnam, Cambodia and Laos, all of which could be either praised or condemned, depending upon one's viewpoint.

v) Kissinger and Secretary of State Rogers

Both Kissinger and Nixon had exceptional knowledge of foreign affairs and favoured by-passing the traditional diplomatic machinery. Nixon chose his old friend and supporter William Rogers to be Secretary of State. Rogers knew little about foreign policy but Nixon told Kissinger that this was an advantage as it would ensure White House control! When Rogers got his first pile of foreign policy papers to read, he was amazed: 'You don't expect me to read all this stuff, do you?'

The Rogers and Kissinger relationship was tempestuous. Kissinger repeatedly stormed into Nixon's office threatening resignation unless Rogers was restrained or replaced. Nixon said:

> I'm sorry about how Henry and Bill get at each other. It's really deep-seated. Henry thinks Bill isn't very deep, and Bill thinks Henry is power-crazy. And in a sense, they are both right.

He put it all down to their egos and inferiority complexes! Years later he wrote that:

> Rogers felt that Kissinger was **Machiavellian**, deceitful, egotistical, arrogant, and insulting. Kissinger felt that Rogers was vain, uninformed, unable to keep a secret, and hopelessly dominated by the State Department bureaucracy.

Key term

Machiavellian
Machiavelli was a sixteenth-century Italian writer who once wrote, 'the end justifies the means' – in foreign policy, that would be considered as *realpolitik*.

Profile: Henry Kissinger 1923–

1923	– Born in Germany
1938	– Family escaped Nazi persecution of Jews; fled to USA
1943	– Became US citizen; studied accounting at City College, New York; served in US Army in the Second World War
1954	– Harvard PhD; became a lecturer
1959–69	– Served as defence consultant to several administrations
1962	– Professor of government at Harvard
1969–75	– Head of National Security Council (NSC); contributed greatly to detente with USSR and People's Republic of China
1970	– Major role in Vietnamisation (see page 164)
1973–7	– Secretary of State; arranged Paris Peace Accords, which brought Vietnam War to an end; awarded Nobel Peace Prize (see page 185)
1974	– Remained Secretary of State when Gerald Ford took over presidency from Nixon
1977	– Left office; became an international consultant, a writer, and lecturer

Kissinger's importance in the Vietnam War context is that he worked closely with Nixon in getting the United States out of Vietnam, supposedly 'with honour'.

vi) The Nixon–Kissinger relationship

Nixon and Kissinger spent a great deal of time together and as Nixon's presidency wore on, Kissinger became ever more influential. Unlike Nixon, Kissinger was always treated with the utmost respect by the media. Such was Kissinger's power that on the occasions when he subverted Nixon's intentions, he got away with it. Led by two such hard-headed realists, American foreign policy became what many people would consider careless of 'larger moral issues' in its emphasis upon the ultimate survival and strength of American power. Nixon himself recognised that it would be called Machiavellian.

b) Vietnam: the problems and solutions

Upon learning of Johnson's bugging and wiretapping in the White House, Nixon said privately, 'I don't blame him. He's been under such pressure because of that damn war, he'd do anything. I'm not going to end up like LBJ … I'm going to stop that war. Fast!' Ironically, although Nixon did stop the war, it ruined his presidency too.

Vietnam was Nixon's greatest single problem. His aim was clear: peace. What sort of peace? Peace through a great victory?

Key terms

Normalisation of diplomatic relations
When the USA disliked another state, particularly a Communist one, it refused to give it diplomatic recognition. It was not until the late 1970s that the USA established diplomatic relations (that is, normalised relations) with China. Once diplomatic relations were established, ambassadors were exchanged.

Madman Theory
Nixon wanted Hanoi to think he was capable of anything, in order to frighten them into making peace.

No. Nixon could not invade North Vietnam or destroy the PAVN. Peace through a straightforward American withdrawal? No. Honour required that Thieu remain in power. Nixon hoped for a Korean-style settlement, an armistice under which two separate states would coexist. How could he get it? He knew that in 1953 Eisenhower had obtained the Korean armistice through pressure on the USSR and China. Nixon would tempt the Soviets with promises of arms agreements and trade and the Chinese with a **normalisation of diplomatic relations**. He also had another ploy, according to one of his advisers:

> I call it the '**Madman Theory**' … I want the North Vietnamese to believe … I might do anything … We'll just slip the word to them that, 'for God's sake, you know Nixon is obsessed about Communism. We can't restrain him when he's angry – and he has his hand on the nuclear button' – and Ho Chi Minh himself will be in Paris in two days begging for peace.

In his inaugural address, Nixon said, 'The greatest honour history can bestow is the title of peacemaker'. America needed peace at home as well as abroad. This was demonstrated in his presidential inaugural parade. Thousands of anti-war demonstrators chanted 'Ho, Ho, Ho Chi Minh, the NLF [the political arm of the VC] is going to win'. Demonstrators burned small American flags and spat at police. Nixon thus had two great tasks as president in 1969. He had to bring peace to America and to Vietnam.

Summary diagram: President Nixon

Nixon + Kissinger = expertise and *realpolitik*

Vietnam War + Division amongst Americans = the need for peace at home and abroad

3 | 1969–71

Although Nixon was determined to end the war, he had to have his 'peace with honour'. It took time and tremendous effort to persuade Hanoi to agree to allow Thieu to remain in power. Nixon had to use great military and diplomatic pressure to gain a settlement in which Thieu was given a reasonable chance for survival, and whereby it could not be said that America had wasted its time and effort in Vietnam. Whilst applying the military and diplomatic pressure, Nixon had also to take into account American left-wing opposition to the war, and right-wing opposition to losing it.

a) Military pressure, 1969–71

i) Military situation, 1969

In February 1969 the Communists launched another offensive on South Vietnam. 'Rolling Thunder' (see page 93) and the American ground offensive of 1966–8 (see pages 98–9) had clearly not worked, so Nixon decided to try an offensive against the Ho Chi Minh Trail (see map on page 82) in Cambodia. Nixon hoped that this would sever enemy supply lines and encourage Hanoi to agree to an acceptable peace. He also hoped to destroy the supposed Vietnamese Communist headquarters in Cambodia – **COSVN** (the Central Office for South Vietnam). In March Nixon secretly ordered the bombing of the Cambodian sanctuaries. The bombing failed to destroy COSVN or slow traffic on the trail, so in late April Nixon escalated it.

'I can't believe', said the exasperated Kissinger, 'that a fourth-rate power like North Vietnam does not have a breaking point'. He advocated blockading Haiphong and invading North Vietnam. Nixon feared domestic opposition to this but deliberately leaked to the press that he was considering it. This was his 'madman' tactic. By the summer Hanoi seemed to be slowing down the fighting.

Nixon thus attempted three solutions to the military problem in 1969: bombing the trail in Cambodia, the 'madman' ploy and Vietnamisation (see page 164). All were designed to gain peace with honour.

Key question
How did Nixon try to end the war through military means?

Key term
COSVN
Central Office for South Vietnam – supposed Vietnamese Communist headquarters in Cambodia.

ii) Military situation, 1970

In spring 1970, having announced the withdrawal of 150,000 American troops from Southeast Asia, Nixon nevertheless appeared to be extending the war to Laos and Cambodia. He was apparently escalating again. Why?

Nixon believed that demonstrations of American power would counter Saigon's pessimism about American troop withdrawals, help to protect the remaining Americans in Vietnam, intimidate Hanoi and gain better peace terms. He therefore escalated the air offensive in January 1970, heavily bombing the trail in Laos and Cambodia, and North Vietnamese anti-aircraft bases. Nevertheless on 12 February the North Vietnamese launched another great offensive in Laos. Nixon desperately needed to do something effective soon in order to get an acceptable peace, especially as Congress was considering cutting off his money. A total of 30,000 American and ARVN forces therefore moved into south-western Cambodia (less than 50 miles from Saigon), but encountered neither enemy resistance nor COSVN. The Vietnamese had just disappeared. Pressure from American anti-war protesters now forced Nixon to make a speedy withdrawal from Cambodia.

What had Nixon's Cambodian offensive achieved? The capture and destruction of vast quantities of Communist war material meant that it was nearly two years before Hanoi launched another major offensive in South Vietnam, which theoretically gave the ARVN time to grow stronger. Nixon claimed that intervention in

Key dates

Communists launched offensive on South Vietnam: February 1969

Nixon bombed Cambodia: March 1969

Heavy US bombing of the Ho Chi Minh Trail in Laos and Cambodia, and of the North Vietnamese anti-aircraft bases: January 1970

Massive North Vietnamese offensive in Laos; US/ARVN invasion of Cambodia: February 1970

Cambodia had occupied PAVN troops who would otherwise have been killing Americans. However, COSVN had not been found. Perhaps it had never existed. The Americans had expected to find a miniature Pentagon, but there were just a few huts. In total, 344 Americans and 818 ARVN died in Cambodia; 1592 Americans and 3553 ARVN were wounded. Nixon's critics said that it had widened the war. The *New York Times* queried whether the offensive had won time for America or just boosted Hanoi by revealing American divisions and the restraints on the president. One totally unexpected result of the Cambodian invasion was that it forced the Communists further inland, where they destabilised the Cambodian government. Furthermore, American bombing increased the popularity of the Cambodian Communists.

iii) Military situation, 1971

By 1971 the morale of the American army in Vietnam had plummeted. This is not surprising. Eighteen-year-olds were still being asked to fight a war that everyone in America agreed was just about finished, in order to allow time for the army of a corrupt dictatorship in Saigon to improve. Nixon warned the **West Point** graduating class that it was no secret that they would be leading troops guilty of drug abuse and insubordination.

Key term

West Point
The top US military academy.

UUUU

American soldiers frequently painted UUUU on their helmets. The initials stood for, 'the unwilling, led by the unqualified, and doing the unnecessary, for the ungrateful'. Black soldiers often wrote on their helmets, 'No Gook [Vietnamese] Ever Called Me Nigger'.

Determined not to be the first president to lose a war and desperate to gain peace with honour, Nixon decided to go on the military offensive again.

The JCS had long been tempted to attack the trail in southern Laos, but Westmoreland had said that it would require four American divisions. From late 1970, the JCS argued that the ARVN could do it if protected by American air power. In Cambodia in 1970 the PAVN had slipped away to avoid meeting the Americans, but the JCS thought that the PAVN could be enticed out if it was to meet the ARVN. American bombing could then destroy them. That should help ARVN morale, show that Vietnamisation was working, cut the trail, and damage Hanoi's ability to stage an offensive in 1971. Nixon gave the go-ahead. Five thousand ARVN elite troops would go into Laos. Rogers warned that Hanoi expected it (there had been leaks in Saigon), and that Nixon was sending only one ARVN division to do a job which Westmoreland refused to do without four American divisions. Why get involved in Laos for that? It would damage ARVN morale. Nixon and Kissinger ignored him.

Key date

Lam Son Offensive by ARVN in Laos: February 1971

The Lam Son Offensive began on 8 February 1971. Initially the ARVN did well, but then the PAVN got the upper hand, thanks especially to new armoured units using Soviet equipment. Within two weeks, the ARVN was routed. Half the force died. American TV viewers saw ARVN troops fighting each other for places on American helicopters lifting them out of Laos. American crews coated the skids with grease so the South Vietnamese would stop hanging on in numbers sufficient to bring down the choppers.

After Lam Son, Kissinger was particularly furious with Thieu, who had refused to send the number of troops the US recommended. 'Those sons of bitches. It's their country and we can't save it for them if they don't want to.'

After three years of offensives and Vietnamisation, Nixon did not seem to have made any progress on the military front.

b) Diplomatic pressure, 1969–71

Nixon hoped that if he applied both military and diplomatic pressure in the correct proportions, he would gain 'peace with honour'.

Key question
How did Nixon try to end the war through diplomatic means?

i) Diplomacy, 1969

On the diplomatic front, Nixon's first initiative was the April 1969 suggestion that, as the Paris peace talks had stalled amidst the public posturing by the representatives from Saigon and Hanoi, there should be secret Washington–Hanoi negotiations. Hanoi had always favoured that option as it excluded Saigon.

Key dates
Nixon suggested secret Washington–Hanoi negotiations: April 1969
Nixon offered Hanoi concessions for peace: May 1969
Nixon started 'linkage': October 1969

In secret talks in May, Nixon offered Hanoi new peace terms. While still insistent that Thieu remain in power, he dropped Johnson's insistence that American troops would only withdraw six months after the PAVN, and offered simultaneous withdrawal. He hinted that America would begin withdrawing soon anyway, as the ARVN was ready to take over. Hanoi was unimpressed. Why should they agree to withdraw if the Americans were going anyway? The North Vietnamese delegation said they were willing to sit in Paris 'until the chairs rot'. Nixon told Kissinger to warn the North Vietnamese in Paris that as America was withdrawing troops and was willing to accept the results of South Vietnamese elections, they must do likewise or Nixon would have to do something dramatic. Kissinger set them a 1 November deadline. Hanoi claimed that they had no troops in South Vietnam and that Thieu must give way to a coalition government.

As he was making little progress with Hanoi, Nixon turned to Moscow. In October Nixon put pressure on the Soviets, promising detente for their help in ending the Vietnam War (he called this exchange '**linkage**'). He warned them not to reject this offer of more trade, arms control and decreased tension. 'The humiliation of a defeat is absolutely unacceptable to my country.'

Key term
Linkage
Linking US concessions to the USSR and China to their assistance in ending the Vietnam War.

ii) Diplomacy, 1970

In 1969, diplomatically as well as militarily, Nixon made no real progress. He had tried changes, concessions and threats, but seemed no nearer to peace. 1970 was no better.

Nixon's goals were clear. He wanted to be out of Vietnam before the presidential election of November 1972, leaving pro-American governments in South Vietnam, Cambodia and Laos.

He also wanted Hanoi to release American prisoners of war (POWs). How was he to get this? His only means of persuasion were 'Mad Bomber' performances and linkage.

iii) Diplomacy, 1971

Key date: Nixon offered Hanoi more concessions: May 1971

In spring 1971 it seemed as if linkage might be working. Nixon's planned rapprochement with both the USSR and China was becoming a reality. There were arms agreements with the Soviets and a Nixon visit to China in the pipeline. This affected Vietnam, as Nixon intended. The USSR and China were urging Hanoi not to insist on Thieu's removal as a prerequisite for peace.

In May Nixon offered to get out by a set date without demanding mutual withdrawal. In return Hanoi should stop sending additional troops or materials to South Vietnam, observe a ceasefire, and guarantee the territorial integrity of Laos and Cambodia (just when the Communists were about to win in both). Thieu would have to stay in power and the American POWs would be returned. Hanoi was unimpressed, especially as there was no mention of stopping the bombing.

Thus, at the end of 1971, Nixon's diplomatic offensives appeared to be as unproductive as his military ones. After three years, he seemed no nearer to obtaining peace with honour. Hanoi just would not give in.

Key question: How did the home front impact upon Nixon and his policies?

c) The home front problem

i) Nixon's tactics for keeping the home front quiet

While Nixon put military and diplomatic pressure on the enemy, he used several tactics to keep the home front quiet.

He made a series of American troop withdrawals from Vietnam, starting in June 1969. He timed the announcements to defuse public opposition, as in September 1969. Anti-war activists and congressmen were preparing to protest, so Nixon announced the withdrawal of 60,000 troops. Kissinger opposed the troop withdrawals, saying it would decrease American bargaining power with Hanoi and would be like giving salted peanuts to the American public – they would just want more and more. Nixon felt that public opinion gave him little choice.

Nixon judged that the heart of the anti-war movement was male college students threatened with the draft. He therefore adjusted it so that older students (whom he presumably considered to be more confident and articulate) were less hard-hit. This temporarily decreased protests and Nixon got a 71 per cent approval rating.

Key dates:
Troop withdrawals began: June 1969
Nixon announced the withdrawal of 60,000 US troops from Vietnam: September 1969
Nixon's 'great silent majority' speech: November 1969

Nixon tried to keep his actions a secret in order to forestall the anti-war protesters, as with the 1969 bombing of Cambodia. When a British correspondent in Cambodia publicised it, Nixon, convinced it was an internal leak, ordered large-scale wiretapping.

Nixon also used speeches to keep the home front quiet and on 3 November 1969 delivered one of his best. He asked for time to end the war:

> And so tonight, to you, the great silent majority of my fellow Americans – I ask for your support. Let us be united for peace. Let us be united against defeat. Because let us understand: North Vietnam cannot defeat or humiliate the United States. Only Americans can do that.

The speech won universal acclaim, but although Nixon exulted, 'We've got those liberal bastards on the run now, and we're going to keep them on the run', protests soon began again. Nixon's speeches were not always truthful. In April 1970 he explained why he had sent American and ARVN troops into Cambodia. He said America had respected Cambodian neutrality for five years ('a whopper', says Ambrose). However, the Vietnamese Communists had vital bases there. Doing nothing would hurt America's troop withdrawal. The Communists might think they could escalate without American retaliation. He explained that the US was engaged in a clean-up operation:

> not an invasion of Cambodia ... If, when the chips are down, the world's most powerful nation, the United States of America, acts like a pitiful, helpless giant, the forces of totalitarianism and anarchy will threaten free nations and free institutions throughout the world.

America's first defeat in its 190-year existence would be a national disgrace. This emotive language was effective. The speech proved quite popular, but again the success was short-lived.

Key dates

Nixon's 'pitiful, helpless giant' speech: April 1970

Widespread anti-war protests; My Lai massacre publicised: October–November 1969

ii) Protests in 1969

Speeches, troop withdrawals, adjustments to the draft and (attempted) secrecy were insufficient to halt the protests. Nixon rightly claimed that the protesters were a minority, but their numbers were growing. In October 1969 the campuses were in uproar and the largest anti-war protest in American history took place. In this '**moratorium**' protesters took to the streets in every major city. Millions participated, many middle class and middle aged. The more radical waved VC flags, chanted defeatist slogans and burned American flags. Although such behaviour proved unpopular, it made Nixon drop the 1 November ultimatum to Hanoi. He backed down to keep the public happy, despite saying that,

Key term

Moratorium
In this context, suspension of normal activities, in order to protest.

> to allow government policy to be made in the streets would destroy the democratic process. It would give the decision, not to the majority, and not to those with the strongest arguments, but to those with the loudest voices. It would reduce statecraft to slogans. It would invite anarchy.

Between 14 and 16 November, a quarter of a million peaceful protesters took over Washington. Thousands of marchers carrying candles filed past the White House, each saying the name of an American soldier. Nixon wondered whether he could have thousands of helicopters fly low over them to blow out their candles and drown their voices. Simultaneously, news of the My Lai massacre (see pages 114–15) surfaced. Although Nixon reminded everyone that the VC often behaved similarly, many thought that if the price of war was making murderers out of American youths, it was too high.

Key date

Large-scale protests throughout US; students shot at Kent State University: May 1970

iii) Protests in 1970

When Secretary of State Bill Rogers finally heard about the planned invasion of Cambodia, he said, 'This will make the students puke'. The Cambodian offensive did indeed cause trouble on campuses across America. In April 1970, Nixon was told that he dare not attend his daughter Julie's graduation, where students chanted, 'Fuck Julie'. On 5 May 1970 four students at Kent State University, Ohio, were shot dead by the National Guard. Some had been participating in an anti-war rally, some just changing classes. Student protests escalated. All Californian colleges were closed down by the state governor. As students rioted, Nixon backed down and declared that he would get American troops out of Cambodia by June. Again, government policy was made in the streets. The military were furious. In New York City, 100,000 pro-Nixon people demonstrated and construction workers (traditionally Democrats) beat up students from the East's leading colleges in support of the Republican president's policies.

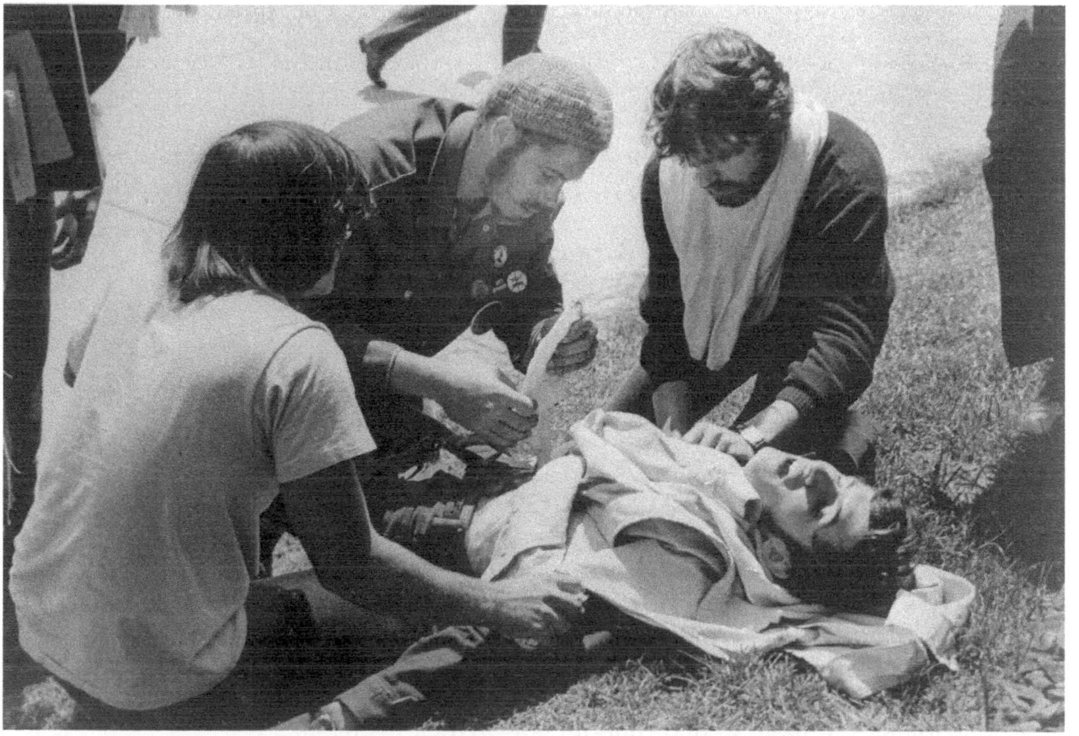

Students give first aid to a young demonstrator shot and wounded by Ohio National Guardsmen on the Kent State University campus.

The protests unnerved Nixon. Security around the White House was stepped up, and Nixon was only half joking when he said that the protesters would, 'probably knock down the gates and I'll have 1000 incoherent hippies urinating on the Oval Office rug'.

Polls showed how the Cambodian intervention had divided Americans: 50 per cent approved Nixon's Cambodian offensive, 39 per cent disapproved. As the Cambodian offensive appeared to be a dramatic escalation of the war authorised solely by the president, it aggravated relations between the president and Congress. Under pressure of the Cold War, America had been developing what many historians call the 'imperial presidency', wherein the president had been acquiring near absolute control over foreign policy. It was inevitable that Congress would attempt to re-assert its power, especially when presidential foreign policy was unpopular. Throughout 1970 and 1971 the Senate enthusiastically supported bills to stop Nixon waging war in Cambodia, Laos and Vietnam. Congress rightly said that the constitution gave them alone the power to declare war and to raise and to finance the armed forces, although Nixon also had a good point when he said that he had inherited a war and the constitution gave him powers as commander-in-chief.

Nixon's time was running out. 'Virtually everybody wants out', said one hawk. Nixon could not get re-elected unless he extricated America from Vietnam, so why was he so slow? He would not be able to save Thieu, honour or peace if he just withdrew. He desperately wanted a face-saving formula that would enable American withdrawal and leave Thieu in power at least for a decent interval. Nixon told Republican senators, 'I will not be the first President of the United States to lose a war'. Vietnamisation and persuading Russia and China to abandon Vietnam were his great hopes, but it all took time and that was what Nixon lacked.

iv) Congressional doubts in 1971

In 1971 Nixon's approval rating dropped to 31 per cent. Congress questioned Nixon about his undemocratic ally, Thieu. Johnson had produced a constitution for Saigon that had decreed a presidential election for October 1971. Thieu held it, but only allowed one candidate – himself! Some senators tried to halt all aid to South Vietnam unless there was a democratic election. Nixon could only say that democracy took time to develop.

v) Nixon under pressure

One of Nixon's greatest problems was his own frustration when he failed to get domestic support. He became increasingly emotional, suspicious and vengeful. During the Cambodian offensive he told a Pentagon employee that the boys in Vietnam were the greatest, unlike the 'bums … blowing up the campuses'. Such language exacerbated American divisions. When his May 1970 attacks on North Vietnamese anti-aircraft facilities became public, he thought Secretary of Defence Laird and Secretary of

State Rogers were the source of the 'leak' and therefore had them wiretapped. Not surprisingly, Hanoi itself had announced it.

The pressure was affecting Nixon's judgement. 'Anyone who opposes us, we'll destroy', said a White House aide. 'As a matter of fact, anyone who doesn't support us, we'll destroy.' As it turned out, the search for leaks would help to destroy both Nixon and South Vietnam.

After three years, then, a frustrated Nixon seemed no closer to bringing peace to America or Vietnam. Public opposition was hampering the military offensives that he hoped would get Hanoi to make concessions at the peace talks. As yet, his diplomatic offensives were not paying off. The USSR and China could not or would not persuade Hanoi to give in. Aware of American national honour and credibility, and fearful of alienating the right wing, Nixon insisted that Thieu remain in power. Hanoi would not agree to that.

Summary diagram: 1969–71

	Military	Diplomatic	Home front
1969	Communist offensive Nixon bombed Cambodia	Madman ploy Secret talks Nixon concessions Linkage	Troop withdrawals Moratorium 'Silent majority speech' News of My Lai
1970	Nixon bombed Laos, Cambodia and North Vietnam's anti-aircraft bases US/ARVN invaded Cambodia Cambodian offensive	Linkage	'Pitiful giant' speech Protests, e.g. Kent State Congress critical of Nixon and the war
1971	Lam Son Offensive	Nixon concessions	Congress critical

4 | 1972 – Getting Re-elected

1972 was the presidential election year. Nixon needed some great breakthrough to ensure that he won. He continued to use his traditional combination of military aggression and negotiation to try to end the war. In early 1972 it looked impossible.

a) Problems in early 1972

Key question
Why did an end to the war look unlikely in early 1972?

In January 1972, Nixon's combination of military and diplomatic pressure still seemed unsuccessful. His bombing offensive on the North antagonised many Americans. Many US pilots were shot down during the air offensive, increasing the number of POWs held by Hanoi. Many congressmen were willing to abandon South Vietnam in exchange for the POWs, but Nixon used their existence and safety to help convince others of the need to continue the war.

i) Hanoi's spring offensive

The USSR and China were pressing Hanoi to settle, to let Nixon out with honour and to let Thieu remain for a while. However, Hanoi did not want to face a superbly equipped ARVN perpetually supplied by America, so the PAVN began a great March offensive against South Vietnam, using tanks and artillery as never before. The ARVN crumbled. Nixon's policy of Vietnamisation was discredited in the presidential election year. He was furious with North Vietnam. He believed that they had used negotiations as a smokescreen for this offensive. He was also angry with the USSR for providing the tanks and artillery.

Key dates

PAVN offensive against South Vietnam: March 1972

Nixon bombed Hanoi and Haiphong: April 1972

ii) 'Defeat not an option'

Kissinger tried to encourage Nixon. He argued that even if the PAVN won while American troops pulled out, at least Nixon could claim credit for ending the war. Nixon said that possibility was 'too bleak even to contemplate'. Defeat was 'simply not an option'. He thought that his political survival was impossible if he failed in Vietnam. He thought that the credibility of American foreign policy would end with failure in Vietnam, and felt that Kissinger underestimated the dangers therein. Nixon therefore ordered bombing of selected North Vietnamese targets: these 'bastards have never been bombed like they are going to be bombed this time'.

iii) Bombing the North as never before

B-52s were used in North Vietnam for the first time since 1968 and inflicted heavy casualties, but nevertheless the PAVN still advanced. Nixon wanted to escalate the bombing. Laird feared the Soviet anti-aircraft defences, congressional reaction and the possible loss of a planned **summit** with the Soviets, but Nixon went ahead. He bombed oil depots around Hanoi and Haiphong, claiming, 'we really left them our calling card this weekend'. Nixon successfully divided Hanoi and Moscow by threatening the latter with cancellation of the summit. On 16 April American bombers hit four Soviet merchant ships at anchor in Haiphong, but the Soviets were so keen to have the summit that their protests were low key. Linkage was working. 'The summit is not worth a damn if the price for it is losing in Vietnam', said Nixon. 'My instinct tells me that the country can take losing a summit, but it can't take losing the war.'

Key terms

B-52s
Large American bomber planes.

Summit
During the Cold War, meetings or conferences between the US and Soviet leaders were known as summit meetings.

Unlike Nixon, Kissinger gave detente priority and on his own initiative hinted to the Soviets that America might consider a coalition government without a North Vietnamese withdrawal. Kissinger knew that concessions were essential if the war were to be brought to an end and was now more inclined to compromise than Nixon. He was being ostracised by old Harvard colleagues, and was terrified that he might suffer the fate of one of Johnson's academic advisers, who on returning to academia was banished to the University of Texas.

iv) Mining North Vietnam's ports

Nixon meanwhile decided to mine North Vietnam's ports. He said,

> If the United States betrays the millions of people who have relied on us in Vietnam … it would amount to renunciation of our morality, an abdication of our leadership among nations, and an invitation for the mighty to prey upon the meek all around the world.

He said that if America was strong, the world would remain half instead of wholly Communist. The Democrats were critical: one spoke of flirting with a Third World War to keep General Thieu in power and save Nixon's face for a little longer. However, it was Nixon who understood the Soviets best. Moscow was tired of financing Hanoi's war. Moscow would not sacrifice the summit to halt the mining of North Vietnamese ports. Nixon had made his position clear to Hanoi and Moscow. He would not destroy Hanoi (there was no talk of using atomic weapons), but he could hurt it. Nor would he abandon Thieu, even at the cost of losing the summit. However, he was hinting to Moscow a new willingness to accept a coalition containing Communists – a great concession.

v) Concessions plus force

Key date
Moscow summit: May 1972

Nixon continued the bombing throughout the Moscow summit (May 1972), illustrating one of the ways in which he intended to get America out of Vietnam 'with honour' – by disguising concessions with simultaneous shows of force. Nixon's approval rating shot up. As the Soviets and Chinese pressed Hanoi to settle, Hanoi rightly accused them of putting their own interests above those of world revolution. However, America was offering Hanoi yet another vital concession: the PAVN would be allowed to stay in South Vietnam, which would be crucial to their future victory.

vi) Hanoi faltering

Hanoi was finally being driven towards a settlement by a combination of American concessions, pressure from their allies, the failure of their offensive to take big cities, Operation Phoenix (see page 114), the destructiveness of the B-52s and the probable re-election of the unpredictable Mad Bomber. After three years, Nixon's combination of military and diplomatic pressure and concessions appeared to be working. It was just as well. He was running out of time and money.

THE END OF OPERATION PHOENIX (see page 114)

Nixon had been delighted by the success of Operation Phoenix, saying, 'We've got to have more of this. Assassinations. Killings. That's what they [the Communists] are doing.' However, when the press exposed the programme, there was considerable American outrage, so Nixon had to cancel Phoenix operations in 1972.

b) Autumn 1972: running out of time and money

Key question
Why was peace 'at hand' in autumn 1972?

By the second half of 1972 Nixon was running out of time and money. Troop withdrawals meant that Congress could no longer be shamed into granting funds to help 'our boys in the field'. Nixon begged them not to damage his negotiating capabilities, and pointed out that just walking away from Vietnam would lead to a bloodbath for former Thieu supporters. Allowing that to happen would be the height of immorality. Polls showed that most Americans agreed with Nixon's bottom line: 55 per cent supported continued heavy bombing of North Vietnam and 64 per cent the mining of Haiphong, and 74 per cent thought it important that South Vietnam should not fall to the Communists. Nixon told Kissinger to tell the Vietnamese negotiator Le Duc Tho he had had enough:

> Settle or else! ... No nonsense. No niceness. No accommodations ... tell those sons of bitches that the President is a madman and you don't know how to deal with him. Once re-elected I'll be a mad bomber.

i) Both sides agree to compromise

Key dates
Kissinger and Hanoi made concessions: August 1972
Kissinger said, 'peace is at hand': October 1972

Despite this tough talk, both sides were compromising. It seemed that Hanoi would let Thieu remain in power while America would let the PAVN stay in South Vietnam and not insist upon a ceasefire in Cambodia and Laos. However, Hanoi insisted upon a voice in the Saigon government and there seemed no chance of Thieu accepting that, despite Nixon's promise that America would never desert him. Kissinger rejected the idea of a coalition government but offered a Committee of National Reconciliation (to be one-third South Vietnamese, one-third Communist and one-third neutral) to oversee the constitution and elections. Kissinger thereby agreed that the Communists were a legitimate political force in South Vietnam, which Thieu had always denied. Kissinger ignored the tearful Thieu, while Nixon reminded the latter of what had happened to Diem and muttered, 'the tail can't wag the dog'.

ii) 'Peace is at hand'

In October, Kissinger thought he had an agreement:

- America would withdraw all its armed forces but continue to supply the ARVN.
- There would be a National Council of Reconciliation with Communist representation.
- The American POWs would be released.
- Thieu would remain in power.
- The PAVN would remain in South Vietnam.
- America would help the economic reconstruction of North Vietnam as a humanitarian gesture.

Nixon said that it was 'a complete capitulation by the enemy', but then got cold feet and rejected the terms. Why?

- He was worried about accusations that peace at this time was an electoral ploy.
- He feared that it would appear he had given in to people like Hollywood's Jane Fonda, who had journeyed to Hanoi to express shame at her country's deeds.
- Some advisers feared that if peace came before the election, people might vote Democrat as the Democrats were supposedly better at peace-time governing, while Republicans were good for foreign crises.
- The American right wing opposed the National Council.
- Most important of all, Thieu rejected the settlement and Nixon shared his doubts. Nixon was not sure that this constituted peace with honour. Thieu wanted the PAVN out of South Vietnam and loathed the National Council. Nixon nevertheless felt that his ally had to make some concessions and threatened him with the withdrawal of American support. 'We're going to have to put him through the wringer ... We simply have to cut the umbilical cord and have this baby walk by itself.' The exasperated Kissinger called Thieu 'a complete son of a bitch'.

Key dates

Thieu rejected Kissinger and Hanoi's agreement: October 1972

Nixon re-elected president: November 1972

Kissinger was as keen as Nixon for the latter to be re-elected. It meant four more years for both of them. On the eve of the American presidential election, Kissinger assured the press that 'Peace is at hand'. A few 'minor details' needed tidying up. That statement infuriated Nixon, who felt that it would make Hanoi and Thieu more intransigent.

Nixon also resented Kissinger gaining the glory from the announcement. Some Democrats were cynical. Why was peace suddenly at hand on the eve of the election? Nixon had had four years to do this. Kissinger pointed out that Hanoi's recent concessions allowing Thieu to remain in power were the difference. He omitted to mention that America had also made concessions. Meanwhile Nixon intensified the bombing to keep the pressure on Hanoi.

iii) Persuading Thieu

In November 1972 Nixon was re-elected, but the new Democratic Congress was not going to carry on funding the war. Nixon had done all he could to help Thieu, but the money would soon run out, so the only way forward was to force Thieu to accept the unacceptable. Nixon had just weeks to finish the war. He gave Thieu his 'absolute assurance' that if Hanoi broke the peace, he would take 'swift and severe retaliatory action'. Thieu knew that any agreement was inevitably going to be a temporary ceasefire, so long as the PAVN remained in South Vietnam and that the American political system could invalidate Nixon's promise of future aid against North Vietnamese aggression. Some of Kissinger's staff were so exasperated by Thieu's stubbornness that they suggested assassinating him! Hanoi's negotiator Le Duc Tho was still willing to accept the October agreement that Nixon and Kissinger had initially considered satisfactory. However, having once rejected that agreement, America could hardly accept it now without looking rather foolish.

iv) Christmas bombing

On 18 December Nixon bombed and mined Haiphong again, confiding to his diary that Hanoi thought 'they have us where the hair is short and are going to continue to squeeze us', so he had to do something. There was no public explanation for this Christmas 1972 bombing; which caused worldwide uproar. Had not Kissinger promised peace? Although American planes tried to avoid civilian casualties in Hanoi, 1000 died. The North Vietnamese shot down 15 B-52s with 93 American airmen, a rate of losses the US air force could not sustain for long.

Key dates

Nixon's Christmas bombing of North Vietnam: December 1972

Paris Peace Accords ended US involvement in Vietnam War: 27 January 1973

Kissinger was cracking: he leaked to the press that he opposed the Christmas bombing, which was untrue. One adviser thought that 'we look incompetent – bombing for no good reason and because we do not know what else to do'. What was the point? Was Nixon trying to reassure Thieu of American strength and support? To weaken Hanoi so that it could not speedily threaten South Vietnam after peace was concluded? Trying to disguise American retreats and compromises in the negotiations? Had he lost control? Or was it a mixture of all those reasons? Given the importance that Nixon attached to military pressure, the first two suggestions were probably the most important. Nevertheless several congressmen and influential newspapers questioned Nixon's sanity and accused him of waging 'war by tantrum'.

v) Peace at last

It is difficult to see what the Christmas bombing had achieved. The accord that was finally reached in Paris in January 1973 was basically the same as that of October 1972 with a few cosmetic changes for both sides. Knowing his funding would soon be cut off, Nixon had to tell Thieu that he was going to sign with or without him. On 22 January Thieu agreed, although he regarded it as virtual surrender.

The 27 January 1973 Paris Peace Accords declared a ceasefire throughout Vietnam (but not Cambodia or Laos). POWs would be exchanged, after which America would remove the last of its troops. The PAVN was not required to leave the South, but had to promise not to 'take advantage' of the ceasefire or increase its numbers. Thieu remained in power, but the Committee of National Reconciliation contained Communist representation, and would sponsor free elections. Nixon secretly promised billions of dollars worth of reconstruction aid to Hanoi.

Summary diagram: 1972 – getting re-elected

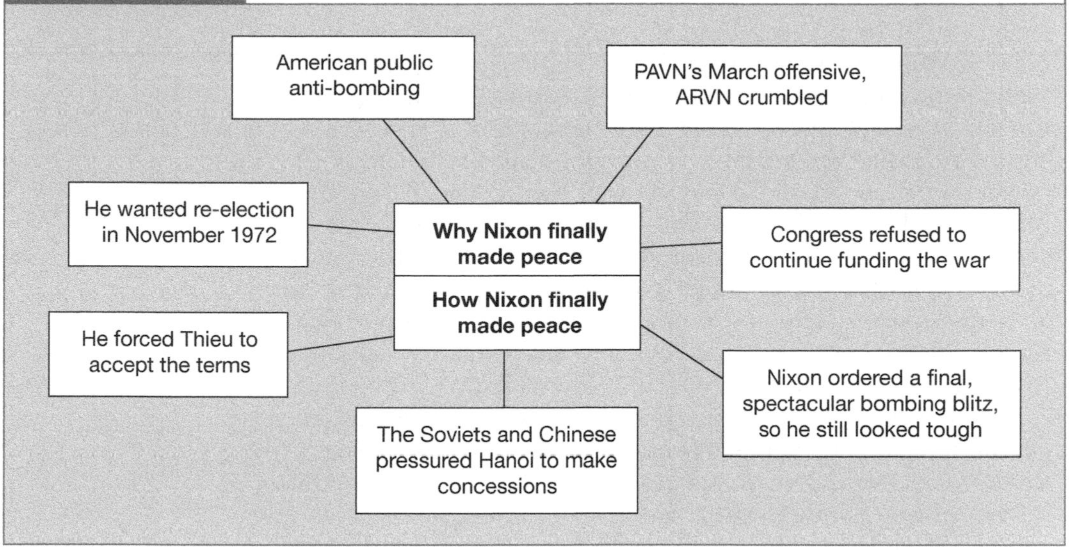

5 | Assessment of Nixon's Vietnam Policy

Key questions
Was Nixon's policy a success or failure?
Can it be defended?

a) Nixon and Kissinger – heroes or villains?

Kissinger and Le Duc Tho were awarded the highly prestigious Nobel peace prize for ending the Vietnam War. Did Kissinger deserve it more than Nixon? It was surely a true team effort. Did either of them really deserve a peace prize? Was Nixon a diplomatic genius or a mad bomber? His sanity was publicly questioned during the 1972 Christmas bombing. A Kissinger aide who quietly resigned over the 1970 Cambodian invasion subsequently regretted his loyal decision not to call a press conference:

> I knew the administration was squalid. But there still was this enormous illusion about Henry. I clung to the delusion that the man was still rational … it was my theory of the limits of the ruthlessness of Henry Kissinger; in truth, there were no limits.

However, looking at all that Nixon and Kissinger did, it is not difficult to find reasons for their actions. They were motivated by the desire to do what they thought was best for America, which for the most part was what they thought was best for themselves also. Although one might not agree with their interpretation, and although one might be particularly upset by what it meant for the victims of their slow withdrawal and saturation bombing, one cannot help but conclude that all was accomplished with rational calculation of what was politically acceptable and best for America and the Western world.

b) Why did Nixon take so long to get out of Vietnam?

During 1968, Nixon had decided that America had to get out, but it took him four years to do it, during which time 300,000 Vietnamese and 20,000 Americans died. Most of the names on the left-hand side of the Vietnam war memorial wall in Washington died during Nixon's presidency, in a war he had decided from the first he could not win. Having decided upon retreat, would it not have been less painful if Nixon had done it speedily? The slow retreat ensured a dramatic drop in the morale of American forces in Vietnam. It antagonised American anti-war activists. Some argue that it created the division, discontent and the presidential paranoia that helped to bring about Watergate (see page 169).

However, Nixon had his own good reasons for simply not getting out. In 1969 Hanoi was unwilling to accept that Thieu would remain in power. Washington was wedded to Thieu because it recalled how South Vietnam had neared disintegration after Diem. This did not seem the time to change governments.

Nixon felt that American honour required that Thieu's South Vietnam be left with a good chance of survival. Why else had America fought at such great cost in men and money? Nixon wrote to Rogers: 'We simply cannot tell the mothers of our casualties and the soldiers who have spent part of their lives in Vietnam that it was all to no purpose'.

American national pride was at stake. The country could not afford to be seen to be defeated. In a November 1969 speech Nixon said he could have ended the war immediately and blamed it all on Johnson. 'This was the only way to avoid allowing Johnson's war to become Nixons' war.' But he had bigger things to think about. He was convinced that a first American defeat would lead to a collapse of confidence in American leadership and to Communist expansion throughout the world. He was adamant that South Vietnam's right to decide its future was not negotiable. He wanted peace, but not at any price. He asked 'the great silent majority' to support him because 'North Vietnam cannot defeat or humiliate the United States. Only Americans can do that.' After that 'great silent majority' speech, Nixon's support soared to 68 per cent.

Although the slow withdrawal was painful, there were clearly many who understood what Nixon was trying to do and sympathised with him. Like so many Americans, Nixon genuinely believed that the USSR and China presented a threat to America and its allies. Given the lack of political freedom within those two countries and Eastern Europe, those American fears were comprehensible and vital to understanding why America got into Vietnam and insisted on getting out 'with honour'. Kissinger said:

> However we got into Vietnam, whatever the judgement of our actions, ending the war honourably … [was] essential for the peace of the world. Any other solution may [have] unloose[d] forces that would [have] complicate[d] the prospects of international order …

> For nearly a generation the security and progress of free peoples had depended on confidence in America. We could not simply walk away from an enterprise involving two administrations, five allied countries, and 31,000 dead as if we were switching a TV channel ... As the leader of democratic alliances we had to remember that scores of countries and millions of people relied for their security on our willingness to stand by allies ... We could not revitalise the Atlantic alliance ... We would not be able to move the Soviet Union toward the imperative of mutual restraint ... We might not achieve our opening to China [if America lost credibility over Vietnam].

Although Kissinger and Nixon believed in detente, they thought that it was dangerous if the Soviets and Chinese thought that America was weak; and they were probably right.

c) Does Nixon deserve any credit for the withdrawal?

At the very least Nixon's critics have to admit that he got the American troops out of Vietnam. He did not always get much thanks for it (doves criticised his slowness) and he perhaps did not have much choice, but it was very significant indeed. It was difficult for any president to preside over the retreat of American power. Perhaps retreat from America's uncompromising and impossibly expensive Cold War militancy was one of Nixon's greatest achievements.

d) Had Nixon gained peace with honour?

Nixon had got the American ground forces out without abandoning Saigon. He had forced Hanoi to agree that Thieu could remain in power with the world's fourth largest air force and an improved ARVN. On the other hand, Nixon had aimed to get the PAVN to withdraw and to nullify the VC in South Vietnam, but he had failed to do so. By late 1972 his freedom was limited: he knew that Congress would cut off his money early in 1973, so he had to make peace on whatever terms he could get, and thanks to his 'mad bomber' and linkage tactics the terms were quite probably better than he could have got in 1969.

e) What did the peace cost Nixon?

It could be argued that the peace cost Nixon the presidency itself. The difficulties of gaining 'peace with honour' in the face of domestic opposition and Vietnamese intransigence accentuated his tendency towards a siege mentality. During 1972 a Nixon organisation, the Campaign to Re-elect the President (CREEP) indulged in dirty tricks and got caught breaking into the Democrats' offices in the Watergate building. The scandal simmered relatively quietly in late 1972, but during Nixon's second term it exploded and brought the president down. Many Americans believed that had Nixon not felt besieged and battered by the Vietnam War, had he not believed that Vietnam might cost him re-election, Watergate would not have happened.

f) Had Nixon really won peace for Indochina in January 1973?

Nixon had not really won peace for Indochina in January 1973. The fighting continued in South Vietnam. Thieu's interpretation of the ceasefire was clear: 'If Communists come into your village, you should immediately shoot them in the head'. Nixon bombed Communist sanctuaries in Cambodia until 15 August 1973 when his money was cut off. Within months, Cambodia had become Communist, and so had South Vietnam. North Vietnam overran South Vietnam in 1975. There was no help from America. Nixon had resigned because of Watergate in 1974. Had he still been president, would Nixon have saved Saigon? Or had he (like Kissinger) just wanted a decent interval to elapse before the inevitable Saigon collapse? In 1977 Nixon said that he did not think he could have saved South Vietnam because Congress was opposed to any more American actions there. Nixon's expensively gained 'peace with honour' was thus untenable. Preoccupied with his foreign policy and international relations, Nixon had failed to engineer the domestic consensus necessary to save the incompetent Thieu.

6 | Key Debate

Nixon felt that, 'History will treat me fairly. Historians probably won't, because many historians are on the left.' He was right in guessing that historians would usually be hostile towards him.

Does President Nixon's Vietnam policy deserve praise?

Kimball (1998) felt that, despite his electioneering promises, Nixon had no new Vietnam policy and never really developed one. He and Kissinger constructed *ad hoc* and often contradictory strategies in reaction to events. The 'madman theory' was the closest thing resembling a consistent approach. Morgan (2002) is particularly critical of the 'madman theory'. 'The use of insanity as an instrument of diplomacy is at best a contradiction in terms and at worst dangerous brinkmanship that could rebound disastrously in a crisis.'

The 'peace with honour' is disputed by most historians, for example, Berman (2001). Many historians, for example, Small (1999), felt that Nixon could have made peace on equally 'favourable' terms in 1969, and saved many lives. 'Because of his faith in mad strategies and triangular diplomacy', says Kimball, 'he had unnecessarily prolonged the war, with all the baleful consequences of death, destruction and division for Vietnam and America that this brought about'. Similarly, Nixon's biographer Ambrose said that Nixon's slow retreat from Vietnam was, 'One of the worst decisions ever made by a Cold War president and the worst mistake of his presidency' (1989, 1991).

Small (1999) contends that the most remarkable of Nixon's feats was not ending the war, but managing to maintain support for his policies for over four years and to win the landslide victory in 1972. Small points out that Nixon used public anger at the 'hippies' in the anti-war movement to get support for his bombing. Since the end of the war, prominent Vietnamese have revealed much, including the fact that Hanoi counted on the American (as on the French) public to tire of the war, and Hanoi believed that the anti-war movement was more of a brake on Nixon than on Johnson.

Morgan declared that Nixon was 'guilty not of losing Vietnam but of trying … to save a regime that was beyond salvation' (2002). Morgan points out that, 'if Nixon inherited the Vietnam war, he did much to create the Cambodian war'. Morgan emphasises the horrific impact of US bombing on Cambodia, blaming Nixon, and disagreeing with those such as Hitchens (2001) who blame Kissinger for being the architect of the policy.

Some key books in the debate

S. Ambrose, *Rise to Globalism* (New York, 1989).
L. Berman, *No Peace, No Honour* (New York, 2001).
C. Hitchens, *The Trial of Henry Kissinger* (London, 2001).
J. Kimball, *Nixon's Vietnam War* (Kansas, 1998).
I. Morgan, *Nixon* (London, 2002).
M. Small, *The Presidency of Richard Nixon* (Kansas, 1999).

Study Guide: AS Questions

In the style of AQA

(a) Explain why Henry Kissinger became a highly influential national security adviser. (12 marks)

(b) How important was the anti-war movement in the decision to end the Vietnam War during the Nixon administration? (24 marks)

Exam tips

The cross-references are intended to take you straight to the material that will help you to answer the questions.

(a) Re-read pages 167–70. There are a number of reasons that can be cited:

- Nixon believed foreign policy to be of prime importance and had a personal need for an adviser in extricating the USA from Vietnam.
- Kissinger was a respected academic and specialist in international relations.
- Kissinger sought power on his own account and provided Nixon with what he needed.
- Kissinger's *realpolitik*/Machiavellian attitude, using personal/secret diplomacy, bypassing traditional diplomatic machinery, made him particularly suitable to a complex situation which involved trying to influence public opinion.

Try to provide a conclusion in which you show how these factors are interlinked and assess the most important.

(b) In order to provide an effective answer, you will not only need to address the anti-war movement, but also balance its part against other factors encouraging an end to the Vietnam War. In this way you can show how far you agree or disagree with the given premise. In support of the quotation you might cite:

- Nixon's concern not to 'end up like LBJ' (Johnson)
- the protests of 1969 and 1970
- the link between the trouble in the streets in spring 1970 and Nixon's decision to pull out of Cambodia (page 177).

Factors disagreeing with the quotation include:

- Nixon's personal concerns and his need for a 'place in history'
- the changing Cold War world (pages 165–6) – there was no longer a monolithic Communist bloc
- the 'unwinnable' war problem (see pages 130–1)
- the military situation and Nixon's decisions prior to the 1969 protests
- US economic problems with the dollar in trouble because of the war by 1972
- US diplomacy.

Once you have decided which way you will argue, work through your points in a logical and linked manner so that your conclusion flows naturally from what you have written.

In the style of Edexcel

How accurate is it to describe President Nixon's handling of the Vietnam conflict as having achieved 'peace with honour'?

(30 marks)

Exam tips

The cross-references are intended to take you straight to the material that will help you to answer the question.

Nixon achieved peace if that is defined as getting American troops out of Vietnam, but you will need to decide what counts as 'with honour'. See pages 186–9 for the issues involved here.

You could plan to deal with the following factors:

- Nixon's view that confidence in American world leadership must be maintained to prevent communist expansion (pages 180 and 186–7).
- The combination of diplomacy plus force enabled him to secure some gains (pages 180–1).
- He maintained support for Thieu and refused to abandon Saigon (pages 179, 182–3 and 187).
- In dealing with these last two points you could refer to the terms achieved at the Paris Peace Accords (page 184).

However:

- North Vietnam overran South Vietnam in 1975 (page 188).
- Many lives were lost in 1969–73 (page 188) and what was the rationale for the Christmas bombing (page 184)?

What is your conclusion? Could President Nixon have made peace in 1969? He was responsible for prolonging the conflict. You could base your final assessment on how far what was achieved in 1973 represented a better peace with more honour than the position in 1969. Re-read pages 186–9 to clarify your thinking here. Again, this is an area of debate amongst historians and not one where there is a right answer to be found. It will depend on the criteria you apply for assessing 'with honour'.

9 Conclusions

POINTS TO CONSIDER

The previous chapters have identified the issues that historians have debated on the topic of America and Vietnam.

- Why did America get involved in Vietnam?
- Which president was mainly responsible for the involvement?
- Should presidents take all the responsibility?
- Why could America not achieve her great aim of an independent South Vietnam?
- Why was America so slow to get out of Vietnam?
- What, if anything, had America achieved?

This chapter summarises those debates, then looks at the effects of the war on Vietnam, the United States and international relations.

Key dates

1975 Vietnam was reunited under Communist rule
1978 Thousands of 'boat people' began fleeing Vietnam
1982 Vietnam veterans memorial unveiled in Washington, DC
1995 President Clinton re-established diplomatic relations with Vietnam

1 | Summarising the Debates

Key question
What do historians consider to be the main controversies relating to the Vietnam War?

a) Why did America get involved in Vietnam?

Successive presidents viewed the world through a Cold War perspective that made a Communist victory in Vietnam seem very significant. In reality though, Ho Chi Minh and his followers were nationalists first and Communists second. They were not the puppets of Moscow or Beijing. However, successive administrations believed that a Communist Vietnam would affect the world balance of power in favour of Communism and cause other Southeast Asian 'dominoes' to fall. Some would argue that American motivation was primarily ideological. Others would say that naked power and greed were equally important.

b) How much responsibility did each president bear?

It might be reasonable to claim that they all bore responsibility. Truman aided the French. Eisenhower was vital in the establishment of South Vietnam and he and Kennedy propped up Diem. Kennedy's complicity in the fall of Diem increased America's obligation to his Saigon successors in the minds of Johnson and others. Once American money and lives had been expended, it seemed a betrayal of all who had gone before to withdraw. It was always hoped that 'just a little more' effort would do the trick. It was very difficult for any president to get out, as his predecessors had bequeathed him a commitment which seemed to have developed into a moral obligation. So, it could be argued that each of the presidents involved should shoulder the same amount of blame.

c) Should the presidents bear all the blame?

All presidents had advisers such as Acheson, Dulles, McNamara and Kissinger who encouraged the commitment to South Vietnam. Congress, the public and the press were supportive for much of the time, which is particularly apparent during Johnson's escalation. However, is there any justification in the argument that the person at the top should always 'carry the can'?

d) Why could America not achieve its great aim of permanently establishing an independent South Vietnam?

Hanoi got invaluable support from Moscow and Beijing. The Communists fought with incredible tenacity. As Kissinger said, 'The conventional army loses if it does not win; the guerrilla wins if he does not lose'. Giap used a judicious mixture of guerrilla and conventional warfare. The guerrillas were never going to give up. They were sufficiently attractive and/or threatening to the Vietnamese peasants to gain the support necessary for survival. The Americans fought a limited war in which their tactics served to aid Communist popularity. Their South Vietnamese allies were usually corrupt, inefficient and unpopular. The American home front collapsed, and the morale of the American army plummeted from 1968 onwards. American politicians decided the war had to stop. So, did America lose the war at home rather than in Vietnam?

e) Why was America so slow to get out of Vietnam?

American power, prestige, credibility and security seemed likely to suffer if the country was seen to be defeated. Retreat would also alienate many American electors, whose (supposed) wishes help to explain the involvement, escalation and withdrawal. Was the American retreat (and the American involvement) dominated by the presidential desire to placate the electorate?

There are other questions that need to be considered. One of the most important of these is, 'What were the effects of the Vietnam War?'

Summary diagram: Summarising the debates

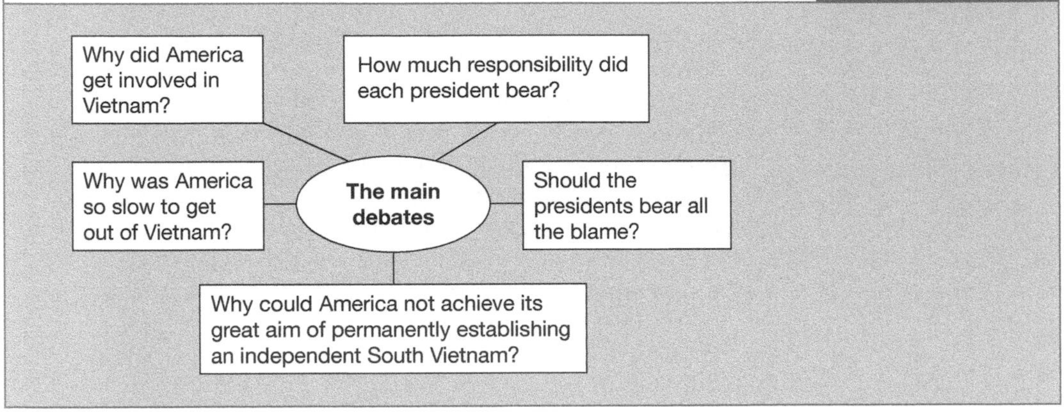

2 | The Effects of the War

Key question
How did the war directly affect the people in Vietnam and the United States?

a) Death and destruction

i) Dead and wounded

- Of the three million Americans who served in Vietnam, about 46,000 were killed in action, 10,000 died through accidents and around 300,000 were wounded.
- Over 5000 Allied troops died: 4407 South Koreans, 469 Australians and New Zealanders, and 350 Thais.
- 137,000 ARVN were killed and 300,000 were wounded.
- Around 400,000 South Vietnamese civilians died and three-quarters of a million were wounded.
- Giap admitted to 600,000 North Vietnamese losses, but America claimed that 800,000 in the PAVN and one million VC died.
- Around two and a half million Vietnamese died and one and a half million were wounded out of the total population of about 32 million.

ii) Mental wounds

For the survivors and their families, many mental and physical wounds remained. 'Now it's all gone down the drain and it hurts. What did he die for?' asked the parent of an American soldier. Divisions and resentment are very much alive in America. A survey of veterans in 1988 suggested that half a million of the three million Americans who had served in Vietnam suffered from post-traumatic stress disorder. Symptoms could appear 10–15 years later, including panic, rage, anxiety, depression and emotional paralysis. Divorce, suicide, drug addiction and particularly alcoholism are higher than average among veterans. One attempt by the veterans to heal themselves and the nation was the construction of the Vietnam war memorial in Washington, completed in 1982. There were bitter arguments about its existence and design. A sombre, long, black slash of marble, like a deep wound in the ground, it contains the names of more than 56,000 Americans who died in Vietnam.

Key date
Vietnam veterans memorial unveiled in Washington, DC: 1982

Vietnam war memorial in Washington DC.

iii) Physical wounds

In Vietnam, there were victims of American napalm who were melted into a kind of gelatine. Some hideously disfigured survivors slunk off to live in caves or remote areas. Vietnam could not afford cosmetic surgery for them. American spraying of herbicides such as Agent Orange had a tremendous impact: the incidence of cancer and toxin-related diseases remains unusually high in Vietnam because of this. Much forest and agricultural land was ruined. By the end of the war, extensive areas had been taken over by tough weeds which the locals call 'American grass'. Since the end of the war, thousands of Vietnamese have been killed by unexploded bombs, shells and land-mines while clearing land or ploughing their fields. Some made a precarious living by collecting this scrap metal, although remaining white phosphorus artillery shells terrified them. If they exploded, the chemical burned through to the bone and could only be removed with something like a metal razor blade.

Key question
What was the impact of the war upon the Vietnamese economy and society?

b) Vietnam's economic and social problems

i) Vietnam's problems in 1975

In 1975, newly united Vietnam suffered from a shattered economy, social and political divisions, exhausted people and ruined urban and rural areas. The tremendous unity of purpose and sense of mission which characterised the North in the war seemed to disappear after it. Giap admitted that the Communist Party leadership was better at waging war than running a country.

For more than 20 years after the Americans withdrew, Vietnam remained one of the world's poorest nations thanks to the legacy of war damage coupled with unsuccessful Communist economic policies.

ii) Unpopular Communist policies

After 1975 the victorious Communists followed the traditional Soviet model and concentrated upon heavy industry, but lacked the necessary capital and skills. Communist economic policies removed the stimulation of money-making incentives. Even Saigon's hairdressers were **collectivised**. The rapidly growing population (which had tripled since 1930) could not be fed. Southern peasants were disillusioned by the collectivisation of farm land, and in the fertile Mekong Delta they preferred to sell their produce on the **black market** rather than hand it over to government agencies. Some slaughtered their water buffalo rather than give them to the government, or let land lie fallow rather than cultivate crops for the government. Even fish became scarce as thousands of '**boat people**' fled the country in fishing boats.

Key terms

Collectivised
Private land ownership was ended.

Black market
Secret commercial transactions designed to avoid paying taxes.

Boat people
Anti-Communist Vietnamese who fled Vietnam after 1975.

iii) 'Boat people'

Vietnamese society was badly dislocated by the war. Many anti-Communist Vietnamese fled the country. The massive exodus of 'boat people' was one of the biggest twentieth-century migrations. Over one million left between 1975 and 1990. Many died from exposure or drowning. Now over three-quarters of a million of them live in America and, one million in other Western countries, but hundreds of thousands spent years in squalid refugee camps in Thailand, Malaysia, the Philippines and Hong Kong. Unless they could prove they fled for political rather than economic reasons, they were often repatriated, especially by the British authorities in Hong Kong. Another quarter of a million ethnic Chinese fled the new Vietnam for China. Some did not get out in time or found it hard to leave. Around 50,000 'Amerasian' children remained as a visible reminder of the American presence. Some blond and blue eyed, some black, all were treated as outcasts and reduced to begging or prostitution. By 1990, 30,000 had gone to America.

Key date

Thousands of 'boat people' began fleeing Vietnam: 1978

iv) Political divisions

Political divisions were hard to overcome. The new government persecuted those associated with the old regime; 300,000 South Vietnamese civil servants, army officers, doctors, lawyers and intellectuals were 're-educated' in concentration camps where malaria, dysentery, torture and executions were common. World pressure meant that by 1990 most of the survivors were released for emigration to the United States. This loss of skilled labour was a national tragedy. Some who had been pro-Communist during the war became dissatisfied in peace-time. When American journalist Stanley Karnow returned to Communist Vietnam in 1990 he looked up many old friends. He was surprised to find that some influential individuals in Saigon had actually been

Communist agents. They told him that their motivation had been nationalism, but that they had become disillusioned with the Communist regime after 1975. One old friend told him how wives of Communist leaders flew from Hanoi to **Ho Chi Minh City** (the victors' name for Saigon) aboard army planes to buy up heirlooms from once-rich families at bargain prices. Karnow said that abuse of rank reminded him of the wives of the Saigon generals during the war. 'Exactly', said his friend, 'this is still very much a feudal society, whatever its ideological labels'.

Key question
How did Vietnam relate to other countries after 1975?

c) Vietnam's foreign friends and enemies after 1975

i) Communist Vietnam and the USSR

During the war North Vietnamese relations with the USSR and China were good, but once the war was over, old Sino-Vietnamese hostilities erupted, culminating in war in 1979. America had got involved in Vietnam partly or mostly to contain China. Ironically, in 1979, the US supported China against Vietnam. This left Vietnam totally dependent upon Soviet aid; 4000 Russians were sent to rebuild the Vietnamese economy. The Vietnamese called them 'Americans without dollars' – poor and bossy invaders. A favourite Vietnamese joke told of Hanoi begging Moscow for economic aid, to which Moscow replied, 'Tighten your belts'. 'Send belts', was the Vietnamese answer. The collapse of the USSR meant the cessation of Soviet aid in 1991, making the Russians the people most hated by the Vietnamese in the 1990s. Ironically again, Hanoi became desperate for improved relations with America, hoping to get trade and aid.

ii) Vietnam and the American MIAs

The resumption of normal relations between America and Vietnam was thwarted by residual bitterness in Washington, fuelled by the supposed **MIAs** (missing in action). Finding the dead bodies of American soldiers who were unaccounted for was difficult with the terrain and climate of Vietnam. Bodies decay rapidly in the tropics. American politicians, the media and families were generally reluctant to give up on these men. After the war, 62 per cent of Americans believed that the MIAs were still being held prisoner by Hanoi. Politicians and the media were probably motivated by self-interest. It was a good story, and politicians were uneasy about the emotions they would arouse if they were to say 'forget it'. The Americans sent teams to search for American bodies buried in Vietnamese cemeteries. Hanoi was willing to allow this as they wanted better diplomatic relations and the Americans paid Vietnamese workers high wages to dig up corpses. However, ordinary Vietnamese were offended when their relations were dug up in the search.

Key terms

Ho Chi Minh City
Name given by Communists to Saigon after the 1975 victory.

MIA
Missing in action: some Americans believe that there are still US soldiers being held prisoner.

International Monetary Fund
An institution that helps to regulate international trade and sometimes gives economic aid to support struggling nations.

iii) US–Vietnamese diplomatic relations

In America it was difficult to overcome the bitter memories of the unsuccessful war with those whom Kissinger called 'the most bloody-minded bastards' he had ever known. In 1991 America stopped the **International Monetary Fund** granting economic aid to Vietnam and a British newspaper said, 'One day Vietnam may overcome the consequences of having won its war against America. The Americans are putting off this day as long as possible'. However, in 1994 President Bill Clinton, although highly sensitive about his own 'draft-dodging' in the war (it was a big issue in his election campaign), moved the process of reconciliation forward. He lifted the US embargo on trade with Vietnam and re-established diplomatic relations in 1995. American businessmen were very interested in Vietnam, but cultural misunderstandings remained. An American plan to open a chain entitled 'Uncle Ho's Hamburgers' was considered highly offensive.

Key date
President Clinton re-established diplomatic relations with Vietnam: 1995

d) Vietnam in the early twenty-first century

Key question
What kind of country is Vietnam today?

When looking back on the wars in Vietnam, it is not always easy to decide what they were about:

- There was a nationalist war of independence against the colonialist French.
- Then, according to Hanoi, there was another war of independence against the imperialist Americans.
- There was also a civil war between Vietnamese to decide what the future of Vietnam should be.

Ho's Communism tapped into the traditional peasant community spirit, but opposing it were the ideas of freer and more individualistic spirits in the South, especially Saigon with its dynamic capitalist urban middle class. In 1975 the communal spirit seemed to have triumphed, partly because of its close association with old traditions, but mostly because of its association with nationalism.

The removal of foreign threats meant a loss of dynamism for the Communist way, and Western tourists seeing the revival of a capitalist economy and the vulgarity of Ho Chi Minh City wondered whether the South had not won after all. In Ho Chi Minh City in the 1990s local Communist chiefs ran brothels and the crime rate was as high as in the old Saigon days.

Influenced by Soviet reforms in the late 1980s and Chinese reforms in the 1990s, Hanoi introduced greater economic flexibility in order to improve their disastrous situation. The market economy, private ownership and incentives made a dramatic comeback. The peasants responded to incentives and Vietnam became one of the developing world's largest rice exporters.

Vietnam also became a fashionable tourist venue. Western tourists were keen to see what remained of its unspoiled 'backwardness' as well as its beautiful scenery. Tourists reported the triumph of capitalistic practices, particularly in Ho Chi Minh City which, apart from the name, was not so very different from its American days. The locals wore American-style T-shirts and jeans, and the black market still flourished. Officials throughout

Vietnam were frequently corrupt and enjoyed giving 'spot' fines to hapless Western tourists, perhaps being made to pay for the sins of their predecessors. Despite tourism, Vietnam remains one of the poorest countries in the world. The situation was not helped by disastrous flooding in 2000.

Key question
What was the impact of the Vietnam War upon the Cold War?

e) The Vietnam War and the Cold War

It is difficult to decide whether the Vietnam War, which grew out of the Cold War, had a marked impact on the latter conflict.

i) Detente

The Soviets and Chinese improved relations with America even as Nixon bombed Hanoi, but the improvement might not have happened had they not known that Nixon was getting the American troops out.

ii) Dominoes

Outside of Indochina, the dominoes did not fall to Communism during the Vietnam War or after it, which might or might not have been due to the American effort. Many potential dominoes prospered. South Korea in particular did very well out of the war, selling vast quantities of goods to the Americans.

iii) Impact on US power

The Vietnam War certainly weakened America. Although America still remains the world's greatest military power, Americans lost some of their unquestioning belief in their nation's cultural rectitude and supremacy. The confidence and optimism born of two triumphant world wars (and to a lesser extent Korea) were lost. Governments and people were more hesitant about future involvement in international relations. The first Reagan administration (1981–5) saw a massive arms build-up and much Cold War rhetoric, but in order to get re-elected Reagan had to take a more moderate line. Polls in the 1980s showed the American public carefully watching Central American events to stop 'another Vietnam'. When the Bush administration got involved in the 1991 Gulf War, Congress debated long and hard and only endorsed entry by a narrow margin. Speedy military success in the Gulf caused a jubilant President George Bush (Senior) to claim that, 'By God, we've kicked the Vietnam syndrome once and for all.' The Gulf War demonstrated that the American military had recovered from the traumatic Vietnam years. However, as it became clearer that the problems in the Gulf had not been totally solved, it seemed likely that Bush's optimism was unjustified.

Summary diagram: The effects of the Vietnam War

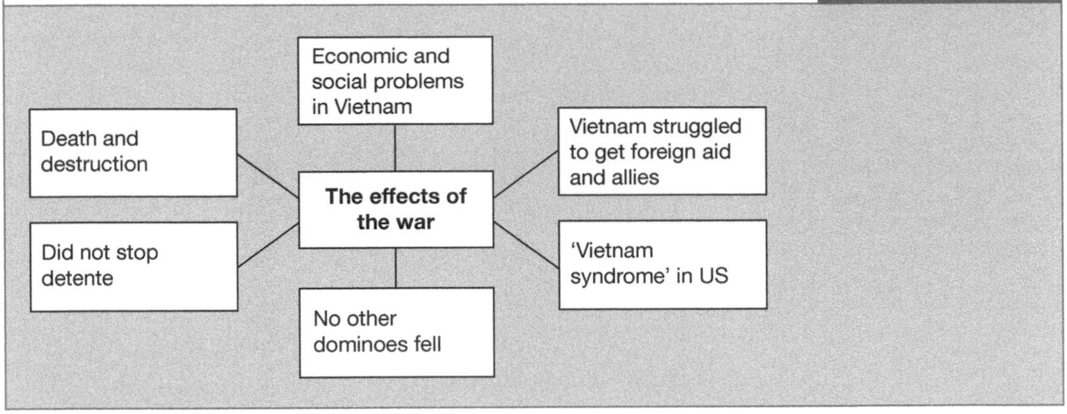

3 | The Lessons of the Vietnam War

The American car manufacturer Henry Ford said, 'History is bunk'. Sometimes people find it hard to understand why anyone should investigate or read about events which happened years ago. Should we study the Vietnam War because there are some lessons to be learned from it? It is not that easy to learn from history. Johnson and his contemporaries thought that they had learned the right lesson from the appeasement of Hitler during the 1930s and that they could apply it to Vietnam. It seems that they were wrong. Is the final tragedy of the Vietnam War that it developed out of a combination of ideas, people and events so unusual and complex that we cannot make sufficient sense out of it to find an agreed lesson to learn from it? At the very least can we say that any democracy should take great care not to get involved in a foreign country without exhaustive domestic debate to ensure consensus, without considerable knowledge of that country and its history, and without detailed study of a war like America's in Vietnam?

Is the US involvement in Iraq in the dying years of President George Bush (Junior), in which many people see great similarities to the Vietnam involvement, the final proof that we never learn from history?

Glossary

Administration Rather than refer to a president's 'government', Americans refer to a president's 'administration'.

Agent Orange A herbicide used by the US in Vietnam, in order to defoliate the trees to destroy enemy cover.

Agrovilles New and well-defended villages set up by Diem's regime to keep Communists out.

Ap Bac An important battle, the first major clash between the Vietcong and ARVN, in which American advisers and materials played a big part.

Approval rating American pollsters continually check the public's opinion (approval) of the president's performance.

Armistice Halt to fighting, but not yet a peace treaty.

ARVN Diem's Army of the Republic of Vietnam.

B-52s Large American bomber planes.

Balance of payments deficit When the value of a country's imports exceeds that of its exports.

Black market Secret commercial transactions designed to avoid paying taxes.

Boat people Anti-Communist Vietnamese who fled Vietnam after 1975.

Booby traps Disguised traps.

Cadres Group leaders within Communist societies.

Capitalists Those who believe in a free market economy with no state intervention – the opposite of the Communist economic philosophy.

Central Intelligence Agency Established in 1947 – responsible for collecting and evaluating intelligence data for the federal government.

Coalition A government containing several political parties; in this case, the Saigon regime would have to include Communists.

Cold War The struggle between the USA and USSR from the mid-1940s to the mid-1980s. US and Soviet forces never met in combat – hence the 'cold' war.

Collectivised Private land ownership was ended.

Commander-in-chief Under the US Constitution, the president is commander-in-chief of the US Armed Forces, giving him a great deal of control (sometimes contested by Congress) over making war.

Commitment trap The theory that each president after Truman was bound to continue the US involvement in Vietnam.

Communist One whose ideology (set of beliefs) is anti-imperialist (against countries that try to conquer or dominate others) and pro-equal distribution of wealth.

Congress The US equivalent of Britain's parliament – passes laws and votes money for the president to spend.

Congressional mid-term elections The presidential term of office is four years; in the middle of that term, some congressional seats are contested.

Congressman Each of the 50 US states elects a number of congressmen to represent them in Congress.

Conscientious objectors Those whose religion (for example, Quakers) made them pacifists and therefore, they said, unable to fight if drafted. The US government allowed some conscientious objectors to avoid the draft.

Containment Truman's policy whereby the US would attempt to contain or halt any further spread of Communism.

COSVN Central Office for South Vietnam – supposed Vietnamese Communist headquarters in Cambodia.

Counter-insurgency When faced with irregular (guerrilla) warfare conducted against the South Vietnamese government by discontented South Vietnamese rebels (insurgents), some Americans urged special tactics (for example, propaganda) to counter those insurgents.

Coup A *coup d'état* is the illegal overthrow of a government, usually by violent and/or revolutionary means.

Court-martialled Tried by an army court for breaking army regulations.

Cross-over point Point at which Americans anticipated that Communists would give up because they were being killed faster than Hanoi could replace them.

DDT An insecticide.

Defence Department The section of the federal bureaucracy with responsibility for US defence.

Detente Relaxation of tension between the USA and the USSR in the Cold War in the 1970s.

Dienbienphu Site of decisive Vietminh military victory over France in 1954.

Diplomatic In international relations, 'diplomacy' means relations between nations; a diplomat represents his nation abroad; nations that fully recognise each other have diplomatic relations.

Doves Those who favoured a less aggressive foreign policy, including an early peace in the Vietnam War.

Draft US equivalent of British conscription; when military service is compulsory.

Egalitarian In this context, a Vietnam in which people had greater social, economic and political equality.

Fragging When enlisted men tried to kill officers by throwing fragmentation grenades at them.

Geneva Accords Agreements reached at Geneva in 1954 by France, China, Ho Chi Minh and the USSR, that Vietnam should be temporarily divided, with national elections held in 1956.

Geopolitical Political positions governed by the United States' geographical location in the world.

Ground troops In March 1965, President Johnson sent the first few thousand regular soldiers (rather than just 'advisers') to Vietnam.

'Group-think' When the herd instinct halts independent thought or disagreement.

Grunt Ordinary ground trooper or footsoldier.

Gubernatorial Pertaining to being a state governor.

Guerrilla A soldier who tries to avoid conventional warfare (that is, one army directly confronting another), preferring methods such as sabotage to counter the enemy's superior conventional forces.

Hawks Militant Cold Warriors in the USA; those at the other end of the spectrum were known as doves.

Hippies Young Americans with long hair, casual clothing and anti-establishment attitude in the 1960s.

Ho Chi Minh City Name given by Communists to Saigon after the 1975 victory.

Ho Chi Minh Trail North Vietnamese Communist supply route going south from North Vietnam through Cambodia and Laos to South Vietnam.

Ideology A set of principles or beliefs. The USSR's ideology was Communism, the USA's, liberal capitalism.

Inaugural address When the US President is sworn into office, he makes a speech setting out his ideas and plans.

Indochina The countries now known as Vietnam, Cambodia and Laos.

International Monetary Fund An institution that helps to regulate international trade and sometimes gives economic aid to support struggling nations.

International trusteeship President Roosevelt envisaged several countries, including the US, guiding post-war Vietnam towards independence.

Joint Chiefs of Staff Established during the Second World War – US army, navy and air force chiefs.

Khe Sanh Crucial battle in 1968 between PAVN and American forces.

Kremlin The headquarters of the Soviet government in Moscow.

Land reform Even anti-Communist Americans saw the need for a more equal distribution of land in Vietnam: an estimated 1 per cent of the population owned all the cultivable land in the south.

Linkage Linking US concessions to the USSR and China to their assistance in ending the Vietnam War.

Machiavellian Machiavelli was a sixteenth-century Italian writer who once wrote, 'the end justifies the means' – in foreign policy, that would be considered as *realpolitik*.

Madman Theory Nixon wanted Hanoi to think he was capable of anything, in order to frighten them into making peace.

Mandarin A high-ranking civil servant.

MIA Missing in action: some Americans believe that there are still US soldiers being held prisoner.

Military Assistance Command, Vietnam Created by Kennedy to co-ordinate US efforts in South Vietnam in February 1962.

Missile gap In the late 1950s, Khrushchev claimed that the USSR had more missiles than the USA.

Monolithic Communist bloc During the 1950s, many Americans believed that Moscow and Beijing were united in their foreign policies; by the 1960s, it was increasingly clear that with the Sino-Soviet split (in which other Communist nations took sides) there was no longer a united/monolithic Communist bloc.

Moratorium In this context, suspension of normal activities, in order to protest.

Napalm bombs Bombs containing jellied petrol.

National Guard US Armed Forces reservists, called up by the president in times of crisis.

National Liberation Front From 1960, Ho's southern supporters gave themselves this name.

National Security Council The 1947 Act that established the CIA also established the National Security Council, to co-ordinate US government work on internal and external security; members included the president, vice-president, secretary of state, secretary of defence, and the chiefs of the CIA and JCS.

National self-determination The right of a people to choose their own form of government in their own country.

Nationalism In the case of Vietnam, patriotic enthusiasm for an independent Vietnam.

NATO The North Atlantic Treaty Organisation was an anti-Communist Western military alliance, established by the USA in 1949.

Neocolonialism Whereas old-style colonialism was usually openly exploitative, neocolonialism had a kinder face as, for example, when France claimed to be granting greater independence to Vietnam after the Second World War.

Neutralised Vietnam Some contemporaries advocated taking Vietnam out of the Cold War context and allowing it to decide its own future, without influence or input from Moscow, Beijing or Washington, DC.

'New look' Republican policy emphasising nuclear weaponry rather than conventional forces for defence.

Normalisation of diplomatic relations When the USA disliked another state, particularly a Communist one, it refused to give it diplomatic recognition. It was not until the late 1970s that the USA established diplomatic relations (that is, normalised relations) with China. Once diplomatic relations were established, ambassadors were exchanged.

Orthodox historians American historians of the Cold War who see their country as bravely and idealistically standing up to the 'evil' of Communism.

Pacification Paying greater attention to the security and government of the South Vietnamese people.

Party convention When delegates from all states meet to decide on their party's candidate for the presidency.

Peace with honour Nixon always claimed he would get 'peace with honour' in Vietnam, by which he meant that Thieu's government must stay in power in a viable South Vietnamese state.

Pentagon Headquarters of the US Defence Department.

People's Army of Vietnam Formal name of Ho's North Vietnamese Army by 1956.

People's Liberation Armed Forces The name by which Ho's southern supporters called their forces after 1960.

Popular mandate Clear evidence that a political leader has the majority of the people behind him and his policies.

Post-revisionist historians Historians who consider the USA and the USSR equally responsible for the Cold War.

Primary When voters in an American state vote for one of several candidates to be their political party's presidential candidate.

Protocol In this context, an agreement between signatory nations.

Quagmire theory Belief that the US got slowly and increasingly stuck in Vietnam.

R&R Rest and recuperation for American soldiers in Vietnam.

Realpolitik A realistic, rather than moralistic or legalistic approach to foreign policy; a belief that foreign policy should be dictated by the national interest.

Reunification Vietnam was reunited in 1975 when the North took over the South.

Revisionist historians American historians who criticise US motives in the Cold War as aggressive and acquisitive.

Rhetoric Stylised speech, designed to impress and persuade.

Rollback The Eisenhower administration talked a great deal about going beyond President Truman's containment of Communism to a pushing back of Communism in places where it was already established.

'Rolling Thunder' Heavy, often non-stop US bombing of Vietnam.

Russian Revolution Began in 1917. It made Russia into the world's first Communist country, called the Union of Soviet Socialist Republics (USSR).

SEATO Southeast Asia Treaty Organisation: defensive alliance between USA, Britain, France, Australia, New Zealand and Pakistan, 1954.

Self-determination When a people has the right to decide how they will be governed.

Senate Foreign Relations Committee Highly influential body of recognised specialists in foreign policy in US Senate.

Sino-Soviet Another way of saying Chinese-Soviet. Sino pertains to Chinese.

Stalemate theory Belief that the US continued to fight an unwinnable war in Vietnam, simply to avoid being seen to be defeated.

State Department The US equivalent of Britain's Foreign Office – the section of the federal bureaucracy with responsibility for US relations with foreign powers.

Strategic hamlets Fortified villages in South Vietnam, similar to agrovilles.

Summit During the Cold War, meetings or conferences between the US and Soviet leaders were known as summit meetings.

Teach-in Anti-war lectures and debates in American colleges.

Tet The Tet Festival was the Vietnamese equivalent of Christmas, New Year and Easter combined. Americans use the word 'Tet' as shorthand for the 'Tet Offensive'.

Third World Cold War era name for developing nations.

Totalitarian An all-controlling, dictatorial government.

United Nations Set up in 1945 to try to keep world peace.

Veterans Those who fought in the Vietnam War (as any other war) were afterwards known as veterans.

Vietcong After 1960, Diem called the National Liberation Front 'Vietcong' (Vietnamese Communists or VC).

Vietminh Ho's Vietnamese nationalist followers were known as the Vietminh after 1941.

Vietnamisation A phrase/policy introduced by the Nixon administration; the policy said that the South Vietnamese government and forces should take the main responsibility for the war against Communism. Previous administrations had wanted and worked for this. They had failed and so did Nixon.

War of attrition Westmoreland believed that US numerical and technological superiority would wear down the VC who must, after losing a certain number of men, finally decide to give up.

Watergate affair During Nixon's re-election campaign, Republicans authorised burglary and wiretapping of Democratic national headquarters at Watergate building in Washington, DC; the Nixon administration tried a 'cover-up'.

West Point The top US military academy.

Wise Men A group of experienced politicians, generals and others who had previously held high office, frequently consulted by Johnson over the Vietnam War.

Working Group A group of experts brought together by President Johnson to study Vietnam and make suggestions for future policies in Autumn 1964.

Index

Acheson, Dean 17, 19, 193
Agent Orange 2, 195
Agrovilles 45, 67
Ap Bac 52, 64–5
ARVN (Army of the Republic of Vietnam) 46, 52, 63–5, 72–4, 97, 109, 111, 120–2, 124, 128, 136, 138, 163, 165, 172–4, 176, 180, 182, 185, 187
Associated State of Vietnam 8, 19
Atomic weapons 47, 139, 146, 163, 181
Australia 19, 41, 137, 193

Ball, George 65, 92–3, 98, 100, 148
Bao Dai 8, 11–13, 16, 21, 25, 29, 32, 34–7, 40–3
Boat people 192, 196
Britain 7, 11, 13, 17–18, 22, 33–6, 39, 41, 47, 49–50, 150
Buddhists 40, 43, 52, 69–70, 73, 78, 120, 135–6

Cambodia 8, 24, 35–7, 41, 62, 116, 128, 162–3, 168–9, 172–8, 182, 184–5, 188–9
Catholics 39–40, 43, 52, 69–70, 95
Chiang Kai-shek 14, 17–18, 26
China 2–3, 5–6, 8, 10–11, 14, 17–21, 23–4, 26–7, 29–31, 34–6, 38–9, 46–7, 52, 55–6, 60–3, 66, 68, 73, 76, 84–7, 92–4, 98, 117, 128, 133–4, 138, 146, 152, 165–8, 170–1, 175, 178–81, 185–7, 192–3, 196–8
CIA (Central Intelligence Agency) 4, 62–3, 65, 85, 87, 91, 98, 127–9, 134, 136, 140, 149
Clifford, Clark 128, 133, 137, 139–40
Commitment trap 4–5, 76
Congress 4–5, 30, 34, 40, 49, 62, 66, 73, 81, 83, 88, 90, 92, 94, 97, 99–100, 114, 128, 132, 137, 142, 146, 148–9, 172, 178–9, 182, 184–5, 187, 193
Containment 31, 52
COSVN (Central Office for South Vietnam) 172–3
Credibility gap 139, 141, 153
Cronkite, Walter 73, 146
Cuba 51, 55, 39, 61–2, 70, 74–5, 77–8

Danang 93–4, 153
Defence Department 4, 21, 57, 60–1, 63, 73, 85, 91, 130
Democratic Republic of Vietnam 8, 10, 15–16, 19, 26, 38
Democrats 18, 31, 52, 83, 85, 132–3, 144, 151–2, 164, 167–9, 177, 181, 183, 187
Detente 170–1, 199
Diem, Ngo Dinh 10, 32, 34, 36–7, 40–7, 49, 51–2, 63–78, 84, 91, 96, 111, 186, 193
Dienbienphu 11, 15, 24, 28–9, 31–5, 38, 42, 47, 49, 163
Domino theory 3, 5, 24, 31–4, 49–50, 33, 73, 76, 81, 91, 98, 192, 199
Dulles, John Foster 31–3, 36, 38, 41–2, 47, 49–50, 193

Eisenhower, Dwight 4, 24–50, 52–3, 56, 76, 81, 94, 100, 163, 168, 193
Europe 17, 19–22, 31, 63, 77, 142, 186

France 1–3, 7–23, 25–8, 30–1, 33, 35–6, 38–9, 41–2, 44, 47, 49, 51–2, 65, 68, 93, 95–7, 127, 150, 163, 193, 198
French Indochina 7–24, 29–31, 33–6, 40, 52–3, 62
Fulbright, William 136, 144, 148

Geneva Conference and Accords 11, 13, 24–25, 30–2, 34–41, 45, 47, 49, 53
Giap, Vo Nguyen 15–16, 24–9, 43, 109, 111, 116–17, 127, 193–5
Goldwater, Barry 89
Great Society 80, 93, 100, 135, 144, 148, 153
Green Berets 56, 63, 124
Gulf of Tonkin Crisis and Resolution 80, 87–90, 100, 143

Haiphong 163, 180, 182, 184
Halberstam, David 67–9, 92, 94, 150
Hamburger Hill 109, 124, 126–7
Hanoi 11, 37, 39, 93, 118, 163, 180, 184

Ho Chi Minh 7–22, 24–9, 34, 38–40, 43–6, 53, 76, 83, 96–8, 100, 133–5, 137, 150, 171, 192, 198
Ho Chi Minh Trail 82 (map), 116–17, 128, 134, 137, 163, 172
Hue 40, 82, 111, 135, 138
Humphrey, Hubert 98, 151, 165, 167

Ia Drang 81, 82, 98, 109, 117
Indochinese Communist Party 7, 10–11, 15, 26

Japan 7, 10–17, 19, 22–23, 26, 32, 40, 125, 142
JCS (Joint Chiefs of Staff) 4, 19, 42, 62–3, 73, 75, 86, 90–1, 98, 100, 113, 137, 140, 149, 173
Johnson, Lyndon 4, 33, 47, 51–2, 55, 58–60, 67, 72, 75, 77, Chapters 5–7 *passim*, 164–5, 170, 193, 200

Karnow, Stanley 63–4, 67, 85, 196
Kennedy, John 4, 40, 45, 49, Chapter 4 *passim*, 80–1, 83–5, 87, 94, 99–100, 133, 136, 164–5, 168, 193
Kennedy, Robert 55, 57, 59–60, 62–3, 72, 74–5, 136
Khanh, General, 86, 91
Khe Sanh 105, 120, 129, 139–40
Khrushchev, Nikita 55–6, 75
King, Martin Luther 132, 144
Kissinger, Henry 163, 167–75, 180, 182–8, 193
Korean War 18–20, 30, 33–4, 60, 66, 81, 89
Ky, Nguyen Cao 81, 95–9, 125, 135–6

Laird, Melvyn 178, 180
Lam Son Offensive 163, 173–4
Laos 8, 24, 35–7, 41, 61–2, 66, 76–8, 109, 116, 120, 128, 163, 169, 172–5, 178, 182, 184
Le Duc Tho 182–3, 185
LeMay, Curtis 86, 98
Lodge, Henry Cabot 55, 68, 70–6, 91, 93

MAAG (Military Assistance Advisory Group) 8, 20, 24, 42–3, 45
MACV (Military Assistance Command Vietnam) 51, 64
Mansfield, Mike 40, 66, 85, 88, 92, 94
Mao Zedong 19
McCarthy, Joseph (and McCarthyism) 19, 52, 55, 85, 168
McNamara, Robert 51, 57–63, 65, 72–3, 77, 80, 85–6, 88, 98, 100, 113, 128, 130, 132–3, 136–7; 141, 143–5, 150, 153, 193
MIAs (missing in action) 197
Minh, General 'Big' the 86, 91, 96
My Lai Massacre 109, 114–15, 163, 177

National Council of Reconciliation 182
National Liberation Front 45
NSC (National Security Council) 63, 72, 170
NATO (North Atlantic Treaty Organisation) 18, 20, 31, 34
Nhu, Madame 67–8, 73
Nhu, Ngo Dinh 67–70, 74
Nixon, Richard 4, 42, 47, 77, 124, 152, Chapter 8 *passim*
North Vietnam 1–2, 5–6, 15, 25, 36, 39, 43, 45–6, 51, 58, 66, 69, 74, 76, 86–9, 92–5, 98, 100, 109, 112, 116–17, 127–8, 133–5, 137–8, 141, 143, 146, 148–53, 162–4, 166, 171–6, 178–84, 188, 193–4

Operation Phoenix 109, 114–15, 181

PAVN (aka NVA) 43, 80–1, 86, 111, 117, 125, 137–9, 163, 171, 173–4, 180–3, 185, 187
Peace talks 51, 58, 66, 69, 79, 93, 150–1, 163, 165, 174, 182–4
Pleiku 80, 82, 92
Press Chapter 7 *passim*
POWs (prisoners of war) 175, 179, 182, 184
Protests 5–6, 142–7, 151, 172, 175–7

Quagmire theory 4–5, 48
Quat, Dr 91, 95–6

Republicans 19, 30, 33, 55–6, 71, 89, 152, 163–4, 168, 177–8, 183
Rogers, William 169, 173, 177, 179, 186
Rolling Thunder 80, 92–3, 99, 136, 150, 172
Roosevelt, Franklin 7, 14, 16, 18
Rusk, Dean 22, 57, 59–60, 62–3, 66, 72, 75, 77, 85, 91, 140, 145, 148

Saigon (now Ho Chi Minh City) 21, 25, 37, 39, 43, 45, 64, 67, 80, 84, 91, 109, 118–19, 121, 125, 128, 143, 172, 196–8
Search and Destroy 5, 120, 127, 128
SEATO (Southeast Asia Treaty Organisation) 24, 30, 32, 41, 49, 66, 76, 88
Second World War 3, 12–14, 16–19, 22, 81, 126, 137, 144
South Vietnam 1–2, 5–6, 15, 24, 30, 32, 36, 38–43, 45–52, 58, 62, 64–5, 67–8, 71–2, 74–7, 80–1, 85–100, 109, 111–12, 116–17, 120, 122, 128–9, 133–5, 137–8, 141, 150–5, 162, 164, 166, 173–4, 178–9, 182–4, 188, 193–4
Stalemate theory 4–5, 48, 100
Stalin, Joseph 9, 19
State Department 4, 14–16, 18–19, 21, 57, 60, 62–3, 66–7, 71, 73, 85, 91, 153, 169
Strategic Hamlets 51, 67, 86, 111

Taxes 132, 145
Taylor, Maxwell 63, 72–73, 80, 86, 91, 93–4, 97–8, 100, 115
Tet Offensive 111, 133, 137–41, 150, 164, 166–7
Thieu, President 91, 96–9, 120, 134, 136, 138, 165, 171, 174–5, 178, 180–8
Truman, Harry 4, 7, 16–23, 25, 30–1, 47, 52, 76

United Nations (UN) 19, 30, 88–9
USSR 2–3, 5–7, 9–11, 16, 18–23, 25, 30–2, 35, 38–9, 46–7, 55–6, 61–3, 76, 84, 86–7, 92–4, 117, 128, 134, 146, 152, 165–6, 170–1, 174–5, 178–81, 185–6, 192–3, 197–8

Vietcong (VC) 10, 45, 52, 64–7, 80, 91–2, 94, 111–15, 117–18, 120, 125, 127–8, 137–8, 176, 194
Vietminh 7, 10, 13, 17, 23, 26–7, 31, 34–6, 38, 41, 43–4, 95, 97
Vietnamisation 164, 168, 170, 173–4, 178, 180

Watergate 169, 187–8
Wayne, John 122, 144
Westmoreland, William 5, 76, 91, 93, 95, 97–8, 115, 121–2, 128–9, 136, 139, 144, 173
Wise Men 133, 145, 149
Working Group 80, 91–2, 95